Form and Method:
Composing Music

Form and Method: Composing Music

THE ROTHSCHILD ESSAYS

Roger Reynolds
University of California, San Diego, USA

edited by
Stephen McAdams
Ircam—CNRS, Paris, France

ROUTLEDGE
New York and London

Published in 2002 by
Routledge
29 West 35th Street
New York, NY 10001

Published in Great Britain by
Routledge
11 New Fetter Lane
London EC4P 4EE

10 9 8 7 6 5 4 3 2 1

Cataloging-in-Publication Data is available from the Library of Congress.

ISBN 90–5755–136–5

Cover illustration designed by Karen Reynolds.

CONTENTS

Part I: The Text

Part II: The Examples

Examples for Essay 1: Form

Examples for Essay 2: Method

PREFACE

In 1992, I was approached by the Peabody Conservatory of Johns Hopkins University in Baltimore and asked if I would accept an appointment as its 1992–93 Randolph Rothschild Guest Composer. The invitation came jointly from the Coordinator of the Composition Department, Professor Jean Eichelberger Ivey, and the Director of Computer Music, Professor Geoffrey Wright. I decided to take this occasion to put into a series of six illustrated lectures a picture of my evolved thinking about the composing of music: both from a more general, overall perspective and from that of the particular moment-to-moment decision making that, gradually accumulating, brings a whole into being.

It always seemed wasteful to me that such explanatory occasions — those on which someone who does things tells others about how s/he does it — more often than not touch only on the surface of matters. My thought was that perhaps in trying to characterize the frame effectively for this occasion, I could at the same time solve the problem for a whole set of subsequent occasions. And by digging into a range of specifics for several subject works, with ample illustration, my whole compositional process could also be usefully glimpsed in operation. In fact, I had undertaken a similar but less ambitious effort on an earlier, parallel occasion. In 1985, I was Senior Fellow of Brooklyn College's Institute for Studies in American Music (established in 1971 by H. Wiley Hitchcock, a musicologist of inspiringly wide-ranging enterprise), and delivered a pair of talks. They became the basis both for a monograph, *A Searcher's Path: A Composer's Ways*, published by the ISAM, and also, differently packaged, for an article "A perspective on form and experience," published in *Contemporary Music Review*, Volume 2, Part 1, 1987, as edited by Stephen McAdams.

There was a (to me) surprising amount of interest generated by these talks about composing, talks characterized by an atypical scope and weighting in relation to this subject matter (my treatment of compositional issues did not dwell extensively, for example, on the already more than abundantly surveyed landscape of pitch structuring). Although there was sometimes notable bewilderment regarding the novelty of my approach — young musicians were indeed responsive. In particular, they often expressed satisfaction with the fact that the formal and methodological perspectives I presented were clearly detectable in the resulting music. That this connection should be unexpected was itself food for thought. I found myself presenting these materials widely: at the Sibelius Academy in Helsinki; at the Ricordi Center in Buenos Aires; Aristotle University in Thessaloniki, Greece; at Ircam in Paris; the Universidade Federal do Rio Grande do Sul in Porto Alegre; the Polish section of the ISCM's International Course for Young Composers at Radziejowice; SUNY Buffalo's June in Buffalo Festival; at the College of the Holy Cross in Worcester; and at Yale, Colorado, Pennsylvania, Princeton, and New York universities. I also brought them back to my own Music Department at the University of California, San Diego, where a quarter-long seminar allowed both presentation and discussion in alternation, week by week. I mention these specifics both to indicate the geographical range of the vetting that these materials have had, and in order to extend my gratitude to the many who listened, considered and — most significantly — provided feedback.

This book is presented in two parts in order to avoid what the author has always found to be the irritating inconvenience of moving back and forth between graphic evidence and textual exploration. The first part contains the narrative commentary, the second the examples.

PREFACE

Referrals from Part I text to Part II examples will be indicated in the form [Example 1]. If the devil is often to be located lurking among the details, so, also, can illuminations be. Footnotes have been kept to a minimum, and appear at the close of the Essay to which they refer.

My gratitude goes out here to all those young musicians with whom I have interacted and by whom I have been alerted to so much that continues to matter. It also goes out to Randolph Rothschild whose inextinguishable curiosity and generosity provided the resource which Jean Eichelberger Ivey and Geoff Wright drew upon. Long-time friend and colleague Stephen McAdams is due deep appreciation for the unflagging clarity, perspective, incisiveness, and wry humor that he brought to the editing of these Essays. Thanks also to Jason Sanyek for his work on one stage of the word-processing, and especially to Eric Dries for the preparation of musical examples. Lastly, a generous helpng of gratitude is allotted to my collaborator, Karen, upon whose stamina, attentiveness to detail, imagination, and vital aesthetic sesibility I have so much depended over our decades together.

Form and Method:
Composing Music

I

INTRODUCTORY REMARKS

It is only fair to emphasize at the outset that I am content with the pragmatic advantages of plausibility rather than attempting to probe in words for anything like absolute principles. My thoughts arise out of and find what validity they have in my work over thirty years as a composer of musical experiences. Theories, I have found, are sometimes interesting but they often tend to become problematic — both disruptive and self-justifying — in application. I don't have theories. I have ways. It is also the case that I don't think consciously about many of the ideas expressed here while I am working. The procedures I have come to trust have for me the immediate effect of off-loading an unhealthy and encumbering level of basic, strategic, and analytical thought while I am composing. They allow the actual engagement with musical tasks to become more immediate, engrossing, and even innocent. My effort, then, has been to devise procedures that not only guide the ongoing composition itself — the evolving web of explicit choices — once it has begun, but also that precede and prepare for this actual composition, thereby freeing me for direct engagement with specific and already delimited choices: which one now? and next?

Form is critical to longevity — redeeming even dated materials — but contemporary factors mitigate against its having a decisive role in determining which music prospers. There is, for example, a drive towards the marketing utility of *premières*, and a work written with the realities of contemporary American musical life in mind will need to be straightforward if it is to be registered accurately (or even serviceably) by a sympathetic listener at first hearing. There is a strong bias toward the conventional shape, a disincentive for bestowing particular attention on any aspect of musical discourse which is unlikely to have its full impact at first encounter. It is evident to me that this tendency, if it continues, will greatly diminish the potential long-term contribution we in our time make both to music and the continuity of its repertoire.

I believe that form is a critical subject requiring our attention all the more now in view of the foregoing. The subject of method, in its turn is uncomfortably situated between the implausibly thorough and the unsatisfactorily informal or slight. Although I have never taught any of the following explicitly, I certainly do teach out of such awareness. Only an occasion such as an appointment as Randolph Rothschild Guest Composer at the Peabody Conservatory of Johns Hopkins University (1992–1993) could have led me to write in these relatively formal terms. Evidently, in one's own workroom it is only necessary to do what one has learned to do. Here, however, my task has been to draw the reader's attention to the landscape of concerns and pathways that are characteristic of my work. I have not tried to write down a fully developed continuity of procedure, only to suggest its components. To do otherwise would have implied the presence of theories which, as I have written, I prefer to avoid.

Let's begin.

ESSAY 1: FORM

DEFINITION/SOURCES OF FORM

Wholeness is the critical *sine qua non* of a musical work. A true composition is not only a remark or stance or display, but a dimensional experience that either leads the listener along a path or proposes a landscape for exploration in such a way that an arc, a trajectory of proposal, engagement, and response has been traversed by its end.

Integrity and coherence arise from the persuasiveness of the sense of belonging one has in the presence of the work's elements, large and small. Integrity can be thought of as a measure of the completeness that accrues to the pattern of objective relationships that underlie a work, whereas coherence relates to completeness within the web of subjective implications aroused. A successful composition addresses both objective and rational as well as subjective and emotional wholeness (cf. Fig. 1).

Each detail is ideally as characteristic of the whole as the impact of the work in its entirety. This has to do with the "sense of belonging" mentioned above. The local event anticipates the macro level in some way just as the overall form invites its detail. If an occurrence at either the micro or macro level does not, in the end, find a plausible place in the listener's overall picture, the form is weakened. If there is insufficient interplay between his grasp of the moment and his comprehension of the gradually accreting whole, the form fails.

Since integration is fundamental, then, how are we to examine an aspect of the whole without at the same time contending with everything? If one is explicating a *composer's*

WHOLENESS

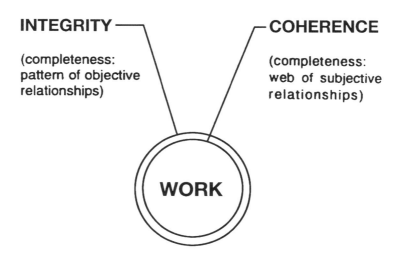

Figure 1

perspective, as distinct from a listener's (whether analytically minded or not), one has an advantage. Fortunately, that is my circumstance here. I am writing about the way music is *made*, and it is clear that musical works are not fully formed expanses to which a composer gains gradual access as, so to speak, the fog lifts revealingly. (One thinks of the melodrama of post-World War II movies: is that the dim outline of a plane? is it the one that promises escape? Everyone sits forward in his chair and squints.)

Rather than being suddenly revealed, whole, a musical work is achieved gradually over time in a manner that doubtless varies for each composer: part discovery, part construction, even, admittedly, part contrivance (and, if poet John Ashbery's *Self-Portrait in a Convex Mirror* is to be believed, also part sheer undirected bumbling). But, in most cases, there is a necessary (though by no means uniform) *staging* involved in the process of completing a musical composition. We can thus inquire into the process recognizing it as a multileveled search for ultimate integration rather than the unrolling of a scroll upon which has been inscribed an already, mystically completed continuity that one needs only to receive. There may have been periods in which individuals (a Mozart) might have gained access to a whole form and its content in this "received" fashion, but ours is not (as certainly Beethoven's was not) of such stripe.

My experience suggests one perspective on the compositional process. Once it is at least tentatively known what the expressive intention of the piece is to be, the issues to be addressed in each project can be reduced to three questions of the following sort:

What kind of overall shape is likely to work?

What are the most appropriate materials?

What procedures will best serve to elaborate the chosen materials toward the large-scale form?

Admittedly, order here is a variable matter. And, of course, the expressive intent of the work is itself an aspect of the desirable preliminary debate. For my purposes, I assume that an expressive intention precedes the address of technical capacity. Nevertheless, one might begin almost anywhere on what is, for me, the closed, interdependent path of consideration between form, material, and method (cf. Fig. 2).

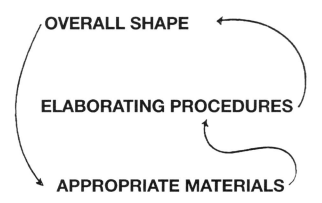

OVERALL SHAPE

ELABORATING PROCEDURES

APPROPRIATE MATERIALS

Figure 2

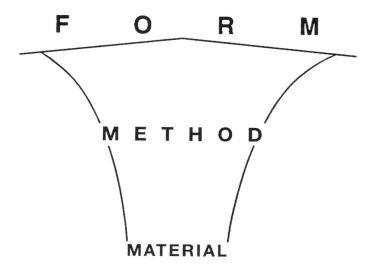

Figure 3

At the most elevated level, I believe, there is form; at the most basic, material; and mediating in the middle there is method, the means by which the composer transforms the small into the large, ensuring that the first two do not become estranged in the process. One can, admittedly, consider these related aspects of composition from the top down or from the bottom up, but my predilection has always been for the former. My expressive intentions seem almost always bound closely to an idea of or commitment to a formal shape. Indeed, until this formal shaping has become whole enough, my intuition resists any effort of the intellect to proceed at all (cf. Fig. 3).

I have used the phrase "expressive intent" several times, and should pause for a moment to add that I intend expression to be thought of in a wide, a metaphorical, regard. It is not mandatory, I think, that a work carry with it the composer's emotions, lay out his narratives, or serve as a simulacrum of personality. A composition may satisfactorily "express" — which in this case is to cleanly radiate — its "manner of operation". Perhaps, ultimately, I am speaking here of an incipient need to make a music, and, further, that this initial adumbration should have at least begun to acquire shape. The composer is then in a position to *intend*, as the dictionary would have it, "to show, manifest, or reveal" something.

In these remarks, I am going to make the assumption that material itself is a sufficiently variable and personal matter that it is less pertinent and useful to discuss it in general terms. In any event, in our time, a musical realist must grant that a composer may very well begin with almost *anything*. Of course, this unruly abundance has a price. The current variability of possible material can confuse questions of form fundamentally.

Material that is audacious, strongly referential, even appropriated, attracts attention to itself, often rendering form impotent or virtually irrelevant since the maintenance of its identity — the identity of the material — is an overriding concern. Intractable, self-justifying materials also disrupt the development of robust method. They are fastened upon precisely because of their assertive and arresting qualities. To render such material subservient to form, to modify it by method is to rob it of its signature, its signal merit. Its relevance tends towards the realm of process (which will be discussed below).

But there are, of course, many other options as one considers materials. It is a straightforward matter to gain access to recorded examples of both Western and non-Western musics of our (or almost any) time. No genre, whether popular and utilitarian or esoteric and obscure is necessarily rejected. No insurmountable restrictions are thought to exist so far as combining musics of different periods or cultures or theoretical persuasions. And in each of these instances of musical behavior, one could fasten upon characteristic fragments with which to begin, or choose to probe for what Xenakis would call their "out of time" antecedents: the privileged groupings, hierarchies or patterns of relationship that precede specific instantiations. Any sound, whether by habit of thought, musical or not, is entertained. So, too, the entirely algorithmic generation of musical elements or textures unmediated by the composer's ear...

Nevertheless, as I assume now and will argue later, unless there is a thoroughgoing and coherent network of connectivity between the chosen material and its designated form, the resulting work is of necessity flawed, less than it could, less than it *should* be.

I suggested earlier that the whole (already fully realized) is not gradually revealed to a composer, but rather sought out in stages: a large span, a relevant detail, an elaborative strategy entering the mind willy-nilly as one works. But I also grant that the way that these things happen is by no means fixed. The three questions I mentioned earlier will be asked on different occasions in widely differing ways. Still, I think that each facet of the picture — form, method, and material — must receive its due.

If the "sense of belonging" is to be considered deeply enough in its relation both to wholeness and to *completeness* on objective as well as subjective grounds, then such consideration will not only result in the possibility of *excluding the somehow inappropriate* but also in *detecting crucial absences* in an evolving musical scenario.

For me, the cardinal issue, then, the one that requires first attention during any compositional process — once, that is, an expressive intent begins to emerge — is that of the large shape, the management of the total experience that the listener is to have. Thus, I will focus here on these high-level concerns (I call them high-level both because their temporal scale is of the largest magnitude and also because they are remote from the explicitness, the sonic immediacy of material). In the second essay in this publication, I will address method, the ways in which I elaborate small-scale specifics onto a global topography. Here it is not the chosen materials or the details of the composer's local interactions with them that concern me, but rather that *appropriate wholeness* that is to be found in effective form.

In beginning to discuss form, I return to intention, for — whether or not the composer has become fully aware of it at a conscious level — it is the *intent* of the work that successful form must satisfy. Since it is usually the case that individual compositions have their own intent, the subject of *global design* is more or less inevitably a matter of *custom design*. I do not believe that, in our time, form should be thought of in terms of categorical patterns, whether old or new.

I want to emphasize that the fitting of the material to the form and the elaborative methods that forge the integrity of their interaction are *particular* responsibilities now because — in a period as fundamentally incoherent and, therefore, as immune from shared conventions, a period in a sense as "unnatural" as ours — this integration does not, cannot occur spontaneously. It becomes the contemporary composer's burden (and, I also believe, his unique privilege) to forge the coherence of each work for himself.

Let us return to the composer's three questions. Assume that he has a notion about what he wants — *not too vague*, but also certainly *not too specific* — he might begin to consider the appropriately shaped formal container. (I ask you to bear with me when I use, rather suddenly, the word "container".) Where will he look?

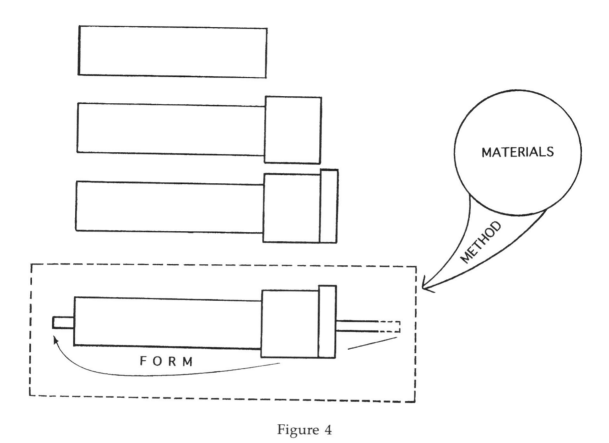

Figure 4

He might find intriguing provocations in *structures* (objects or phenomena from the physical world) or, perhaps, in *processes*. Although neither of these terms is particularly attractive, they will do here, adequately pointing to the two potential sources for formal modeling that I want to consider. For whether one thinks out from the experience of the past (which is to say from the perspective of conventionality) or from the more fragile but flexible perspective of the moment, one is likely to settle either on something *object-like*, a shape in some metaphoric sense, where essence, challenge, opportunity are to be found in the identity of parts, their positions and relationships to one another; or else upon the unitary trajectory of a sufficiently absorbing or gripping process, *a way of proceeding* in which the experience of the whole is to be found in the nature of the journey through it.

Consider the successive fitting of parts together schematically indicated by the progressive diagram in Figure 4.

Many of the formal schemes that I have used have arisen out of some external model or influence. In the case of what I am calling *structural models*, indebted forms involve the relationships of portions of the whole to one another, where these "portions" are individually distinctive. Forms based on *processual models* focus on unbroken evolution of premises such that suddenness of change, distinctive demarcation is subordinated to an unbroken, if varied, unfolding, a continuous aggregation of implication.

It seems to me that, in the West, the vast majority of formal schemes has been based upon what I am calling "structural models". They may be understood as "objects" of a special sort because they exist in the space of time. Perhaps this tendency in our tradition is implicated

STRUCTURES:	PROCESSES:
SECTIONS:	CONTINUITIES:
IDENTITY POSITION RELATIONSHIPS	EXPERIENCE OF 'A WAY OF GOING'
WEST:	JAPAN:
RESISTANCE TO NATURE	ACCEPTANCE OF NATURE
(Containers → Awareness of Space)	(Process → Awareness of Time)

Figure 5

in Toru Takemitsu's perspective: "In contrast to Western architecture, which occupies space in resistance to nature, Japanese architecture possesses a tendency to occupy space in common with nature." He continued, "The Japanese live within an essentially temporal world. While one is made strongly aware of space in the West, one is more likely to be conscious of time in Japan."[1]

Resistant space. Containers. Architecture. *Structural models* on the one hand.

Consciousness of time. The empathic surrender to the character of temporal flow in a given situation. *Processual models* on the other hand.

Consider for a moment the contrasted pairings in Figure 5 (structures/processes, sections/continuities, West/Japan, resistance/acceptance, space/time...) as a rudimentary matrix.

While aspects of the two sources of formal models that I have posited might potentially coexist, it is useful to delineate them in discussing their relationship to musical form, and I will proceed in that way.

The inclination toward either arises ideally from a small generative source or seed. I like to refer to this as the "impetus" of the work, the concentrated, radiant essence out of which the whole can spring and to which, once composition has begun, the evolving whole is continuously made responsive, even responsible. Again one encounters a bidirectional perspective. The impetus acts, from formal heights, to guide the coherence of the whole while simultaneously driving the integrity of the accumulating detail (cf. Fig. 6).

For a time, the "process" option (the most obvious references might be to Ravel's *Bolero*, or Reich's early phase pieces beginning with *Oh Dem Watermelons*) enjoyed a seductive currency. Although I think it has a more limited application than do structural models in the context of composition (because it has a less varied and satisfying range of results), it is nevertheless of continuing interest. Its potentially revitalized dimensionality stems now from the availability of computers. They allow one to conveniently extrapolate and sonically model the long-term implications of various generative assumptions. One should also not forget Feldman's suggestive late work. It combines a choice of material and a compositional process which admit the impression of sectional identities without appealing to their formal potential. But his music also moves forward without appealing more than incidentally to the directionality or accretive attributes of processes.

IMPETUS

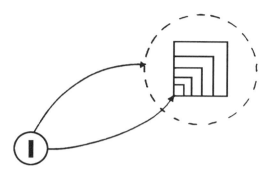

Figure 6

Dimensionality is a measure I associate with intellect, while *depth* I associate with the emotions. They are distinguishable attributes and both are equally desirable (cf. Fig. 7).

The dimensionality of an experience is a function not of how deeply engrossed we may become in the identity of a singular evolutionary trend, but rather of the way in which our listening perspective resituates itself during a performance: at one moment thoroughly *engrossed*, at another *reflective* (what does this remind me of? where am I?), at another *comparative* (is this the material I heard at the beginning?), at yet another *anticipatory* (how long will this continue? where will the music turn next?).

Depth, on the other hand, seems to admit far less of calculation, consideration, comparison. As with any realm of experience, an emotionally gripping musical occasion by nature rivets one's attention. The deeper the emotional engagement, the less one is able to assess one's experience. Though the tenor of an emotion can evolve, perhaps even with astonishing swift-

DIMENSIONALITY　　　　　　　　**DEPTH**

intellect　　　　　　　　　　*emotion*

changing perspective　　　　　**constancy of perspective**

.

.
engrossed　　　　　　　　　　**absorption/**
reflective　　　　　　　　　　**involvement**
comparing
anticipating

.

Figure 7

ness, its presence in any substantial degree is not a matter of the varied and quasi-objective perspectives of the intellect but of empathic submission. It is harder, I think, to consistently manage a creditable depth than to, at least momentarily, engage the intellect.

If the utility of a process itself is to be measured primarily by the degree to which one is able to empathize with it, to submit to its ways, then in order to achieve what I am calling the dimensionalizing effect of multiple perspective as one listens, it would be necessary to combine several distinct processes. But as soon as complementary processes are placed in superposition, the singularity of immersion (and its substantial pleasures) are necessarily disrupted. We find ourselves again veering into the realm of contrast: the alternation of attention and a subsequent variation in the contour of the listening experience which is of an unpredictable nature. This is at the least the world of counterpoint, where the proportionality of redirected attentiveness presses itself forward as a compositional concern. These characteristics bespeak the world of structural models and their identifiable parts, not the quintessence of what I understand as *process*.

At this point, then — while having no intention of dismissing the significance of alternate ideals — I will proceed to treat form as though it were separable from the materials that give it voice and, further, as though it may usefully be thought of in terms of what I have called "structural models".

ATTRIBUTES OF FORM

One can expect to find a number of attributes in the sorts of forms I am addressing. Again, for the sake of convenience, I will where possible separate the objective from the subjective (which is more the province of "coherence" and "depth" as I have defined them earlier). Emphasis on the objective side is intended to characterize aspects of my practice that might be more readily shared, mechanisms that can be more easily adopted, adapted to the requirements of other sensibilities. It is also, not incidentally, the case that there is very little vocabulary, little in the way of established discourse, that would allow the subjective aspects of musical art to be unself-consciously addressed. I would like to see some serious effort exercised in this regard, but will not undertake it here.

From an objective perspective, we may begin to build or to describe a form by identifying its parts or sections. Identity is dependent upon a number of factors, as shown in Figure 8.

At some level, any bounded musical area fulfills these conditions: it possesses length; a certain consistency of procedure (linear, chordal, contrapuntal), some level of harmonic consistency, temporal norms, characteristic sonorous identity, and a physical disposition (enforced by the positioning of the musicians or more flexibly established through the generalized projection of sounds from loudspeakers).

Note that my list of relevant factors is directed at organizational domains themselves, not at the idiosyncratic ways the composer may decide to use them. It is also worth emphasizing that "sections" may be thought of almost entirely from the building perspective, have significance as a means of organizing the composer's work without his requiring them to be heard. "Sections" in this sense help describe not the experience of hearing the work but rather that of creating it. The term "section" suggests a bounded, delimited circumstance, and this is surely inadequate. Without elaboration, I will observe that the inverse notion of a "domain", which describes a locus of characteristics that is strong at its center and gradually loses cohesive force as it radiates outwards, might be just as useful as a discussion point.

IDENTITY (in design)

of sections/parts . . .   **/ domains**

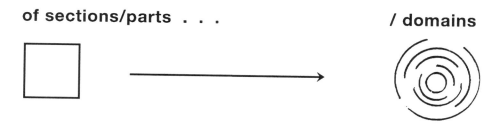

duration
texture
pitch vocabulary + harmonic conventions
tempo (speed) + rhythmic vocabulary
density profile
timbre
spatial character

Figure 8

What I will, for convenience, continue to call sections are related not only by proportion (however the identity of proportion is established) but by their numerousness in relation to the scale of the overall form. A form articulated by a rather large number of smaller subsections will place a differing weight on their pattern of relationships than will one whose identity is dependent on a few larger subsections (cf. Fig. 9).

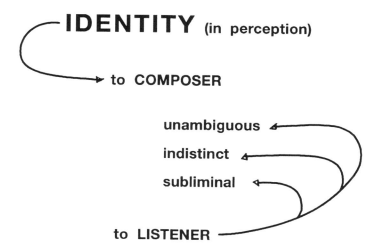

IDENTITY (in perception)

to COMPOSER

unambiguous

indistinct

subliminal

to LISTENER

Figure 9

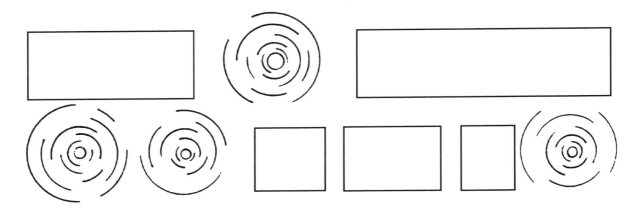

Figure 10

The *palpability* of these sections and other formative factors is also, of course, variable:

   a section can be unambiguous, virtually self-evident;
   it may be suspected but remain indistinct and/or uncertain;
   it may function only subliminally.

(In mentioning palpability here, I am *not* addressing matters of interpretation, but rather perceptual thresholds. I am addressing not how a section is understood in relation to the whole, but whether and how accurately and vividly its existence is detected.)

If a musical form is comprised of several coexistent layers of material, each with its independent sections, weakness of boundary definition and hence of the identity of sections may occur not only because there is too subtle a level of differentiation, but because events in one layer obscure or otherwise disrupt one's ability to register the sectional design of another. Such interference is, of course, far less likely in more straightforward narrative successions, but they are, in turn, less dimensional. Consider how many-faceted the relationships suggested by the arrangement of sections and domains in Figure 10 could become.

It is important to bear in mind that there is a place in the experience, and therefore in the consideration of form, for both the clear and also for the elusive. Almost at the same moment that a work insists on the primacy of one point, it may be surreptitiously whispering the contrary. On a less conspiratorial note, there is also something — a good deal in fact — to be said for the position that the most intimately absorbing effects are produced by organizational factors that *may not be consciously registered* by the listener. One thinks in this connection of religious and mythic dimensions which do not at all fail in their impact as a result of imprecision or allowance for ambiguity.

Aesthetic consistency is always a function for me of the presence of constraints but equally — if the consistency is to be aesthetically effective — of the subtle adjustment, the modification of these limiting conditions in application: what I have called the practice of "sensitive adjustment within a world of constraint".[2]

I don't believe that music which is strictly bound to procedure is likely to have admirable dimensionality, nor do I believe that effective form can be reliably achieved by submission to formula, however subtle and refined. There is in my experience no music that derives its merit and certainly even less its emotional persuasiveness from strict adherence to rule, whether that rule is philosophical, stylistic or procedural. The function of guiding principles, of *whatever* aspect, is to enforce a norm, to provide a scaffolding for integrity and a climate for coherence. The playing out of these norms is optimized not by total submission but by inspired inflection.

In beginning to discuss form, I spoke of its essence being found in "the identity of parts, their positions and relationships to one another". Now, whether one speaks of "part" or "section" or "passage" or "domain" or in some other way characterizes a particular portion of a whole that is less than that whole, is a matter of taste. I do not assert that these smaller-than-the-whole domains should have any particular description, rather that, unless they are somehow characterized, they cannot be reasonably said to exist as aspects of perceived form. It is also not *necessarily* the case that one needs to think of what I am calling "sections" as being identified by beginning with their outer boundaries and working inwards. As noted above, I would be interested in discussing "sections" as domains, fields of conformity or influence that radiate outward from some center. Still, there are economies in speaking of a whole as being composed of parts.

That there will be sections of the whole, and, in all probability, further subsections within them as they are reinterpreted as lower-level wholes, seems likely, indeed, almost certain. I defer here to English psychologist Eric F. Clarke, whose views are often persuasive though sometimes carried to conclusions that might be unpalatable to the dedicated 20th-century composer.

In his article "Levels of structure in the organization of musical time",[3] he notes that, "Despite the considerable antagonisms between different theoretical perspectives, the issue of temporal hierarchization is one on which virtually every current theory is in agreement."[4]

In discussing the perceptual dimensions of temporal structure, Clarke goes on to observe (with a certain unexpected surprise) that, "… our experience [of form] in music does seem to be rather different from that of note-to-note and small group relations."[5] Here by implication he differentiates as I have the local domain of materials and method from the global realm of form. He finds the psychological explanation of this difference in "the distinction between perception and memory." "What divides one from the other", Clarke writes, "is the upper limit of the *perceptual present*".[6]

While "perception can be characterized as experience that is initiated by sensory information which may originate inside or outside the body… The primary characteristic of memory… is that a retrieval process is involved"[7] (cf. Fig. 11).

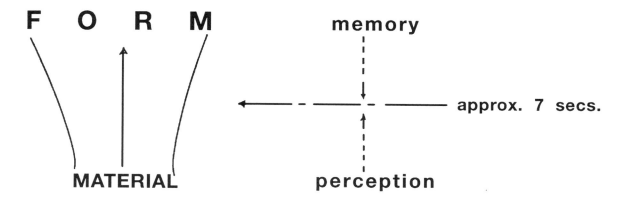

Figure 11

The perceptual present, discussed particularly well by Paul Fraisse[8] and J. A. Michon[9], may be understood as the upward limit of duration for an interval of time in which we are neither distracted by awareness of the past nor — through dissatisfaction (as Fraisse would have it) — with the anticipation of the future: an interval, that is, during which the duration of the present moment stretches on without spontaneous subdivision. This interval is variously estimated to be between 7 and 10 seconds.

This duration, then, is the lower limit for any element that is meant to function formally in my music. It is, of course, probable that any segment of such brief extent is itself a part of a larger subdivision within an overall form, though not necessarily so.

The awareness of form operates not at the level of precision, but as an evaluative, a comparative process that draws necessarily on memory (and potentially on anticipation as well). Proportion, thus, matters as it describes general or potential relationships of weight and succession, not in terms of precise and complex ratios or of durational measurements of unrealistically explicit resolution.

What characteristics then define the section as a function of the elementary fact that they occupy or characterize its duration? I have made some informal suggestions above. Stephen McAdams refers to such attributes in his article "Psychological constraints on form-bearing dimensions in music".[10] He addresses "the form-bearing *capacity* of the perceptual dimensions that are used in music" by proposing that, "A dimension can bear form if configurations of values along it can be encoded, organized, recognized, and compared with other such configurations."[11]

But not all musical characteristics have equivalent utility. This, McAdams continues, "depends on some additional factors. A dimension that affords a greater number of perceivable configurations is more valuable to a composer than a dimension along which only a small number is possible."[12] (He compares the dimensions of vibrato rate and spatial location unfavorably with those of pitch and duration.)

Finally, McAdams writes that, "a potentially form-bearing dimension should be closely correlated with the sensory dimensions that affect perceptual grouping, whether it be of a simultaneous, sequential or segmentational nature. Current research indicates that the dimensions of timbral brightness, pitch, duration, dynamics, and spatial location have this capacity."[13]

I draw your attention to the fact that, in effect, what McAdams argues for here, is the same sort of accountability and integrity that I am espousing. Though it might seem unnecessary to labor the point that a composer would do well to spend his time on the dimensions of music which it is possible to hear, and subsequently to comprehend and remember, the fact is that they do not always do so. (Occasionally germane as well is the observation that a composer may be combining materials, methods, and formal schemes in fundamentally self-contradictory fashion. Orderly ways in themselves do not assure completeness in the pattern of objective relationships that a composition offers to a listener.)

Since the process of devising effective form cannot proceed on entirely objective grounds, I at this point admit a second array of factors meriting consideration, even though they are *far* harder to forge into a logical succession, and even though nothing so convenient as "temporal hierarchy" or "form-bearing dimensions" can be summoned up in elaborating them. I treat them here rather in the fashion that was formerly used for considerations of *timbre*, as a catch-all category for what remained after what could be conveniently categorized had been.

Surprise and its place relative to the conventionality of expectations

If there is not a well-established continuity as a work unfolds, the listener is not free to give himself to the detail of the argument (however the composer has conceived it). Surprising turns are essential to deepening engagement — to eliciting wonder — but must not themselves be the seeds of a conflicting conventionality of dissociation.

The plausibility of succession

Whether the chronology of subsections is or is not related to some, however metaphorical, thread of narrative, the listener must not too often resist the passage from one section to the next as implausible. If he does, the form fragments and its coherence is damaged.

The frequency and degree of contrast

Like the preceding points, this is a general criterion, applicable at all levels from the details of a phrase to major sections of the whole. The iconoclastic critic Peter Yates once commented in the 70's that my forms were like seal-skins: no edges, too few corners. One needs always to be aware of and to be enlarging the range of excursion in balancing continuity and change. This leads, in turn, to...

the balance between transformation and invariance

What has already been heard returns, but in different guise, rendered fresh, but not tilting over too far in the process towards something that strikes the listener as essentially foreign. The remembered model, the link to an earlier experience is essential to formal impact, and, in this regard,...

the degree of tolerable transformation...

is also affected by the "distance" — measured in time and also as a function of distraction — between subsections that are meant to be heard as related. Invariance is a measure of the degree to which the identity of something is maintained as it undergoes transformation, but comparisons are made in contexts of differing cohesiveness.

Landmarks and their memorability

Not necessarily relatable to sectional identity, these are moments that occur in startling relief from their surroundings, moments which may be *apparently* incongruous, and which stick in the mind... are anticipated in later hearings, perhaps, without being fully comprehended. We find our way in new or complex terrain in part by means of "landmarks" (cf., for example, Kevin Lynch's *The Image of the City*[14]).

* A source of proportional integrity
* More than one set/series of proportions superimposed
* "Core" thematic elements are composed as, in effect, intermediate-level materials:

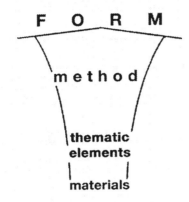

* Proportional sections populated by derivations from thematic sections
* Direct manifestation of models
* Bias towards nested, hierarchic formal relationships

Figure 12

FORMAL STRATEGIES

Now that some remarks about form and its attributes (those more and also less objectifiable) have been laid out, I will outline the practical considerations that have become primary for me (cf. Fig. 12). Of course, these do not constitute a formal agenda. They are, rather, the factors that are, for the moment, likely to arise as I carry through the process of actualizing the formal plan for a new composition. I mention eight concerns, though there may be others in any given work. A parallel survey at some different time in my life would almost certainly contain a different collection.

A source of proportional coherence is required

If one accepts sectional design and identity as useful concerns, the next question is how their durations should relate. To what standard might one appeal for plausible guidance in this matter? I determined in the early 70's that, since the human nervous system is attuned to change, I would adopt progressively expanding norms (e.g., the Fibonacci series 1, 1, 2, 3, 5, 8, 13, 21,...) in devising formal relationships. Several categories of such series have been useful.

Logarithmic series

I have employed logarithmic proportions as a basis for determining section lengths for more than twenty years now, and most frequently array them in sequence. Using such proportions in this most formal and straightforward way, I have normally applied the following constraints:

A series of numbers is established by laying a straight line across a sheet of semi-log graph paper. Such sheets are logarithmic along their vertical axis and linear along the horizontal one, thus it is possible to obtain a logarithmic series of numbers by reading the vertical Y-values at equidistant steps along the X-axis. A logarithmic series grows (or diminishes) in a non-linear way, thereby approximating, metaphorically, the effect of a musical ritard or acceleration.

The series, once determined, is used sequentially. The successive repetition of values is minimized since repetition suggests a static condition. As indicated above, I have come, rather, to feel that trended change is a more natural and engaging address to the perceptual system than constancy.

No permutation of order is allowed (that is to say, non-contiguous successions are avoided) for this could create the impression of arbitrariness, rather than necessary, coherent trends of growth or diminution.

Evidently, all forms devised according to these criteria tend towards accordion-like connectivity, and carry with them a sense of dynamic inevitability: in fact, no impression of sectional disruption is *possible* from this proportional perspective. One essentially trades off the advantages of directness against constraints upon formal novelty.

I have utilized logarithmic series of varying extent: brief successions (with as few as four terms), and longer ones (thirteen or more). Since they can be used recursively, reading forwards and backwards continuously, in part or in total, a fairly small series still allows for considerable flexibility. It is also important to note that changes in the slope of the lines drawn on semi-log paper will radically affect the *degree of difference* between successive terms. All of this will be demonstrated when we begin to examine specific examples.

It can be noted, in passing, that it is problematic to use numerical magnitudes that vary too widely in describing the domain of local rhythm — values effecting the organization of time *in the perceptual realm*. I will return to this subject in the following essay on method.

Other sources of proportional coherence

Whatever plausibility there is in adopting continuously expanding and contracting proportions as a formal reference, other norms will also have their own impact, and should be considered.

In several works, I have derived proportion from measurements of average durations for spoken phonemes. In *The Emperor of Ice Cream* (1961–62) for eight singers, piano, percussion, and contrabass, I utilized a table of average phonemic timings and applied them to a Wallace Stevens poem, calculating the predicted durations for words, phrases, and stanzas, and then translating them directly into formal proportions by multiplying the predicted timings by some constant factor to augment them consistently. In another instance, *Shadowed Narrative* (1977–1982) for violin, clarinet, piano, and cello, I carefully rehearsed readings of a García Márquez text and used the timings from several recordings of it as the formal determinants of phrase and sectional lengths. The hope in these instances was that there would be, inherent in the manifestation of language as speech, some elemental bond between content and appropriate duration, whether objectively considered (as with *Emperor*) or dramatically realized (as with *Shadowed Narrative*) so that interpretive factors modulated the pattern of more objective proportions.

Recent explorations of *chaos theory*, in particular the character of attractors (which is both centered and yet unexpected), provide an intriguing realm of behaviors that range between periods of strictly constrained, and others of virtually unlimited, differentiation. Accessing chaotic or other relatively indeterminate behaviors as a reference involves, however, a logical irritant: while, in theory, the appeal to a (variously) unpredictable source is intriguing, I have found that one needs to listen long and hard to find a particular sequence of values that is *varied in an interesting way*. In other words, randomness in itself is essentially gray, and one should, I think, resist giving the essentially arbitrary the role of arbiter.

I have utilized cross-sectional samplings of the Hénon attractor to derive a set of numbers which have an explicit, mathematically demonstrable origin yet give rise to proportional relationships that are not evidently *nested* — as can be the case with those that are logarithmic — and are, in addition, *apparently eccentric*. The attraction of the non-multiplicative organization of dimensions is that values will not be related to a common factor (as, for example, the conventional 4-bar unit is implicated in its 8-, 16-, and 32-bar extensions). A significant further advantage of "chaos-derived" proportions is that they can give rise to radical discontinuities in the lengths of successive sections. Here is a procedure which is objectively grounded, but circumvents the smooth variation of sectional length that is implied by the logarithmic conventions outlined above.

There are unexpectedly wide variations in sectional length, but they have a basis, an origin that might carry some as yet unobjectified significance. (There is a shadow of the impetus notion here.) More to the point, the geometry of, for example, the Hénon attractor allows families of similar but not identical proportional irregularity (cf. discussion of *Dionysus* and then *Odyssey* below, Exs. 6–12).

Normally, more than one series of sectional proportions is simultaneously in effect in a musical structure.

The bias in my use of proportions is towards the assumption that *change is the norm*. This is, in turn, based upon the physiological fact that the human nervous system is attuned to change, that, indeed, the nervous system soon becomes indifferent to any constant input. Beginning with *Again* (1970–74) for pairs of flutes, sopranos, percussionists, trombones, and contrabasses with 4-channel tape, I determined to embrace irregularity as the norm, sectional or iterative regularity serving as an occasional contrasting, an inflectional, device of limited scope. Regular reiteration, that is, took on in my music the inflective role that changing speed (rit., accel.) traditionally has in Western music.

At the same time, it also became clear to me that the traditional assumption that music should manifest a unitary continuity, one narrative at a time, however elaborately instantiated, was also at odds with the experience of daily life, where several more or less independent streams of events coexist sometimes in stirring fashion (the weather, the passage of the day into night, transport from one place to another, movement from public to private contexts, anticipation of a dreaded encounter or the savoring of an unexpected pleasure). As a result of this observation, I have tended to resist dependence upon mono-dimensional musical textures. I have focused more upon formal schemes that include a detectable interaction between coexistent layers of activity. *I have tended, in other words, to value contrapuntal norms both on the local and also at the formal level:* in my music there will normally be more than one thread or aspect of an overall argument proceeding at the same time, and the formal plan will foresee the pattern of this coordinated evolution.

If one is going to entertain more than one independent stream of events at a time, the completeness and continuity — the nature of the self sufficiency — of each becomes a major concern, as I have observed before with regard to sectional definition. If coexistent streams are too vigorous, never giving way to one another, the result can be an impenetrable cacophony. If a stream is lacking in self-definition or assertiveness, it loses its independence, merging with a stronger continuity in a subsidiary role.

Several layers of (potentially) self-sufficient musical materials may be used simultaneously to conjure up a multileveled experience (e.g., *Archipelago* for 32 instruments and 8-channel tape, *Transfigured Wind II* for solo flute, orchestra, and quadraphonic computer processed sound, etc.).[15] Ives probably provides the best known precedent for this, in *Three Places in New England*, or in the second movement of the *Fourth Symphony*. These works contain, in parts, not only a montage of independent thematic elements, but fully realized yet separable musics in exhilarating or evocative simultaneity. An added feature in Ives' case is the contextual identity that his layers, or independent musical streams, bring with them: the church, the picnic or parade...

Using a multilayered compositional approach, several processes (e.g., differing algorithmic extrapolations of thematic elements) can interpenetrate one another, and still be formed into a resultant continuity having more the quality of kaleidoscopic reformulation than that of a braided rope or a Burgess Shale (e.g., *Variation* for piano, *Autumn Island* (1986) for marimba, *Coconino... a shattered landscape* (1985; revised 1993) for string quartet, or *The Behavior of Mirrors* for solo guitar).[16]

In my work, this situation arises, for example, when several algorithmically extrapolated layers are generated and superimposed upon one another to create a new field of potential. The composer, having woven (in a relatively autonomous fashion) a tapestry of opportunity, then mediates between alternative possibilities, resolving conflicts and forming a viable, coherent, overall pathway that is responsive to several independent arguments. This will be illustrated in later examples (particularly in the case of *The Behavior of Mirrors*, Exs. 4 and 5).

"Core" thematic elements are composed for each specific occasion.

These elements must serve not only an immediate expressive function, but assert an identity that will respond well to the transformational procedures that the larger design of the piece requires of them. Each potential section in the overall plan is evaluated *vis-à-vis* its anticipated function in the context of the whole. Each large stratum must have an expressive logic.[17]

"Core" elements are composed according to strict methodological standards, whatever this may mean in a given piece. Their rigor is particularly important because of the fact that they serve — at least in my case — as the reservoirs of orderliness for the work as a whole. The algorithmic procedures that I use often disturb temporal proportion and succession radically. Overall consistency in the composition, then, requires that each derived fragment of the original whole, wherever it is found, should itself be a reliable product of the underlying orthodoxies (and, hence, bound effectively to their formative influence).

Let us consider a more specific perspective. If a transformational algorithm shuffles segments of an original thematic element such that portions of the end are mapped onto portions of the beginning, one must have foreseen whether the resulting composite needs to be homogeneous or heterogeneous in character in order to best serve the purposes of the larger form. There may, then, be *second order* as well as primary functions for any core thematic element. Anticipatory decisions are made in preparation for the later application of optimal transformational strategies.

Formal designs are filled out by derived variants of the core themes.

These derived forms (or *variants*) can serve primary functions — introductory, thematic, cadential — or some other, secondary roles — transitional, contrasting, accompanimental — and can come about as a result of a wide variety of procedures, some non-traditional in concept and requiring the utilization of new technologies. In any case, these derived materials populate the proportional sections of the overall form.

Recomposition can alter the weight of organizational dimensions (by changes in dynamics, transposition, articulation, with retrogrades, inversions, permutation...) or modify expressive character without altering scale. Shortly, in reference to *Archipelago*, I will discuss the categories "nascent" (variants that precede a "core" statement) and "heightened" (for those that follow it). In the formal conception of *Personae* (cf. page 34), what was in earlier works thought of as a continuum of statements and their responses became an interactive dialogue in which elements sometimes overlap and at others are separated in time, either following or preceding their referents.

Extension can be accomplished compositionally, by hand, using straightforward or variable augmentation of given durational values. In a more perceptually revealing fashion, it can be brought about with a computer by phase vocoder analysis and resynthesis techniques, wherein the dynamic nature of even brief transitional states (the movement from one finger position on the cello A-string to another remote one) are revealed for our empathic appreciation.

The *algorithmic derivation* of new and normally longer sections will be treated in the second Essay on method. These new sections can be characterized according to the needs of the form by the adjustment of the algorithm's parameters. They become, as a result, more or less dense, weighted centrally or at the edges, and so on (preliminary to a full discussion in the second Essay, see the comments below regarding Ex. 4).

Reorchestration or, through computation, *analysis* and *resynthesis* can be employed to alter the timbral dimension of a thematic element with minimal impact on its other dimensions.

Spatial "orchestration" can alter a core element solely with regard to successive positions in acoustical space (note to note, phrase by phrase...) or by the illusion of continuous movement trajectories.

Direct *manifestation* can also be a goal.

Here, function within a form is asserted not by thematic directness nor by what amounts to musical variation, but phenomenologically: a section is characterized by certain novel and obsessively dwelt-upon methodological or textural norm. A dominant facet of some model is played out in some directly persuasive fashion. The idea of direct manifestation appeals both to the notion of the impetus and to what was called earlier the process basis for form. A defining aspect of an impetus is, in effect, translated directly into sound, and since the behavior itself is the subject, the immersion, the empathic surrender which I identified with process is implicated.

There is a bias towards hierarchic and nested relationships.

While the assumption under which I worked for many years was that the various hierarchic levels of an overall structure should share a common proportional character, this is not necessarily the case, and it now interests me to assume that hierarchy may still be influential without being rigorous. (Because, let us say, the large-scale sections of a work were in the relation of 3:2:5, it does not necessarily follow that the 5 subdivides into smaller parallel units of 1.5, 1, 2.5.) The numerical absolutism of the 50's produced examples of rote architectonicisms which were as much in need of consideration from an experiential perspective as are the more recently spawned self-similar sirens of Benoit Mandelbrot. The quixotic search for imperatives that will somehow relieve the creative process of unseemly effort while insuring elegant and dimensional results is not unique to our time, of course. For me, some level of normative proportionality continues to seem useful.

The same proportional series of numbers that guides sectional dimension may also influence local temporal and even rhythmic character, and more on this will follow, as I have indicated. But, although the numerical range necessary for guiding the shape of a whole work can be rather wide — including the setting of sectional dimension both by small and rather large values — consistency and a more intimate level of proportionality for rhythmic detail and local phrase length is important to "flow". And this quality is better achieved by a limited set of integers that do not vary widely in magnitude. My procedure is to examine number series or collections that apply at the structural level and then to reduce them to some manageable yet diverse collection with, perhaps five to seven members. This derived number set is then used to generate rhythmic detail. The local and the global are in a general sense proportionally compatible, then, though they are not strictly hierarchic. The connection between them is managed with an appropriate pragmatism.

In some cases (e.g., *Transfigured Wind II* and *Personae*), the reflexive dimensionality of hierarchic parallels, of the sense of self-similarity at differing formal levels, seems appropriate and is explored. This will be illustrated, but here it is sufficient to say that there is normally a flexible relationship between parallel positions (among replicated sectional proportionalities at different hierarchical levels), whether with regard to the identity of the material that reappears at parallel places from level to level or their expressive or functional character. Sometimes direct connections are usefully made, while at others such routine parallelism would congest or burden the form.

I am convinced that return, that the experience of familiar material reappearing, is a critical element in effective form that cannot be discarded without unacceptable loss. But it seems equally true that *the routine resorting to identical or nearly identical repetition* is a vestige of earlier times and their simpler realities. It is not trivial, of course, to determine what degree of alteration may be introduced in the restatement of a musical idea without sacrificing the identity that the experience of return requires. This is, formally, a criterion of psychological *invariance*, an area needing careful study.

Sections of the whole form with identical durations are treated as privileged.

However it may happen to occur — often as an unforeseen result of particular numerical procedures — when sections of the overall form have identical lengths, they may be given closely related, even identical content. One should not look askance at the many potential gifts that arise from orderly behaviors, yet one must also remember that there is no obligation to accept an invitation just because it is extended. This sort of occurrence, an apparent result of happenstance rather than of the routine pursuit of accepted conditions, is related to what I called before the role of surprise or landmarks in form: It is an opportunity to perhaps startlingly inflect the prevailing probabilities. It can also act rather as a pivot chord might in modulation, leading one unexpectedly from one hierarchic level to another.

Finally — perhaps most significantly — the character of the form must appropriately reflect the composer's intent.

Whether the composer is reaching for a primarily expressive, conceptual or combined effect, the aggregate impression left by the strategies he uses must nourish his ends. Naturally, such a judgment is based both on what the mind grasps and also what is *felt* where conscious thought cannot securely venture, that is, on the composite criterion of dimensionality and depth. All the above practical strategies with regard to composing structure reflect the ways in which the preceding more general attitudes about form were being projected in the music I produced during recent years. Some will doubtless remain compelling for me whereas others will be replaced by new criteria.

EXAMPLES FROM MY WORK

In the following pages, we will move to a more explicit level of consideration. From higher-level concerns, and pragmatic positions on the basis of which I can act consistently while composing, I come now to a number of particular instances. As will be seen, they are not strictly parallel. Rather, the emphasis shifts, the perspective alters with the project depending on its goals.

Archipelago (1982–83) for 32 instruments and 8-channel computer processed sound.

This work, written at Ircam in Paris, served as an occasion for me to rethink attitudes, ways of working that had become habitual: in particular, form and the fashion in which variation techniques could serve formal purposes.

I had been using logarithmic proportions since the early 70's so that a sense of convergence upon or expanding out from key points in the overall form could be asserted. In *Archipelago*, this approach was extended to a maximum of complexity, for there are fifteen independent, converging or expanding layers. Not all of these are in effect throughout the entire work, though during the 22nd minute, for example, twelve separate series are in play (cf. Ex. 3c).

The form of *Archipelago* is treated in some detail in a monograph entitled *A Searcher's Path: A Composer's Ways*.[18] I will not try to summarize that discussion here, but rather focus on several points.

Variation form has traditionally included among its assumptions the following:

the theme to be varied occurs at the beginning of the series of variants,
the variants follow upon one another directly,
only one theme is treated at one time.

In *Archipelago*, these and other assumptions are suspended. Treating a thematic element, a "core", as the essential model to which variants refer, I have placed it sometimes at the beginning of the related collection, but at other times in the middle, or even at the end of a series. Such a "core theme" is a complete texture, not only a motive or thematic unit, and, in *Archipelago*, ranges between 18 (Solos) and 42 seconds (Quintet) in duration.

Those variants[19] that precede the core are thought of as "nascent", as embodying some significant aspect of the actual core, but at a rudimentary level of realization. Those which follow the core are in some sense "heightened", and here an effort is made to intensify in an explicit, phenomenological way some aspect of the core. The former class of variants then will tend to be inarticulate, inferential, and vague, the latter detailed, explicit, and extreme or obsessive.

Because the formal aim of *Archipelago* arose from the impetus of the title image, a chain of islands in the sea, I also realized that it was not necessary that the elements of my series be immediately adjacent to one another. They were spaced out in time so that both the length of each variant in a series could tend towards larger or smaller durational values, and also the temporal gaps separating them could be graded in logarithmic proportion.

The separation of variants in a series from one another had two important results. First, there was less direct masking and other sorts of interference by one layer of the whole upon another layer — and in fact the arraying of elements in each series such that the aggregate relationship of all elements at all times was optimized became a contrapuntal task played out at a formal level. It was necessary to fit series with particular numbers of terms (and sets of durations) into a logarithmically defined matrix of possibilities, and this involved a very large number of trials indeed.

Second, the demands on memory — and therefore the degree to which the listening experience dimensionalized the formal (in contrast to the perceptual) aspect of the work — were significantly increased.

Not only did an interval of time intervene from one element in a series to the next, but usually a number of competing variants from other series did as well. Memory has to hold one (or more) evolving series of variants in an arrested state of evolution while becoming acquainted with or revisiting other series.

It was, of course, essential that the identity of each core theme be optimized (which is also to say differentiated) in all the regards listed above: pitch, tempo, rhythm, phrase proportion, texture, instrumentation, dynamics/articulation, embellishment, and space. Let us look at some of the ways in which differentiation was considered and then at the context in which these individual core themes or variants found themselves.

Example 1
Early consideration of theme types in *Archipelago*.

Example 1 is an extract from my compositional notebook in 1981, showing early efforts to consider the types of themes (solo, duo,...). In a sense, this inquiry sought the expressive potential of each core type: the virtuosity and expressiveness of the solo, the cooperative interchange of the duo, and so on. Various other more objective matters were also initially defined: overall duration, number of sections, textural norms, instrumentation.

Example 2 (a–b)
Formalizations of theme types in *Archipelago*.

Example 2 shows the later formalization of the suggestions first broached in the notebook sketch. Here, proportional design (according to logarithmic series), familial likeness, the textural/behavioral parsimony of the entire aggregate of core elements, and so on, were laid out. It should be emphasized that the categorization of textural types and how they were distributed among the thematic elements (shown on the right side of Example 2b) arose not out of any effort to control such matters from a methodological perspective, but rather as a formal imperative for maximal differentiation of materials. Opportunity was created by establishing a framework of norms within which invention would be nourished.

It would not have been practical, I believe, to have attempted a formal design of this sort without the added levels of discrimination and thereby differentiation possible both through computer processing to produce textures and timbres unavailable with strictly instrumental approaches, and also the ability to enhance spatial characterization (which McAdams includes as one of the potentially "form-bearing dimensions" discussed previously on page 14).

Variant series were made distinct from one another in part by sectional definition according to the above list of criteria, by means of basic textural and behavioral types, and also by the number of sectional subdivisions of each: there are five solos each with two sections, four duos with three, three trios with four subsections, two quartets with five, and one quintet with six.

One should keep in mind that, for example, a "solo" is a collection of attitudes as well as opportunities: tending toward flexibility, idiosyncratic behavior, flamboyance, and so on. From this perspective, two or more musicians could — albeit with some difficulty — participate jointly in projecting what was conceived as a "solo". And they do so in *Archipelago*.

Example 3 (a–d)
The overall plan for *Archipelago*.

Referring to the overall *transformational mosaic*, which is the term I have used to describe this form, it can be seen that certain element series (especially Quartet 1, Trio 1, and the Quintet) tend to frame the 32-minute span of the whole while others anchor the central area. Principal among the latter is Duo 2 which occurs first at approximately the 7:30 mark. A fragment of it is reprised as a component of the concluding Quintet some 23 minutes later — although one can see that this was not originally specified in Example 3d. Rather, I decided that the inclusiveness of the Quintet core element in its greatest extension (126 seconds) could accommodate this concluding reprise of the duo's expansive lyricism.

The Duo 2 series came to consist of the core form and five variants for a total of six elements (the other Duo series have only five). The first three representatives of Duo 1 are "nascent" because they precede the fourth which is the core for the series. The last two members are "heightened". The durations of the primary series elements converge:

240, 126, 68, 36, 19,

while their intervening silences expand:

20, 124, 188, 256.

Thus, as the elements become concentrated into their most essential forms, they become, in this instance, more distant from one another in time.

The Behavior of Mirrors (1985) for guitar.

Example 4
The overall plan for *The Behavior of Mirrors*.

This is a concentrated, 6-minute work for solo guitar. Its form is related to that of *Archipelago*, but is far simpler. There are three thematic elements and each is extrapolated into other derived sections algorithmically so as to make up three superimposed layers. Referring to the overall plan: the first thematic element begins the top layer series and has three derived sections; the second ends the lowest layer series (at the 284" mark) and is preceded by four related sections; the third, which defines the middle layer, ends the work and is preceded by three sections. Thus, all sections of the three layers are contiguous within their layers; the top continuity expands from a thematic element while the bottom two converge upon their sources. Evidently, the form of this work is less concerned with extrapolation from the known than with the discovery of wholeness. The listener hears fragments of the second and third core themes in heterogeneous and irregular passages long before encountering them in their integrated, original continuities, in their "core" forms.

In the case of *Archipelago*, the complexity of the formal design and the frequent gaps between variants required concentrated material and careful attention to effectively characterized identity. In *Behavior*, the derived areas of the piece (composites of several layers) are not variants in intention or effect, but rather reservoirs of characteristic detail that contribute to the changing flow of materials which bridge and link the three core thematic sections. Also, the derived composites are presented in unbroken succession so as to emphasize the impression of interpenetration.

The algorithmic processes that generate the derived sections allow control of density, as has been indicated, and in this case, the aim was to produce a field of fragments (though a field that had a particularly characterized profile). The field was not a mosaic of clearly delineated, variant "tiles", as was the case in *Archipelago*, but an optimized world of potential within and from which I could select, eliciting the specifics of the work as a sculptor might find a form he has envisioned in a block of wood. To reinforce the parallel, this sculptor would also respond to unpredicted details in the material as he encountered them: grain, knots, cracks, and so on. Here, the composer mediates between an abundance of potential elements and the actual continuity of the final passage which employs some eligible fragments and omits others. Everything that happens in the piece results from formative processes, but not everything generated as potential survives the mediation process. At this point, then, we are considering sectional identity from the builder's more than from the user's perspective. A listener might well be more aware of something like domains or zones of influence, for, while the composer may choose to emphasize boundaries, he may just as easily ignore them in the pursuit of a subtly emerging trend. *The Behavior of Mirrors* is the only example presented in this essay of the "domain"-oriented use of materials. When discussing method in the second Essay, I will treat *Variation* in detail. It is a more elaborate work which takes a similar "builder" rather than "user-centered" perspective to that discussed here.

Examining the overall plan for *Behavior*, one can see that there is a flux of contributory influence from beginning to end.

The work opens with the theme of the top layer alone.

At the 38" mark, its first derived section follows.

At the 61.5" mark, the first derived section of the lower layer begins, mingling with what is already in process.

These layers are both joined at 161" by the first section derived from the theme that closes the work.

Until the 284th second, the 3 themes interact through the interpenetration of fragments from their derived sections.

At 284 seconds, the second thematic element (ending the lower layer) occurs, temporarily obscuring both other layers.

From 298.5" to 360", the top and middle layer materials continue to interact.

And at the 360" mark, the final thematic element occurs, concluding the piece without incursions from the other layers.

Formally, then, the composite is made up of three strata, each of which is sectionalized. Certain of these sections are clear and dominant (the three themes) while the others are much more elusive to the questing ear. The layers are, in effect, *fields of potential influence*. The compositional process involves the algorithmic derivation of a set of subsections from each theme, their temporal alignment (according to the formal design based on logarithmic proportions), and then a process of selection, of mediation which brings about a new continuity indebted to the fields of influence that are in play at each moment. Example 5 indicates with colored arrows (green = top layer, blue = middle, and orange = lower), the degree to which materials from the fields in play are interleaved and joined.

Example 5

A page from the score for *The Behavior of Mirrors* showing the interweaving of derived fragments from the three core themes.

Without at this stage describing the workings of the algorithmic method that fragments and then elaborates themes into expanded sections, I can say that each derived section has a variable density and coherence as a result of how the source materials (in this case, the themes) are fragmented and reordered: in *Behavior*, the beginning and ending of the derived sections contain, by my precompositional design, strongly contrasting materials while the middle section is more homogeneous. This does, of course, draw some attention, potentially, to those moments in the form that correspond to sectional boundaries. This higher level of characterization is available to the composer but he is not obligated to use the opportunity.

Combining, then, the effects of derivation and layer organization, the overall form reflects the following flux of influences:

a play between heterogeneity and homogeneity of materials,

a play between order (correct sequence of thematic fragments as produced by the algorithm in some situations) and disorder (shuffled sequence as produced in other situations),

a play of fields of potential by section, each with its own character and emphasizing succession and / or superposition depending on layer alignment.

The algorithm is applied in such a way that the resulting fragments may be as evenly arrayed over time as desired or concentrated in certain ways (though this is a function of the durations of both the core element and the derived section). Thus, before the mediating stage, the level of conflict between layers could have been minimized by controlling the overlapping of fragments generated by the algorithm. The compositional goal is the creation of a derived music which is a compound of the component themes, and the listener is not, as in *Archipelago*, faced with a formal task that taxes memory in so formidable a fashion by maintaining multiple, widely separated and independent series of variants. Still, the kaleidoscopic weave of fragments, each potentially carrying with it the evocation of another differently conceived continuity, is itself novel to the mind as well as to the ear.

Although this point will be addressed in the second Essay, I mention in passing here that the methodological approach used in this piece is particularly attractive, allowing response to (often) unanticipated conjunctions of material. As one composes, one finds oneself before a field of choice where — though the variety of influences and the numerousness of elements can be arbitrarily greater or lesser — there exists a reliable consistency and shape to the distribution of possibilities. There is created here a *principled* world, a world within which invention and taste can be exercised with an assurance not totally dissimilar to the sensation that one can imagine a composer might have had in a common practice period.

Dionysus (1990) for chamber ensemble.

From a formal perspective, the signature quality of the converging or expanding trends in sectional proportion is fluidity. While the accumulative and dissipative trends that are projected to the listener by these methods can be satisfying, even compelling, they mitigate against formal surprise in the critical matter of sectional duration. Expanding or concentrating sections are normally prepared for in the sense that previous sections have predicted the current condition. While attracted by such geometric change in defining successions of sections each of which is more than 7 seconds in duration (over the threshold of "the perceptual present" mentioned earlier), I have been dissatisfied with the fact that conservative use of this strategy *precluded* sudden change in sectional duration.

What was needed was a source of authority for more unpredictable, even apparently eccentric behaviors. "Chaotic" phenomena offered such potential: characteristic bifurcation diagrams that reflect the behavior of liquids with increasing levels of turbulence, or in the fluctuation of biological populations, for example.

Example 6

A bifurcation diagram from the realm of chaos theory, showing the change in the value of a non-linear function over rising values of the critical variable.

The general pattern is that as turbulence increases there is — at intuitively unpredictable moments — a sudden "clarification": instead of having an enormous, chaotic range of values, all equally likely, the variable being graphed suddenly has only 2 or 4, 8 or 16 possible values, each specific. Then, as the value plotted (turbulence, for example) continues to increase, there is, also quite unexpectedly, a return to what we normally think of as the incomprehensible prolixity of "chaos". This process is indicated in Example 6. The "self-similarity" feature — wherein local behaviors mimic global ones — can be seen by comparing the right-central rectangle with the expanded version in the box at the lower left. There is an evident familial relationship. Note the unpredictable — the "chaotic" — change in the values along the vertical axis given by this graph: there are 2 at, say, the horizontal axis reading of 2.4; an innumerable range of values at 2.7; but only 3 at the higher reading of 2.83.

I should emphasize, if it is not already evident, that I am not implying (because I do not believe) that the direct translation of physical concepts or their mathematical representation into musical terms holds much promise for most composers. My goal, my interest in such things, is far more limited: *a certain plausibility*, an "acceptable" proposal to which useful aesthetically directed responses can be made. Evidently, anyone can simply sit down and *invent* an eccentric pattern of relationships. Anyone is free to do so. What I have found is this: if one can identify an external source of proportions, a resource that is acceptable, it may carry with it valuable bonuses. In particular, as with an *impetus*, an external authority for proportionality can also harbor a variety of valuable attributes in ways and at levels initially unsuspected. It not only initiates but can continue to guide as composition proceeds.

Thus, in summary, a resource that is found in some external context (musical or otherwise), and felt to be attractive and acceptable, frees one to indulge in the pleasure of submission:

"That's one thing I don't need to think about", one says. But, of course, one has already "thought about it" — if one has made categorical and framing decisions. The point is that one is able to think about different aspects of creation at different stages, not in one, unmanageably congested here and now. Still more important, though, is that pre-compositional decisions of the right sort provide a bridge to aspects of an impetus' home context which one may find useful in unforeseen ways. (Consider an archipelago, mist, an aerial view, the effects of a boat ride, wandering among them so that perspective causes scale and order to permute.) Finally, an accepted resource — whether an impetus, or a proportional consistency, or even a pre-compositional strategy — can reasonably provoke a whole family of responses, that is, a succession of different but related compositions. No behavior, unrehearsed, is likely to be optimal. One needs to do everything important again and again. And again.

Dionysus is an octet for two contrasted quartets of instruments. The impetus in this work was the figure of Dionysus as depicted in Euripides' *The Bacchae*. I was much struck by the implacable polarities at work in this character. God and man; violent and sensual, arrogant and seductive, feminine and masculine. Dionysus is an extraordinarily fecund source of always unresolved conflict. The piece that I wrote, not surprisingly, was conceived in two layers, each itself moving at explicit, gradually changing rates of sectional articulation (occurring often, then rarely, then often again). From an overall perspective, strongly asserted and conflicting layers of chordal sequences are occasionally interrupted by brief islands of ejaculatory thematic behavior. (These, too, are contrasted: the piccolo is intense to the point of hysteria, the trumpet, at first alarmed, becomes brooding and soulful.)

Example 7
An alternative, cross-sectional representation of a bifurcation diagram.

Formally, I utilized what could be thought of as cross-sectional samples from the bifurcation diagram. Referring to Example 6, one can see that, if vertical cross sections were taken (at uneven intervals), moving from left to right, that at first one value (1.9–2.0), then two values (2.0–2.46), and so on, would be determined. In Example 7, cross sections of this sort are displayed successively from top to bottom. They then became the source of quasi-hierarchical subdivisions in the overall form for *Dionysus* which appears in Example 8. One can see that the irregular branchings in this figure result in the successive complications of increasing demarcation, from the simple bipartite subdivision of the top line to the increase in clustered cross hatches on the lower lines. What one can also see is that these sets of proportions — if, as I decided to, one accepts them as related durational successions — are not strictly hierarchical (though hierarchy is, as it were, loosely implied). Very large and small subsections neighbor one another here, and, therefore, the element of surprise, even eccentricity, has been brought into the picture.

Example 8
The overall plan for *Dionysus*.

In specific terms, I devised a plan for the piece that included provision for the long-term exploration of trends (in the "central plains") as well as for brief outcroppings of thematic exposition at beginning and end. The eccentricity of the piece is not confined to sectional proportion, or to the relative paucity of thematic substance, but resides perhaps most of all in the unreasonable relentlessness of the clash of reiterated chords that define the two layers (one low and dark, the other higher and brighter) as their contrasted speeds converge upon one another. The extremity of duration of the central sections is used as an occasion for obsessive behavior, something approaching the *direct manifestation* discussed above. The goal of the convergence at the center is, of course, not resolution — not in the case of *Dionysus* — but a still disruptive ratio of 4 against 5.

The image of duality is served here (at the 467" mark) by the reversal of instrumentation relative to the pitch resource characteristic of the two component layers (indicated by the oblique and horizontal line textures). The pitch aggregates carried by the flute, clarinet, piano, and contrabass are assumed by the trumpet, horn, bass trombone, and marimba, and vice versa. At the same moment, the chordal texture of the first half is suddenly replaced by deconstructed aggregates arrayed successively as ostinato motives expanding in time, leaving trails that reconfigure their interactive harmonic worlds.

Examples 9–10
Pages 27 and 28 from the published score of *Dionysus*.

Logarithmic proportions are still used here as the basis for the proportional subdivision of the two very brief thematic elements. But these numerical relations are derived by approximation from the proportions of the whole (which were, in turn, derived from the bifurcation diagram). They control not only durational relationships but the whole iterative design of the complete work. I will return to this in the Essay on method.

As the second half of *Dionysus* plays itself out, another disruptive element asserts itself in the form of two also clashing, asynchronous sequences of outbursts from the pianist and the percussionist. Though highly animated, they are determinedly non-thematic. My intent in this work is to give "thematic" behavior — one might metaphorically say the operation of lyrical reason — a very special and fragile status in a world of outrageous and unmanageable emotion. The spacing out of these two disruptive sequences is logarithmic, converging just before a cumulative section at the end.

Example 11
Page 37 from the published score of *Dionysus*.

Before moving on to the next Example, I want to refer, in passing, to another representation of chaotic behavior, the Hénon attractor. This is a mathematical simulation of a non-linear process which is not modeled upon a natural phenomenon. In writing a work for Ircam, from 1989–93 (the 75-minute *Odyssey* on Beckett texts), I used selected cross sections from this elegant form to determine a quasi-hierarchical structure that presents a satisfying level of sectional variability. Because of the asymmetrically nested, boomerang-like shapes of this form, its cross sections have family characteristics: several small values, an extremely large one, then another concluding burst of definitions. The changing cross sectional dimensions of this figure taken at different points along a centrally-placed axis suggest further nestings which can complicate without dramatically altering the basic trend.

Example 12
The Hénon attractor shown with cross-sectional proportions.

Symphony[Myths] (1990) for orchestra.

The formal designs presented so far are all, in effect, abstract structures, though informed by idiosyncratic goals or more specifically by an animating impetus. I will now turn to a form that is more explicitly wedded to its subject, that actually attempts the direct *musical manifestation* of a physical model. Here, the impetus is taken so literally that its physical nature and dimensions (as well as the attributes that have, over centuries, been accorded it by observers) come directly into play.

Example 13

A photograph of the Japanese rock formation *Futami ga ura*.

Along the eastern shore of Honshu in Japan, there is a striking rock formation called *Futami ga ura*. One doesn't need to know about Amaterasu (the central goddess of Japan's creation myth) or the practices of the Shinto religion (which is the source of the distinctive geometry of the *torii* gates, one of which is atop the left rock, while another is indicated by the huge ropes that join the two), one needs no interpretative apparatus, in other words, to be struck by the iconic force of this scene.

I did explore, however, the various tales told about the formation, and surmised the following picture:

The two large rocks represent male (left) and female (right) gods, brother and sister, who became separated and have been symbolically, rejoined by the triple-stranded rope that stretches between them.

Between the two monumental rocks is a third, smaller and often hidden beneath the surface of the sea. This is a *kami ishi*, or "spirit rock", in which the essence of the Goddess Amaterasu is thought to reside.

The Japanese formation was central to *Symphony[Myths]*, but something else, not unrelated, had lodged itself in my memory independently, an image from George Herriman's "Krazy Kat" comic strip.

Example 14

George Herriman's drawing of a rock formation, "a pair of Lithic mittens".

The vitality of this image — its antic improbability — cried out for explanation. Eventually I located a reference to the story of the "clashing rocks" (*symplegades*) from the tale of Jason and the Argonauts. This pair of massive formations were fated to crash together periodically, crushing any vessel that attempted to traverse the narrow straight between them. Jason's stratagem was to release a bird which triggered the *symplegades*, and then to slip his ship through as they recoiled. Unable to restrike quickly enough, and having failed to destroy their prey, they were then immobilized.

Example 15

A Greek vase depicting rocks that define a narrow passage.

I began work on the symphony by sketching an initial three-part structure with massive beginning and ending sections joined by a lyrical, linear span which was itself marked in imitation of the ornamental ties distributed along the triple strand of rope. There is also, in the sketch, provision for an intermediate spirit rock. It was clear to me from the outset that the literal impetus of the *Futami ga ura* formation would also serve as the source of the entire symphony's three-movement form: a massive and relatively static first movement, a brief lyrical, intentionally pregnant, central intermezzo, and a clashing multilayered final movement from which arises a superimposed lyrical aspect broached in the intermezzo. The second large movement of the overall form, however, is based on a parallel myth involving two rocks, the *symplegades*. These rocks, incessantly clashing, are finally frozen in separation as a result of Jason's clever strategies. The whole work evolves from a dual impetus, then, the image of one pair of stable rocks seeking union and another pair of clashing rocks that could be thought of as seeking rest.

Example 16
The first sketch of the overall form of *Symphony[Myths]*.

Example 17
A second more refined laying-out of the overall form of *Symphony[Myths]*.

Primarily the first movement concerns us here. The early, casual sketch was formalized little by little, using the now familiar logarithmic proportions as a way of fixing the size of the form's parts. In this case, note that they are *not* in an ordered sequence.

Two of the largest divisions of the series (180 and 118 seconds) were taken as the measure of the first and last major parts of the movement (the male and female rocks) and the remaining 27 elements in the total were arranged so as to delineate sectionally the other aspects of the three-movement form. There will be further discussion in the second Essay of the 29 proportionally related sectional units (cf. Exs. 79–87). What is significant here is the fact that refining the form involves a process of alternating proposal and adjustment. The basic shape of the form is set out in Example 16. Example 18 shows the in-process effort to fit the available proportional units into plausible positions relative to the overall design which becomes gradually more explicit. It is rather like a jigsaw puzzle where a number of pieces are placed into relationships that effectively serve a larger, known picture. My assumption is that the tension generated by this process encourages engagement and speculation in a way that benefits the result.

Example 18
The formalized plan for *Symphony[Myths]* with proportional specifics.

Let me emphasize that the goal in the first movement especially was almost literally *form as manifestation*. I attempted to represent over an interval of time the sense of vital massiveness that these rocks — which I first saw in 1966, almost twenty-five years before the piece was written — impressed upon me. (As an aside, I also had in mind a first attempt at enlarging the sense of "the perceptual present" to an expanse far greater than the accepted 7–10 seconds; this is something I plan to return to in a later composition.)

The rocks were conceived as thirteen-layered ostinati. Their design will be discussed in detail in the next Essay. For now it is sufficient to note, for example, their staggered layers, each of which has a distinctive substructure. The detailed specification of each ostinatic succession made allowance for three differing norms:

an initiatory flourish followed by an ostinatic succession,

an ostinatic alternation broken midway by an energetic staccato patterning and then resumed,

an ostinatic succession ending with a fanfare-like series of rapid, repeated notes.

Example 19
First movement plan for *Symphony[Myths]*.

Example 20
The design of the "female" rock with 13 strata.

Example 21
The design of the "male" rock with 13 strata.

Example 22
A detail of the "male" rock design.

Although the preceding detail regarding the construction of the two rock elements is not relevant in itself to the present discussion of form, I want to draw attention to the fact that it is precisely the level of differentiation between layers, the assertive nature of the figuration within layers, the decisions about and the design of the overall pitch relations within and between layers that admits the possibility that the phenomenon of the section itself can be both form and content. Nothing is stated in a traditional sense, nothing developed, nothing countered or returned to, except that a second, similar large structure occurs at the movement's end. There is for me a quite unique aspect of the formal here: the phenomenalistic masses at either end of the movement, though they do nothing but assert their essence, are substantive, whereas the central section, which is thematic and contrapuntal in a traditional sense, is felt as a transitional, almost incidental, span.[20] The sense of content has been shifted from argument to manifestation.

Transfigured Wind II (1984) for solo flute, orchestra, and quadraphonic computer processed sound.

We return in this instance to the world of *Archipelago* in the sense that the transformational resources of computer processing are important to the dimensionality of the form itself. In 1983, I began work on a series of concerti. In them the basic approach is to generate a solo statement in one or more sections and then to use an instrumental ensemble and the computer in a multilayered structure of response. The solo materials constitute the foundation for the whole, so that instrumental and computer processed responses are directly based upon their pitch and rhythmic vocabulary as well as their spirit and character. It is appropriate to refer first to *Transfigured Wind*, written just after the more complex *Archipelago*, in 1983–84, before subsequently treating *Personae*. This will allow me to establish linkages between the first of the concerto series and its more recent relative. It will also indicate *Transfigured Wind*'s relationship to its forerunner.

Example 23

The initial sketch for the overall form, *Transfigured Wind II.*

In the overall plan for *Transfigured Wind II,* the solo-centered formal perspective is represented by two logarithmically expanding series with four terms each (0.84, 1.39, ... for the solo flute, 1.39, 2.93, ... for the ensemble). In their expanded state, they are simply interleaved. A solo statement from the upper series is followed immediately by an ensemble response from the lower series. The second sketch for this form carries the process further.

Example 24

Second sketch, overall form for *Transfigured Wind II.*

There are still two source series, each logarithmically expanding, and each with four terms, and the expanding character is accentuated — each solo longer than the previous one and each response itself relatively elongated. New layers are also generated here, however, as a result of the fact that each instrumental response (e.g., the first, 1.39 minutes long and beginning at the 0.84-minute mark) is itself subject to a response. There develops a subsurface layer of formal "echoes". The first response generates a series of four echoes of expanding length (2.15, 2.57, 2.8, and 2.93 minutes). The second spawns 3 echoes, the third 2, and the last (which consumes the final 13.16 minutes of the 32-minute whole) has what might be thought of as a single "pre-echo". [The sets of three words in line with the top four rows of boxes (e.g., WARPING, STRATA, SPREAD), indicate proposed transformational processes.]

A primary purpose of the string of examples I have been presenting is to indicate the flexibility of this approach to thinking about form. The scheme for the flute concerto was an extrapolation from the *Archipelago* form: the same 32-minute duration, but a simpler structure of a slightly different nature. Though each of my works is responsive to the approaches and then to the experience of its predecessors, one can introduce rather fundamental new considerations without any radical change in the component steps. The aim is always to generate a musical structure appropriate to the expressive intent, the impetus, the materials and methods of each compositional occasion.

Instead of 15 themes, in *Transfigured Wind* there are 4, but they are extrapolated in a more inferentially intertwined fashion than is the case of *Archipelago.* Here, there is a *responsorial norm* in addition to the basic idea of a theme and its variants. The basic structure is set up so that each solo statement is immediately followed by a response, and that the responses are themselves "echoed" in the form as strings of variants (in order, as John Cage reported regarding the problematic effect of evil in the world, "to thicken the plot").

Again, it should be emphasized that the relevance of computer processing to forms of this multiperspectival nature is that it raises the level of resolution in three of the "form-bearing" dimensions that McAdams lists: duration, timbre and spatialization. Without the perceptual enhancement that computer processing offers, there might well be insufficient differentiation of materials, layers and their sections to make forms of this sort viable. But with these new resources, a level of formal exploration becomes possible wherein multiple, simultaneous yet independent streams of sound can coexist fruitfully. In effect, what has been the province of multiple lines in *local contrapuntal texture* can be extrapolated to multiple musics in a *global contrapuntal form.*

Personae (1990) for solo violin, chamber ensemble, stereophonic or quadraphonic computer processed sound.

Now let us begin a more specific examination of *Personae's* form. In 1990 I completed a third concerto, *Personae*, for violin and chamber ensemble. (The second was *The Dream of the Infinite Rooms* (1986) for solo cello, orchestra, computer processed sound.) The accompanying diagram (Ex. 25) can be explained as follows. The top line describes the evolving structure of the solo materials. An opening statement of 80 seconds duration; a second of 78"; a third which is a symmetric collection of 8 elements, 200" long; and a fourth which covers a span of 530" with four nested statements that can be seen to mimic the large-scale structure that precedes it (both sectional durations and intervening silences). What is emphasized here is *nesting* or *hierarchical reflection*: a proportional structure initiated at one level in the overall form is reflected on a different scale (smaller or larger) in the same or in a different layer.

Example 25
Overall plan for *Personae*.

Returning to the overall *Personae* plan, one can see that the first solo is followed by a 48" ensemble response and that this is, in turn, echoed by a 29" element on tape. The orderliness of this first sequence, however — a solo statement followed immediately by an ensemble response and then one from the computer on tape — does not become the norm. The second solo is overlapped by its computer-derived parallel, while the ensemble response follows the computer's. The disjunction of parallel elements in the three layers increases with the 3rd solo element and converges again with the last, since, evidently, the end of the work at roughly 22 minutes must terminate all three strata.

The fourth solo reprises the form of the whole in a multidimensional accumulation. The material of the opening 80" solo is represented by a 23" element at the 380" mark in the ensemble layer, at the 850" mark in the solo layer by an 18" element, and again at the 1148" mark (also in the solo layer) by an 11" element. Although the tape, or computer section representing that layer's response to the fourth solo statement, begins at the 796th second and extends over 584", it does not follow the nesting trend, but rather takes a more cohesive approach that will be examined in a moment.

Example 26
Derivation of the proportional relationships between *Personae's* three strata.

Example 26 contains material more completely discussed in the second Essay (Exs. 109–110). One can simply note at this stage, the fact that various parallel families of proportions have been laid out, and that adjustments are made in order to space these so that they serve an integrated formal intent.

Before taking the investigation of *Personae's* form further, it is worth summarizing some of its aspects:

There are several related but independent series of formal elements occurring in a *contrapuntal* mosaic form.

The series are conceived of as layers where the primary one is germinal.

The solo violin materials for the first three sections of the solo layer become the materials, as well, for the instrumental response layer, though they are recomposed in their new context. This is true also for the computer processed layer which uses recordings of the solo elements as its sources for processing.

The fourth solo begins in a recapitulatory vein, referring to the three earlier solos (but, of course, their materials appear in a newly recast form that reflects the nature of the Solo IV "persona"). Towards the close of this element, newly composed material extends its spirit and content to end the piece.

I intend the form of *Personae* to operate on a number of levels. No section of the plan is shorter than the 7" upper limit of the "perceptual present", but, at the other extreme, one is just short of nine minutes in length. Such extended sectional duration can only be supported in a contrapuntal form by strong dimensional reinforcement. In this case, the basic material is a composite "line" of sustained violin notes culled from the first solo element. The pitches in this line are differentially augmented by phase vocoding techniques to fit a proportional design for the fourth element of the computer processed layer. The spectral character of phase vocoded expansions as well as their gestural limpidness assert a unique and palpable identity for this element in the form. To further this impression, the results of the analysis aspect of the computer program are parsed so as to separate the odd from the even partials of the individual pitches (which, in their extended form, have become drones). Each double-stranded drone is now further characterized by placing its paired aspects on symmetrically mirrored spatial paths. In particular, for example, if the left loop of one of the four distinct path pairs shown in Examples 27–28 is used to carry the odd partials of a particular tone, then its complementary pair would be used to process the even partials. The result is to literally focus and defocus the physical density of an instrument's sound spectrum.

Example 27
The open path segments for spatialization from *Personae*.

Example 28
The closed path segments from *Personae*.

Example 29
The assignment of spatial paths to drone pitches from *Personae*.

In performance, the solo and instrumental layers can coexist with the computer processed one in ways that are mutually supportive and do not involve competitive perceptual strategies on the part of the listener. Naturally, the composition of the solo and instrumental materials for this final section took into consideration the nature of the computer processed layer, so that the solos emerged as more animated and rhythmically disrupted while the ensemble writing became more slowly evolving and iconic, emphasizing in turn the string, percussive, and wind choirs.

Ideally, the echoing of materials in different timbral and textural worlds and on different temporal scales calls into play perception and memory in newly resonant fashion. Materials might be thought of, and over repeated listening felt as, initiatory statements, memories or premonitions. The tasks emphasized in the case of *Archipelago* are primarily the retention of the identity of multiple core themes in transformed variants that are distanced from their models in time, and also coping with the interference of distracting elements that intervene or overlap. In *Personae*, the task involves less the retention of models and more the registration of hierarchy (solos reflected at some metaphorical remove in the medium of the ensemble and, again, yet more remotely, in that of computer processed sound). It also entails the registration of function in the chronology of the whole form (Is a given element initiatory, recapitulatory, or prefigurative?).

In *Personae*, four roles are posited as the bases for the four solo sections:

The Conjurer
The Dancer
The Meditator
The Advocate

Each is characterized not only by norms of pitch, rhythm, and sectional proportion, but by a "behavioral reference" that shapes the nature of the musical material and its interpretive aims. In this case the original overall impetus — consideration of an individual performer's attitude towards his task, even the recognition of and manifestation of personality traits — proliferated into four local impetus categories. I hoped that the tracking of solo materials from layer to layer or hierarchic stage to hierarchic stage would be facilitated by the idiosyncratic spirit of the materials. The Conjurer's solo is exhibitionistic, rising to various registral high points as the performer attempts to amaze. The Dancer's section involves an athletic traversal of a structure of simultaneous, asymmetric ostinati — the performer pauses from time to time to regather before beginning a newly challenging phrase. The Meditator moves recursively in slow, controlled cycles over a repetitive intervallic field, occasionally indulging in flashes of rising embellishment meant to suggest a flicker of enlightenment. The last, the Advocate, draws together in a final solo all the previous threads in a fervent exhortation that rapidly, unpredictably moves from one kind of presentation to another, including numerous, breathless parenthetical asides. One can observe the ways in which I considered the identities and comparative characteristics of the four personae by referring to Examples 30 and 31. It was through such parallel categorizations — even when they did not, in the end, assume importance — that the foregoing overall picture clarified itself.

Example 30
Exploration of the four basic personae.

Example 31
Categorizing the personae.

The long final section was ordained to be sporadic in its rapidly changing references by the nature of the plan, and it seemed important, therefore, to alter the basic nature of its tape-layer response so as to promote continuity and closure, not to further the proliferation of fragmenting references. Examining the formal plan of *Personae*'s final minutes, one can see the interaction of all three layers and the role that the more than 9-minute long continuity of computer processed drones should have in solidifying the close of the work.[21]

Personae is neither the longest nor the most complex formal organization I have attempted using instruments and digital sound, but it is the most multidimensional. The notion of referring to personality or behavioral types as sources of identity which could supplement and modulate the objective form-bearing dimensions allowed, I found, a more reverberant sectional characterization. The domains associated with the four source solos are more consistently and persuasively argued than would be likely if one were thinking primarily in objectively musical dimensions. (More than, for example, the characterizations, in *Archipelago*, of Solo, Duo, etc.)

Ariadne's Thread (1994) for string quartet, stereophonic or quadraphonic computer generated sound.

During the period 1991–94, I was engaged in writing two large-scale works, both intended to set, to respond to, powerful texts: *Odyssey*, on bilingual writings of Samuel Beckett, and *last things, I think, to think about*, utilizing writings of John Ashbery. Just as I had been attempting to gain more variability of section design by accessing sources of proportional coherence that were less predictably smooth than logarithmic proportions, I also felt a need for a more complex, a less reasoned field of stimulation while composing. This tendency had been fore-shadowed in the dual center of *Symphony[Myths]*, as well as in the four subclasses of impetus at work in the conception of *Personae*.

When working closely with other strong-minded artists or their materials, one inevitably encounters elements of the work which — while effective, self-consistent and, intuitively, admirable — simply do not make sense. At least, one cannot immediately grasp their justi-fication. At such moments of genial perplexity — if one is not to simply evade the issue — one has to make a leap, *to accept what occurs within one*, however incompletely it may seem to have been acquired, however incomplete the security of the intellect.

Against the background of decades of working in the ways I have been discussing, and having written dozens of compositions with them, it occurred to me that it might now be possible, in a sense, to "compose" an impetus. A good text provides a deep and dimensional resource of specific relationships and evanescent allusions. My new thought was that, in the case of purely instrumental work, a composite impetus might generate a similar rich climate. *Ariadne's Thread* is the first work in which I explored this possibility. Here is a brief listing of three contributing factors and their practical correlates:

The phenomenon of line

The thread which Ariadne uses in the myth to assure Theseus of escape from the labyrinth after battling the Minotaur. This provided the argument for the unbroken line of the composition.

The linear, *graphic input to the UPIC synthesis environment*[22] that guides both wave shaping and the evolution of textures over time. The conception of all textures and the design of pitch materials throughout the work were linearly based.

The use of *line in drawings* by a set of five great draughtsmen: Rembrandt, Klee, Matisse, Pollock, and Johns. These were used as graphic stimulants, as notation to elicit from the members of the Arditti Quartet, characteristic sound materials. And these, in turn, guided the computer synthesis. They also suggested, in a more inclusive sense, categories of musical texture.

The labyrinth

The metaphoric trail into and out of the maze which was designated by the thread also involved, necessarily, the retracing of steps. A *primary pitch line* was devised and then replicated, in retrograde; nested in this line were iterated motives (and their retrogrades) suggesting the retracings involved in searching for the way.

The *mirroring in the temporal proportions* of the form's sections of mounting *apprehension* about arriving at the center and of gradually increasing *expansiveness* (and hope) upon passing outwards again.

The *manifesting* of the *labyrinth*'s massive, intransigent *physicality*. A regular temporal unit was established that controlled both the spacing in time and the duration of very assertive blocks of computer synthesized sound. These sometimes join with but also often *intrude into* the linear continuity of the form.

The myth

Its numbers: the sacrifice of seven youths and seven maidens; a 9-year cycle of such tributes to the Minotaur; two maidens secretly replaced by youths; Theseus intervening in the horrific pattern of sacrifices on its third cycle: hence the number collection 9, 7, 5, 3, 2.

The concept of surreptitious and daring substitution which recurs in the myth.

The character of and mythic relationships between the four primary players: Theseus, Ariadne, the Minotaur, Dionysus.

The overall plan for the structure of *Ariadne's Thread* can be seen in Example 32. It has three aspects: the lowest line of subdivided boxes describes the seven primary sections of ensemble music, the central set of four boxes establishes the shape of individual solos, and an upper series of seven spread out boxes specifies the appearances of computer generated sound. Each aspect has a distinctive temporal nature. The lowest is defined by a logarithmic series irregularly ordered and similarly subdivided; it shapes the dramatic flow of the primary line which — in general — compresses as it approaches the 56-second fourth section (defined by the computer and metaphorically signifying the central labyrinth) and then expands outwards from it. Example 33 shows the origins of the closing in and opening out proportions of the piece.

Example 32 (a–b)
The overall plan of *Ariadne's Thread* showing the structure of interaction between the thread, the characters, the labyrinth.

Example 33
The logarithmic proportions utilized in formalizing the overall plan of *Ariadne's Thread*.

Each of the central line of boxes, offset to clarify the identity of the pre-labyrinth pair (violin II and cello) and also the post-pair (viola and violin I), has seven sections. These compress according to logarithmic proportions. Notice that they are — as true independent solos should be — idiosyncratic in their temporal alignment with the primary sections below. At the top of the page, there is what might be thought of as a $4 \times 7 = 28$-second "clock" pulse — a clock that, not surprisingly, beats 28 times. It controls the occurrences of periodic intrusions from the tape and also assertive flourishes, outbursts of energy from the soloists. There is, evidently, a more heterogeneous character to this formal design in keeping with the less-focused dimensionality of the multiple impetus. As indicated in the discussion of *Ariadne*'s composite impetus, line is active at many levels here. A Jasper Johns drawing (Ex. 34) was one of seven I used as sources. Example 35 gives the component element which I extracted while the following one analyzes its potential.

Example 34
A drawing by Jasper Johns.

Example 35
One graphic element from the Johns drawing as used as a notational stimulus in *Ariadne's Thread*.

Example 36
An analysis of the element in Example 35 and its possible uses.

The Johns drawing might be thought of as a loose structure of cross-hatching, and, in attempting to manifest its energies, I schematicized it while adapting it to a musically realizable form. Example 37 shows a formalization of the adapted texture, while Example 38 carries the parallel families of lines into the realm of explicit frequencies (determined on the basis of originating and terminating harmonies). The pitch structures of Example 38 were precisely reproduced in the UPIC domain (which allows the user to enter frequency values numerically).

Example 37
Sketch for a textural parallel to the Johns drawing in Example 34.

Example 38
Pitch specifications for the relative-pitch textural design in Example 37.

In order to achieve component glissandi that were more sonically satisfying, the UPIC user must retrace repeatedly so that each basic line becomes a variable weave of lines bundled together. Example 39 shows the overall graphic effect of the input that the UPIC System received to define its synthesis. Note that I added the boxes to indicate where the live string quartet was to be substituted for computer sound, and they are, of course, not on UPIC's graphic specification. One can see the braided lines better in the detail of Example 40.

Example 39
The linear modeling of the Johns drawing represented as patterns of heavily retraced linear elements input to the UPIC System.

Example 40
A detail from the UPIC specification for *Ariadne's Thread*.

Example 41 reflects the ways in which other linear sources than the Johns were characterized, contributing in their own ways to the shaping of the resulting musical form. Similarly, in Example 42, for the phenomenon of the labyrinth.

Example 41
A categorization of five artists' linear practice; from an early sketch for *Ariadne's Thread*.

Example 42
A consideration of the overall form of *Ariadne's Thread* as it relates to the labyrinth; from early sketches.

The peril in such a procedure as the composite emphasis is, of course, that there may develop not a supportive cohesiveness but an incoherent muddle that unproductively blurs one's focus. This is why I say that such an impetus is itself a compositional project.

Versions/Stages I–V (1986–91) for quadraphonic computer processed sound.

The final example involves a work in which the intent was literally experimental. If a form — described in terms of time and position — could be identically repeated but was, meta-phorically, "illuminated" by differing sound materials, would one hear the formative structure independent of the sounds which rendered it audible? To state it directly, is form separable from content?

The thought of such an experiment arose in my mind as a result of experience with Monet's series paintings, particularly those of the face of the Rouen Cathedral done at various times of the day and in varying seasons. In these works, an array of basic geometric elements is experienced to dramatically differing effect as a result of the way color and light are associated with it (Exs. 43–44).

Examples 43–44
Two contrasted representations of the Rouen Cathedral by Claude Monet [*Rouen Cathedral, West Facade, Sunlight* (1894) and *Western Portal of Rouen Cathedral — Harmony in Blue* (1894)].

Working with similar approaches to those used in the compositions I have just been discussing, I created a paradigm that was seeded by five different segments of sound one minute in length. The result was a set of five 5-minute movements which were identical in the following senses:

At a specific number of points in time, a "window" of specific length is opened.

The windows each have a particular position in a space.

There are four "host" spaces in which a window can occur and they are defined by size and resonant character (from bright and intimately scaled, to mellow and large).

Given the spaces used (one illusory spatial character was assigned to each of the formal scheme's four layers), a window has not only a starting time and a duration, but an azimuthal angle (this angle places it, for example, centered ahead of the ideal listener or displaced to the right or left of center by less than 180 degrees). Each window also has an assigned distance from the listener. The determination of what sound would, as it were, radiate through the window into the illusory space computed by the program was made by applying a particular sequence of algorithmic transformations to a one-minute sound source. The algorithm subdivides the "input" source in accord with the values that seed it. It then takes each of the resulting fragments and assigns it to a specific moment in time, as a part of an "output" structure of events.

Thus, through each window, a sound of a certain duration can be heard if there is a sound at the corresponding moment in the source that the algorithm accesses. Whatever is in the extracted fragment (whether sound or silence) will occur during the time window specified, in a particular host space, and in the particular spatial position designated (by angle and distance).

In this work, *Versions/Stages*, the form is a structure of potential. It is not only a formal pattern in a general, categorical sense as is, for example, sonata form, but in a *literal* sense. The control of at least two form-bearing dimensions — one of them, time, arguably the most basic of all — is reliably, precisely repeated through the five movements.

Example 45
The overall plan for *Versions/Stages I–V.*

The potential scope of this formal pattern, or scheme, then, is a result of the way it interacts with the structure of its one-minute sources. These might be graded in terms of their congruence with the design of the formal plan and in terms of the degree to which they are themselves organized. The five moments utilize, in order of input complexity:

cello materials composed precisely to an eight-sectioned proportionality on which the overall formal paradigm is based,

a Japanese actress as Dionysus, reciting a speech from a Japanese-language version of Euripides' *The Bacchae,*

a fragment of text by Tadashi Suzuki where repetitive lines are spoken by a leader and echoed by a chorus,

a period during which waves pound the Pacific shore,

the sound of a delicate waterfall whose stream shifts slightly, unpredictably over time.

My conclusion is that form can quite clearly be apprehended independently of its content. But, as with the Monet paintings upon which my series was modeled, the cohesiveness of the whole experience (in particular, the ways the form and its material modulate and reverberate relative to one another) is a necessary condition of success.

With *Versions/Stages*, I complete a general description of a variety of formal plans, all of which arise from a collection of basic assumptions differently applied. As I have indicated, the primary motivation in laying out the shape, dimension, and nature of a work's overall course is to be found in the freeing of local invention for more intuitional vibrancy. One is not seriously engaged at the same moment with the persuasiveness of a detail *and* its formal functioning.

Before concluding these remarks about the large-scale considerations in my compositions, there are two further points to be made. The first concerns the important question of how clearly, accurately or persuasively temporal proportions can be heard in music. Evidently, this is a serious issue meriting careful investigation. Informally, one realizes that the speed at which events pass as well as their intricacy influences our judgments about the passage of time. But experience itself and subsequent evaluations of it may not parallel one another, and thus perceived time in music is certainly a complex and inconstant phenomenon. Accepting these difficulties does not negate the utility of temporal planning, however. Designing form in the ways that I have been describing has the fundamental merit of directing the composer's attention specifically to the issue of large shape and to the listener's overall experience.

Since a music which eschews contrast is surely one which sacrifices one of its most salient and potent characteristics, demarcation of some sort is virtually inevitable. One could say, simply, that if demarcation exists, then *some* divisional relativism also comes into play. If this is true, in turn, then surely it is better that one attempt to influence, even manage, this aspect of one's music, rather than have it remain arbitrary and, perhaps, detract from one's expressive intent.

The second remark addresses rather the question of the authority which is appealed to in specifying proportionality. Is there special merit in one series of numbers or perspective over another? To pose the question more generally, is it the particular *identity* of proportion or rather the fact of attending to the sectional design in a composition and its relation to the whole that is likely to have the most importance? In my mind there is little doubt. I believe that while plausible notions about form and its contents are necessary, they are certainly not sufficient to confer inevitable merit. It is the quality of and the reasonable coherence of the many small decisions and adjustments the composer makes while working that lend to the music its ability to engage us dimensionally. While the framework evidently precedes its use, no unadjusted prescription, whatever its source, is likely to rise above the mundane.

Gaining the ability to manage the choice and the evolution of materials relative to a pre-ordained form is not straightforward. But it is a useful skill. It parallels the visual artist's capacity to accommodate the structure and expressive intent of his work to a chosen canvas already sized.

Having set out my way with forms, it is now appropriate to go into a more detailed examination of how method can help a composer to fit local materials to these larger conceptions.

Notes

1.   Toru Takemitsu, "My perception of time in traditional Japanese music", *Contemporary Music Review*, 1987, Vol. 1, pp. 9–13.

2. This phrase is the title of an article regarding the relationship between rational procedures which frame and intuitive modifications that complete the process: "L'ajustement de la sensibilité à un ensemble de contraintes", in *Inharmoniques*, 8/9, Ircam, 1991.

3. Eric F. Clarke, "Levels of structure in the organization of musical time", *Contemporary Music Review*, Vol. 2, Part 1, 1987, pp. 211–238.

4. *Ibid.*, p. 211.

5. *Ibid.*, p. 228.

6. *Ibid.*

7. *Ibid.*, p. 229.

8. Paul Fraisse, *The Psychology of Time*. (New York: Harper and Row, 1964).

9. J. A. Michon, "The making of the present: a tutorial review". In J. Requin (Ed.): *Attention and Performance VII*. (Hillsdale, New Jersey: Erlbaum, 1978).

10. Stephen McAdams, "Psychological constraints on form-bearing dimensions in music", *Contemporary Music Review*, 1989, Vol. 4, pp. 181–198.

11. *Ibid.*, p. 181.

12. *Ibid.*

13. *Ibid.*, p. 195.

14. Kevin Lynch, *The Image of the City*. (Cambridge, Mass.: MIT Press, 1960).

15. Cf. Exs. 1–3 for *Archipelago* and Exs. 23 and 24 for *Transfigured Wind II*.

16. Cf. Exs. 46–77 for *Variation* and Exs. 4 and 5 for *The Behavior of Mirrors*.

17. Cf. the following discussions of *Archipelago*, *The Behavior of Mirrors*, *Personae*, and also *Variation* in the second Essay.

18. Roger Reynolds, *A Searcher's Path: A Composer's Ways*, I.S.A.M. Monographs Number 25 (Brooklyn, Institute for Studies in American Music, 1987). A slightly reframed, parallel discussion is available in the *Contemporary Music Review*, 1987, Volume 2, Part 1, pp. 277–308, under the title "A perspective on form and experience".

19. I use the term "variant" to place some distance between the traditional formal *variation* of a "theme and variation" and what I am doing here. Those variants that precede may, in fact, *must*, be incomplete in some way relative to the core theme, as must those that follow. One can address an aspect of the core state which will carry its identity appropriately into some moment in the overall progress of the work without feeling the necessity to maintain others.

20. Incidentally, I decided to place a distinctive "landmark" in both the initial and final large "rock" sections: *ff* tam tam strokes which occur at bars 14 and 127 of the published score: C. F. Peters Corp., New York, 1991.

21. There is a "landmark" event during this section of *Personae* also (cf. footnote 20) involving the tam tam (reinforced) and announcing the entrance of Ensemble IV at 914 seconds (bar 333, published score: C. F. Peters Corp., New York, 1992).

22. The UPIC System (the acronym stands for Unité Polyagogique Informatique du CEMAMu which is the Center for Studies in Mathematics and Automation of Music, founded by Xenakis in 1965) was developed by Xenakis in 1977 with the intent of providing a deeper and more direct relationship between graphic invention and sonic behavior. It allows one to directly create a potential musical texture with lines inscribed on a computer screen in a two-dimensional, frequency versus time field.

ESSAY 2: METHOD

Starting from the overall picture of formal structure, as developed in the preceding Essay, let us now examine how an accumulation of musical material and its extrapolation through appropriate methods can bring these differing levels of the creative process into a coherent and dimensional relationship. This Essay will proceed by examining sequentially a series of Examples drawn from my compositional sketches.

Variation (1988) for solo piano.

The first sketch I did in preparing to work on *Variation*, a large-scale solo piano piece, is shown in Example 46. This page reveals a number of features originally posited: expanding (and contracting) logarithmic proportions utilizing a now familiar set of numbers, a three-layer mosaic of "sections", textural norms for the necessary three "core elements", and a rationale for how these normative behaviors might be seen as a succession which implied cycles. Some of these features were retained as work progressed, others discarded.

Example 46
Early sketch for *Variation*.

The conceptual evolution of thematic elements: A (Figurative) → B (Linear) → C (Chordal) is seen to be a natural evolution where scattered flourishes connect into line, and line thickens into chordal weight. But, from the outset, the coherence of the thematic material's origin was abandoned, *in presentation*, so that the structuring of the work itself became the first act of variation. It would seem that the Linear material was judged a more assertive way to begin than the relatively unformed essence of Figurative as imagined.

The first proposal in the sketch occupies the area just above the midline of the Example. Here each stratum has a core (shaded in the Example) and two variants; the placement of the core is either initial (second layer), central (bottom layer), or final (top layer). While this is neat, it is also too reductive, and the form below this sketch has already markedly shifted the proportional balance (moving, for example, the central core towards the beginning), assigned textures to strata, and begun to take account of the need to conform this approximation to some geometric, numerical series (i.e., proportional considerations such as "a" and "b" now emerge). Although there are still three elements in each stratum here, this can be seen to have evolved by comparing Examples 46 and 47. In the final form, the strata have, top to bottom, 6, 5, and 8 elements, and patterns of expansion and compression have been more strongly asserted without sacrificing balance.

Example 47
Formal plan for *Variation*.

The final formal plan is a framework onto which and within which related detail is mapped out.

There was — incidentally — no extra-musical impetus at work in this composition, only the making of a musical statement within a certain realm of constraints. A particular perspective on the process of musical variation was itself the impetus. My aim was to make a dimensional fabric of variational elements (musical atoms), not to think in terms of projecting specific variant sections derived from the thematic "cores". The landscape here is best thought of as domain-like.

"Section" is almost solely significant from the building (that is to say from the composer's) perspective. A listener might well sense the shadow of certain of the subsections laid out in the plan, but the ear is not intended to hear many formal demarcations of a sectional sort. Rather, one experiences an unforeseeable amalgam of fragments from coexistent algorithmic reservoirs in kaleidoscopic reformulations. The composer's ear, in turn, is led by intuition and serendipity in the process of mediation between competing possibilities.

The proportional structure of each of the three layers involves the series 23.5, 38, 61.5, …, 260.5, which controls the duration of thematic sections, algorithmic variants in each stratum, and the silences between them. Since a number of methods are applied in evolving the desired fabric of variation, it is useful to deal with them in turn rather than all at once. I have just mentioned "algorithmic variants". This is a reference to the fact (discussed below in relation to Examples 65 and 71) that I have developed several quasi-autonomous methods for subdividing and redistributing in time, the materials of a composed musical cell. The two algorithms, SPLITZ and SPIRLZ, are loosely analogous to the familiar notion of canon, where, having conceived a suitable subject, the composer can play it out canonically so as to realize an entire section of a work on the basis of suitable replications of a single line. Note that the plan also considers which algorithm should be applied in each section and in what way (e.g., the SPIRLZ in ③ is to be heard backwards — from small fragments to larger ones in successive cycles; the SPLITZ of element ⑮ uses only the E (even) fragments output by the algorithm. The actual meaning of these details will emerge below; for now, the point is simply to observe the emergence of an overall design from initial notions to definitive compilation). Some thought is also given at this stage to what tempo is likely to prevail from section to section.

Example 48
Describing the "core" textures for *Variation*.

An initial exploration of the "textural norms" which characterize the three strata in *Variation* is shown here from my notebook. The basic textures, Linear, Chordal, and Figurative imply in the most general way music that is centered on line, on harmonic succession, and on rapid passage work that lies somewhere between these essentially horizontal and vertical ideals. Example 48 is concerned with the ornamental enhancements of each normative texture.

It is critical that the three norms be strongly characterized:

In composing each core element, special care is given to consistency of the materials and invention within it. Their fragments — those that result from algorithmic subdivision and restatement in derived sections — need to carry identifying character with them in spite of their brevity.

Identity is established by various dimensions, but because of the essence of the two algorithms (discussed in detail in relation to Exs. 65 to 78 below), the musical texture itself is of particular significance here. In *The Vanity of Words* (1986), a stereophonic tape composition also achieved (exclusively) by means of the algorithms SPLITZ and SPIRLZ, I used vocal materials of three sorts to underscore the form of the piece: dramatic declamation, an unemotive intoning, and whispering. In this case, vocal types delineated the operations of the algorithms just as musical textures are meant to in *Variation*. Ideally, from even a very small sample of a normative texture, the ear could identify it reliably.

Note that there are ornamental subcategories within the three primary textural norms, e.g., under the second category in Example 48, Linear, four particular ways of marking its character are noted:

Linear:
    stutter
    flourish
    feint
    distant ally

The first of these involves rapid, freely staggered iteration; the second a multidirectional succession of different pitches; the third the notion of distracting attention to a subtly articulated and longer lasting event by associating its attack with a forcible chord; and the last the practice of locating a single grace note, or ally, at a surprising registral remove.

Example 49
Simultaneous tempi and their coordination in *Variation*.

Since the overall plan involves simultaneous presentation of materials from each of the three categories, and it cannot be clear which influence will predominate until the opportunities offered by the algorithmic process are evaluated; it is not possible to know which tempo will most practically apply in heterogeneous sections until they are actually composed out. All materials must be capable of fairly accurate restatement in alternative tempi since their fragments must often alternate very frequently as well as combine with one another in complex interweavings. This aspect of the mediation process will become clear in relation to Examples 70 and 77.

The three core themes (Chordal, Linear and Figurative) move, respectively, at MM 54, 81, and 108, or in a ratio of $2:3:4$. Example 49 examines, by absolute duration in seconds, the equivalence (or near equivalence) of each tempo's subdivisions to those of the others. The values are obtained by determining the duration of the basic pulse (the quarter note) at each tempo (e.g., $60/81 = 0.74074$ sec.) and subsequently its further subdivisions (e.g., $0.5556/6 = 0.09/\eighthnote^6$).

Examples 50–52
The proportional structure of the three "core" themes in *Variation*.

These Examples show the proportional structure of the themes. In order to off-load the task of developing flexible, appropriate, and perceptually effective sectional proportions in *Variation*, I used a, for me, familiar numerical sequence that had been developed earlier, especially in the context of computer music compositions: 3.5, 5.5, 9, 14.5, 23.5, 38, 61.5, 99.5, 161, 260.5. All primary subdivisions of core elements involve arrangements of this repertoire of standard values. Note that the nested numerical character of this series facilitates elegant subdivision.

Figurative: 3 parts ($3.5 + 14.5 + 5.5 = 23.5$)
Linear: 4 parts ($3.5 + 5.5 + 23.5 + 5.5 = 38$)
Chordal: 5 parts ($14.5 + 9 + 14.5 + 9 + 14.5 = 61.5$)

The subdivisions are not in the tempo proportion 2 : 3 : 4, but rather reflect the logarithmic nature of the repertoire of standard values adopted here with progressive allowance for internal symmetry as the core elements become longer and more sectionally complex. Let us examine the Linear theme as an instance. Each subsection within each core type is further subdivided in an hierarchical replication of the whole as decimal fractions. In the Linear case:

$$3.5 \quad : \quad 5.5 \quad : \quad 23.5 \quad : \quad 5.5 \quad = \quad 38.0$$
$$0.092 \quad : \quad 0.145 \quad : \quad 0.618 \quad : \quad 0.145 \quad = \quad 1.00$$

For example, the total duration of 38 seconds is divided into four parts in the proportions of $0.092 : 0.145 : 0.618 : 0.145$. In the case of the 23.5 subsection, $23.5 \times 4 = 124$ sixteenth-notes. Apportioning these according to the decimal fractions 0.092, 0.145, 0.618, 0.145 gives durations for the smallest formal units here of $11 : 18 : 77 : 18$ sixteenths.

Just below the major subsectional proportions in seconds (3.5, 5.5, 23.5, 5.5) are given the number of beat subdivisions of a particular rhythmic grain ($14 \, \flat^3$, $22 \, \flat^3$, $124 \, \flat$, $22 \, \flat^3$) that will approximate the absolute durations specified.

Note that precision of proportion is a less important priority than the plausibility of beat structure (and metrical simplicity) within a given tempo. A familial similarity of proportion between hierarchical levels is enough to establish relatedness at the level of memory, and this is all that the formal level requires. The local level, however, should be spared unnecessary convolutions, and felicitous roundings-off may therefore be in order.

As is normal in the evolution of my work, one can see evidence in these Examples of the constant interplay of the rational process with more intuitive positings and adjustments. At the bottom of Example 50 there is a momentary involvement with the numbers that have arisen as a result of the hierarchical application of proportionality along with the subsequent conversion into an appropriate rhythmic subdivision: the numbers that occur as a function of $\flat^3$ and $\flat$ subdivision, 3, 11, 4, 8, 32,... are arrayed progressively as 3, 4, 5, 7, 9, 11, 12, to explore their potential value in other contexts. In Example 51, textural aspects of the design are carried further, as the qualities first proposed in Example 48 are assigned as strata norms.

Example 53
The row chart for *Variation*.

The pitch resource for the core elements is strictly established by using a 12-tone series. Black notes are used for the first hexachord of the reference set and white notes for the second. This facilitates the informal tracking of related forms. The transpositions proceed from top to bottom in accord with the intervallic structure of the row itself.

A particular series — chosen according to an intuitive consideration of an appropriate harmonic climate and also the requirements of idiomatic piano writing in this work — was decided upon and a chart showing its 24 transpositional forms made. Although a very considerable amount of time goes into exploring alternative rows, the process by which one possibility is discarded and another is more extensively searched remains for me a very personal one, resistant to objectification.

There are groups of five forms of this row that exhibit near complementarity; for example, relative to the C Original form: E Mirror, G♯ Mirror, A♯ Retrograde, D Retrograde, and F♯ Mirror Retrograde. These relations help to maximize or to minimize harmonic consistency while composing.

Example 54
Overall pitch emphasis in the core elements of *Variation* by section.

In addition to using the various forms of this row directly and in "braided" composites to organize note-to-note successions of pitches in the composing of the core themes (cf. Ex. 62, below), focal harmonic successions were also established so that there was a certain fundamental connectedness in the harmonic chronology across each of the core elements. In the early stages of composition, I had planned to present the three core elements as a connected theme, played in its entirety before the work, proper, began. In this case, the composite was to have been arranged: Figurative, Linear, Chordal. At a later stage, I decided to forego such double exposure of the basic material.

Taken in order of increasing duration, structural and textural complexity, the three-part core element (Figurative) has 3×3-note verticalities; the four-part element (Linear) has 4×4-note verticalities; the Chordal element has 5×5-note chords. The use of four row forms in sequence is straightforward. These harmonic fields are expressed as fixed-pitch fields (e.g., Ex. 57 from the middle section of the 3×3-note distribution (Figurative) displays the imprint of the 3_2 harmony from Example 54, with 2 high G♯'s, mid-register G♯'s, and one low E♮).

Once the algorithmic processes have generated the derived sections specified by the overall plan (in Ex. 47, numbers ②, ③,...; ⑦, ⑨,...; ⑫, ⑬,...), final pitch choice is governed by intuition as the evolving identity of the final music is determined through mediation. That is, as I make specific choices from the field of potential generated by the larger aggregate of processes — the formal design and the algorithmic extrapolation of core themes — some potential harmonic implications are suppressed and others emphasized. Two Examples below (70 and 77) provide windows into the details of the mediation process.

Example 55
Planning the textural detail of the Figurative and Linear core elements in *Variation*.

As I have said, the identity of the core elements is a critical matter in the richness and integrity of *Variation*, and the textural design is, in turn, important:

for absolute identity: the sense that an individual theme is both consistent with an ideal and yet dimensional within it;

because appropriate textural variation influences the outcome of the algorithmic operations. For example, because the algorithms tend to map fragments of the closing of a passage onto its opening, interleaving them in the output, the listener will feel the impact of transformation on the *derived* materials more if the opening and closing textures contrast, and less if they are closely related.

The textural design of each core theme is done in accord with its ideal (Linear, Figurative, Chordal) and with attention to local emphases and their appropriate diversification (considering, for example, distinctions between openings and cadences, the significance of symmetry). Textural design is done in a relative pitch-time plane, without consideration yet of the actual pitch choices which will follow although relative high-low contours are suggested. The texture-type subcategories "directional blur", "insistent", "mobile masses" are evident in the Figurative plan, as are "flourish", "feint", and "distant ally" in the Linear plan. The effort to foresee texture is not simply schematic, but precisely detailed (cf. the following Exs.).

Example 56
Textural detail from Figurative in *Variation.*

Consider the detail of textural design in the central subsection of the Figurative element's primary middle section 14.5/8.98. The "mobile masses" ideal from Example 48 is used (albeit, influenced by the "feint" subcategory of Linear.)

Component motives are thought of as made up of "principal" elements (more stationary and lasting, indicated by small white notes) and "introductory" elements (more preparatory and fleeting, indicated by small black notes).

A gradual complexification of groupings is generated:

  a. a 1-note introduction to a 1-note principal,
  b. a 1-note introduction to a 2-note principal,
  c. a 2-note introduction to two, successive 1-note principals,
  d. two 2-note introductory notes to three 1-note principals,
  e. two 1 + 1 + 1-note introductory events to (1 + 2-note principal) + (2 + 1-note principals) + (3 + 3-note principals).

This level of heterogeneity, again, is called for by the known fate of the core themes: that they will be minutely fragmented and that these small resulting parts need to be categorically related yet still distinguishable from one another. The textural planning shown here includes also various reminders involving global considerations and details to be resolved at the moment that actual pitch choices are made. The same kind of ongoing, working dialogue between logical and intuitive concerns on this page are noted above in regard to Examples 50 and 51.

Example 57
The realization of the textural design from Example 56.

Example 57 is a detail of the realization of the 14.5/8.98 element of Figurative. Note the persistence of the textural design's original groupings. Those indicated in Example 56 are exactly carried out except for the final group on the page where several musical accommodations were required. Note also the influence of the fixed-pitch field, as discussed under Example 54, above.

A set of four small integers (3, 4, 5, 11) was loosely derived by approximation from the overall proportional design of the form. (This process whereby a convenient integer set is extrapolated from formal proportions will be traced in detail in the following discussion of *Symphony[Myths]*.) The rhythmic design of this subsection results from fitting together some combination of these integers which equals 32 ♪'s: the rhythmic total that corresponds to the calculated time duration for the subsectional subdivision of 8.96 seconds at MM 108 (cf. Ex. 50). The passage in Example 57 is one-half of the total: 5 + 3 + 3 + 4 + 3 + 3 + 5 + 3 + 3 = 32 ♪'s. The order of these elements is decided flexibly, but not arbitrarily. The textural plan specifies nine groupings, so nine numbers are required, but differing proportions, using another collection from the integer set (3, 4, 5, 11), could have been used here. There is a normative range of component durations and a set frame-length. The opportunity is to invent a musically effective combination.

Example 58 (a–b)
Textural design for the Chordal "core" element (in two parts).

The textural design for the Chordal theme of *Variation* is shown in Example 58. The proportions of sections and subsections are given along with equivalent numbers of basic rhythmic units (e.g., $\flat^{6}$'s or $\flat^{5}$'s) that are required:

$60/54 = 1.1111$ (the duration of $\downarrow$ at MM 54)
$1.1111/6 = 0.1852$ as the duration for each $\flat^{6}$

The first subdivision of the 14.5-second subsection shown in Example 52 is 18 $\flat^{6}$'s long. Therefore, $0.1852 \times 18 = 3.333 \approx 3.4$ seconds, which is the correct approximation of the overall subsectional proportions $14.5 : 9 : 14.5 : 9 : 14.5$ (e.g., 3.4 corresponds to 14.5 and 2.1 corresponds to 9, etc.).

In addition to proportionality and order, the textural sketch shows:

A variety of types of textural subcategories (already indicated, in general, in Ex. 48 above):

    f. snapped
    g. distended
    h. ostinatic weighting
    i. snapped
    j. distended
    k. snapped
    l. ostinatic weighting

all marked (f, g,..., l) beneath the first 14.5 subsection, far left of Example 58a.

Similarly varying pitch densities, considered by subgroups, from the left (Ex. 58a):

    9, 4, 5
    7, 3, 4
    8, 5, 3
    etc.

The influence on harmonic tension between successive chordal elements of changing spacings in relation to pitch content: closed/tense, relaxed, moderate, tight, spacious,...

Later, in a second 14.5-second section, there is a parallel to the grouping criterion followed in Examples 56 and 57; this time applied to the *iterative weighting* subcategory of the Chordal texture.

Example 59

A detail of the Chordal texture design, with iterative weighting *(Variation)*.

The iterative texture is specified by a consideration of several factors:

I.   number of iterative elements,
II.   density order within elements,
III. maximum density within the whole element.

In Example 59, this gives the following (second section from the left, marked 3.4):

	I	II	III
m.	4	1 2 3 1	3
n.	3	1 3 1	3
o.	2	3 3	3
p.	3	2 4 2	4
q.	4	1 1 5 1	5

Example 60

The musical realization of the textural detail from Example 59.

In the case of (m), for example: the vertical harmonic unit E, A, D♯ contains four iterative elements, an initial D♯, an A/D♯ dyad, the E/A/D♯ triad, and a further isolated E. Their successive density pattern is, evidently, 1, 2, 3, 1, and the maximum in the overall picture is 3. In the actual realization, when specific pitches were introduced, the (p) element (3; 2 4 2; 4) was changed to (3; 2 **3** 2; 3).

The small integer set guiding rhythmic design here is: 2, 6, 9, 10 (which contrasts with 3, 4, 5, 11 in Figurative). The series of rhythmic articulation points in this 14.5-second section, using the basic unit $\flat^6$, has two strata. They begin:

$$(18 + 11 + 19 =)\ 48\ =\ 2,\ 6,\ 2,\ 6,\ 2 \qquad 9,\ 2 \qquad 9,\ 2,\ 6,\ 2$$
$$[9,\ \ 9\ \ ]\ \text{null} \qquad 2,\ 9 \qquad 2,\ 6,\ 2,\ 9$$

Note that this rhythmic realization is inelegant as a result of the density of events and the corresponding necessity of logical compromise.

Example 61

The sketch of the Figurative core element from *Variation*.

An examination of the sketch for Figurative reveals how the various aspects of the overall method shape the decisions about detail.

The guiding integer set's 3, 4, 5, 11 influence hovers over the subsectional divisions. Referring to Example 50, note that the initial 3.5-second section is subdivided — using a basic unit of $\flat^3$ — into durations of 3, 11, and $4 \times \flat^3$. 3.5 divided by 0.5556, (the duration, in seconds, of each beat at MM 108) equals approximately 6.3 beats divided into $\flat^3$'s $\Rightarrow 6 \times 3 = 18\ \flat^3$ beats. 3 + 11 + 4 groups of $\flat^3$'s = 18. But the integer set also assumes detailed control over the rhythmic placement of events, acting as a reservoir of allowed note-lengths from which an appropriate sum is worked out, (for example, the rhythmic design shown in Example 57 below the double stave).

All rhythmic values are responsive to the central norms provided by the basic set of integers, although the numbers are flexibly used. Their purpose is to shape and establish a local orthodoxy which constrains to a norm, but within which the opportunity for choice still welcomes invention.

Example 62
A detail of the opening bars of the Figurative sketch *(Variation)*.

The pitch world is guided by the serial resources introduced in Examples 53 and 54. The detail in Example 62 shows that series forms are employed in straightforward succession, although flexibility is provided for by overlapping of row forms (the 10th pitch of D♯M is also the first of GMR), and that there is braided intermingling of several row forms (pitches 10–12 of GMR are inserted between 5 and 6 of G♯O). It is my intent to seek consistent linearity of row presentation (as much as possible while meeting other demands such as those of the textural sketches) because the algorithmic process that will later be applied is certain to further fragment, dissociate, and rearrange this normative succession.

The three fixed-pitch fields assigned to the three primary sections of this theme also constrain and shape the possible flow of choice. In sum:

> texture,
> proportional phrase lengths,
> rhythmic unit repertoire,
> harmonic fields,
> pitch succession

all *shape* the exercise of choice, but also, at the same time, generate opportunity of a coherent nature.

Examples 63–64
A page of the Chordal core element sketch with a detail from its opening *(Variation)*.

Examples 63 and 64 provide a parallel overview to that given in Examples 61 and 62, guided now by the 2, 6, 9, 10 integer set. The fixed-pitch fields here inform but do not necessarily describe the actual harmonic choices. Compare the specifications from Example 54 with what actually happens in the detail shown in Figure 13.

Again, in spite of the sectional alteration of the basic rhythmic unit ($\flat^6$, from the first beat of the first bar → $\flat^5$, first beat of fifth bar → $\flat^6$, first beat of eighth bar → ...), the integer set asserts its multiple influence on proportion (in the matter of subsection duration), and also on rhythmic unit repertoire, as a strong but not inflexible norm.

Example 65
A schematic view of the operation of the SPIRLZ algorithm.

Two "editorial" algorithms are essential to the methodological consistency of *Variation*. They are algorithms in the sense that, once boundary conditions are established in the form of

Example 54 (5₁)   from Example 64

Figure 13

appropriate choices for variables, the output of the process is entirely automatic. If one listed the choices available in the case of canon (apparently the only established algorithmic device in the Western music tradition), the factors to be determined would include:

transpositional level,
rhythmic point of entry,
factor of augmentation or diminution, where relevant
numbers of simultaneous voices.

If these decisions are appropriately made, a multivoiced canon can be constructed almost by rote. Naturally, the process of making such decisions is in fact interactive, involving trial and error, because in traditional contexts a higher order of musical concerns must also be met, e.g., tonal harmonic imperatives. In a way that is similar to the musically successful use of canon, an array of conditioning concerns also weighs on the effective use of the two algorithms that influence *Variation*. As with canon, the goal is to achieve a new passage that enlarges and enriches a preexistent theme or core element.

The word "editorial" is introduced to underscore the fact that these algorithms do not add information or, indeed, transform the materials upon which they act except in terms of continuity. That is to say, SPLITZ and SPIRLZ both operate by:

subdividing,
replicating, and
reordering

the content of a subject phrase. The result (or "output") of the SPIRLZ process involves a direct, contiguous representation of the extracted samples:

a, b, c, d, e, f, g, h, i, j, k,...

In the case of the SPIRLZ algorithm, the process can be imagined as involving a knife circulating (spiraling) out from the middle of the subject towards its outer limits, all the while cutting out a series of equal segments that alternately sample the later and earlier portions of the subject symmetrically. When the subject has been subdivided once, the knife returns to a central position and begins to spiral outwards again, this time taking segments that are once again of uniform size, but smaller than those extracted during the initial cycle. In the instance illustrated here, the result of this process involves a gradual, staged granularization of the subject. Perceptually, the effect of listening to the succession of resulting cycles, each presenting smaller, hence more rapidly occurring, fragments, should be of a palpable sense of convergence.

Each cycle is terminated when it reaches an outer limit (at either the beginning or ending) of the subject, and the total number of cycles is limited by the choice one has made about the lower limit of size for the smallest allowable extracted segment duration. Examining the schematic diagram in Example 65 will clarify the process. At the top is a four-segment representation of a musical motive ten seconds long. The first cycle of cuts begins at the subject's 5th second, and extracts samples 2 seconds in duration. The second cycle begins later, at 7 seconds, and its segments are only 1.0 second in length, etc.

SPIRLZ is a flexible algorithm that, in general, produces a single line of converging (or, when the process is reversed, expanding) fragments in incessant alternation, forwards and backwards in the original subject. The immediate future and past of the chosen starting point is cyclically sampled so that, at first, a kind of compressed antiphony is asserted, a regular rocking. Then, as a result of cyclic stages, a virtual melding of future and past can be achieved in a seemingly irrational blur of alternating samples (as the sample size becomes smaller and smaller, tending toward its lower limit).

Without describing the functioning of the algorithm in detail, the factors that must be decided on before the automatic process is definitively unleashed are:

the point in the subject phrase at which the first sample will be taken,

the size of the samples to be extracted in the first cycle,

the positioning of successive samples,[23]

the relative change (if any) in the location at which each successive cycle of spiraling samples taken will begin,[24]

the factor by which the duration of samples in successive cycles will differ from those of their predecessor (they may be smaller, as in Ex. 65, or larger).

Example 66
The graphic output from a computer run of the SPIRLZ algorithm, displaying its product.

This graphic output represents how a run of the SPIRLZ process could dissect and reorder fragments from an original subject. There are three cycles and they draw, in turn, from the beginning, center, and close of the subject. The length of the samples in successive cycles is markedly smaller and they are also non-contiguous. Note that the portions of the original unrepresented by **b** and **a** are touched upon by **o** and **m** of the second cycle. A converging impression of cadence is suggested for the output redistribution, a cadencing flavor which will parallel any such tendency in the subject.

Example 67
Overall plan for *Variation* indicating SPIRLZ example.

The second derived section in the Linear layer of *Variation* occurs at 260.5 seconds and is produced by applying the SPIRLZ algorithm to the Linear core element. Note that the algorithm is used in reverse here.

Example 68
A portion of the computer generated "note list" produced by the SPIRLZ algorithm, used in *Variation*.

When values for the various factors discussed above are fixed, the algorithm generates a set of numbers that describe the ways in which it fragments and redistributes the given subject. Here, SPIRLZ was used to generate a 38-second long section whose influence is felt beginning at the 260.5-second mark of the overall plan.

The fourth column of Example 68 shows the duration of the fragments in the three cycles that make up this particular application of the algorithm: 6225 samples at a sampling rate of 8192 samples/second = 0.76 seconds; 3112 samples = 0.38 seconds, and 1556 samples = 0.19 seconds.[25]

The next two columns give the beginning and ending points for the extracted fragments in each cycle. At the far right, the "begin times" have been converted into seconds, by dividing the sample count at the beginning of the extracted segment, 155648, by 8192 (the number of samples per second). It is evident that the times for the odd-numbered fragments gradually increase (19.0, 20.3, 21.62,...) while those for the even ones decrease (17.7, 16.38, 15.1,...) as would be expected, reflecting the fact that, beginning at some midpoint, odd fragments are taken successively towards the end of the subject while even fragments are extracted successively towards its beginning.

Example 69
The Linear core element from *Variation*, with superimposed timing for SPIRLZ extractions.

Below the staves of the Linear element are rough indications of clock time calculated according to the fact that, at MM 81, a quarter-note beat = 0.74074 seconds. These allow one to locate algorithmically identified fragments from the subject.

Since, at MM 81, 0.7404/4 = 0.1852 seconds for each sixteenth-note, and a 0.19-second fragment duration is used by the algorithm in its third cycle (but, because the algorithm is run in reverse, the third cycle segments are heard first), the fragments extracted by the SPIRLZ process are assumed to be approximately one-sixteenth in length. Example 70a shows — on the smaller, lower stave system — a sequence of sections cut from the source music (Linear) by the SPIRLZ algorithm. The first is cut from 32.1 seconds into the subject (cf. Ex. 69) and the second from the 37.6-second point. The succeeding fragments follow, moving respectively forwards and backwards in time incrementally, and, since this SPIRLZ application is reversed, moving from small segments to large.

Example 70 (a–c)
Three pages from the sketch for *Variation*, showing the mediation from raw fragments to finished continuity.

These examples show the raw information provided by the SPIRLZ algorithm and how it was shaped into an acceptable final form. [I have selected a passage that required a rather large amount of mediation. This is often true in the very fine-grained situations produced in a by-hand application of the algorithm. The difference between direct computer applications of the process (which involve transients, resonances, intersections between several events, etc.) is considerable: harmonic and practical factors dominate the latter.] As indicated in the first Essay, algorithmic processes are used to provide an intermediate level "market of opportunity" which the composer then selects from to achieve a final result. Comparison between the actual material provided by the algorithm and its recasting on the larger staves above reveals just how much reshaping must sometimes be done. *It is also important to observe the general relevance of this situation to others involving the intersection of autonomous processes with musical imperatives. The process only proposes, the composer decides what will find its way into the score.*

The overall effect of the passage (which appears in the printed version of the score from page 5; line 1; measure 1 to page 5; line 4; measure 1) is to move outwards from an energetic, secco regularity, in expanding cycles which — as though a flower were opening its petals — allow more and more of the character of the subject material to emerge.

The musical grain of the SPIRLZ process begins at ♪, steps after little more than a bar to ♩ and, again doubles to ♩ a little more than a bar from the end of Example 70b.

The interaction between the regular alternations resulting from the algorithmic knife and the unexpected fluctuations of material that are juxtaposed, provides a vitality of textural evolution that one would be unlikely to achieve intuitively. Yet the experience derives from orderly relationships and procedures that continue to be sensed by a listener, even though it is safe to say that their specific nature could not easily be deduced.

Incidentally, notice that in the following passage (at MM 108 shown in Ex. 70c), the sparseness of the algorithmic output is mitigated in the final version by scalar passage work derived directly from the row that is basic to the pitch structure of *Variation*. These sorts of augmentations occur very rarely, but, on the other hand, whenever they are musically necessary.

Example 71
A schematic view of the operation of the SPLITZ algorithm.

The second editorial algorithm, complementary to the monophonic SPIRLZ, is SPLITZ. It is conceptually polyphonic and produces a characteristic profile which moves from a heterogeneous mapping of the end of the source subject onto its beginnings, towards a more homogeneous mapping of portions of the middle of the source onto itself, and then returns to heterogeneity as the beginning of the source is mapped onto its end. Thus, while the beginning and end of the output are likely to produce a variegated result, its center will be more "recognizable".

Examining the diagrammatic depiction in Example 71 will clarify the procedure. In the case of the SPLITZ algorithm, the source (represented, again, schematically by a five-segmented line at the top) is divided into a prescribed number of segments (the number of segments must always be odd, and in this case it is 13) by a sequence of numbers called a *proportional series* (here: 1, 1, 2, 2, 3, 4, 4, 4, 3, 2, 2, 1, 1). This sequence happens to be symmetrical, but need not be. The odd segments (here: a, c, e, g, i, k, m) are presented in chronological order, with interspersed silences that grow gradually longer. The even segments (b, d, f, h, j, l) occur in reverse chronology in the output of the SPLITZ program. The even segments begin after the first odd segment and end before the final odd segment is completed, so that they are, as a group, symmetrically indented. The even segments also have interspersed silences, but these gradually diminish in size, reversing the trend in the stratum of odd segments.

In Example 71, the first operation expands the total duration only marginally, but fragments and shuffles the ordering of the original. At the bottom of this example is a more spacious version. The difference here is caused simply by specifying a longer overall output result. The algorithm then inserts proportionally longer silences between what is an identical set of fragments, ordered in the same way within the two basic strata (the odd and even fragment sequences) but *altered in their composite chronology* as a result of the differently enlarged silences.

The factors which must be decided upon before applying the SPLITZ algorithm automatically include:

the duration of the output to be achieved (for purposes of this discussion, the duration of one of the derived sections specified by the overall plan for *Variation*),

the proportional series of integers (often comprised of an arrangement of numbers from the same basic integer set that guides the rhythmic invention of core materials during composition),

a decision as to the way in which the two sets of interspersed silences are to grow or shrink (this is established by the "slope" of the function that prescribes their values),

the number of times this process will be repeated. (A derived section may have one "pass", consisting of a stratum of odd and another of even segments; or it may have two or three or more passes, creating a nested "echoing" structure where several identical series of fragments will interact in a polyphony of shifting, kaleidoscopic relationships.)

Example 72
The overall plan for *Variation*, highlighting a section of the whole which involves material derived from all three strata.

The overall plan shows that the section which bridges between the core Linear and Chordal sections is planned to mediate between materials derived by the SPLITZ algorithm from the Figurative and the Linear core themes.

Example 73
A "note list" produced by the SPLITZ algorithm.

This Example shows the output of the SPLITZ program used to create the derived section ⑫, which begins the Figurative stratum of the overall design. The application of SPLITZ here produces three passes (or a total of six "polyphonic" layers, in pairs, labeled "half-passes"). The second column indicates the time point in the musical output at which the odd fragments will be positioned (0", 2.132", 6.132", etc.). The fifth column (0.280, 0.280,…, 0.559,…) gives the duration of the segment to be extracted. These durations are then converted into their nearest rhythmic equivalent (at MM 108, 0.28" approximates an ♪, 0.56 a ♩). At the far left, an added column converts the clock time of the successive placement positions in the output to beats at the appropriate tempo (note that these converted values apply to the tempo of the derived section, in this instance ⑫ at MM 54).

The numbers inscribed in column 4 identify the odd segments (①– ⑬ in Example 74, not Example 72) and the even (⑭– ㉕). The sixth and seventh columns show the beginning and ending sample numbers (in case the source material were in a digital sound file), and one can see that these numbers in columns 6 and 7 rise in the odd sequence, showing that successive fragments come at later and later points in the source. Complementarily, the even source fragments are reversed, beginning from large numbers (late in the subject) and becoming smaller (or nearer the beginning).

Example 74
The Figurative core element from *Variation*, with superimposed rhythmic values showing its proportional subdivision.

The line running above each of the three staves of the Figurative theme shows the rhythmic positioning of successive fragments resulting from the particular 25-term proportional series used in this SPLITZ application. The first of the 13 odd segments, 0.28 seconds long, is extracted as an ♪, the final (even) segment, ㉕, specified as 0.699 seconds is next at ♩♪ in length. The second odd segment is also ♪ long and follows immediately. The placement of these segments at appropriate positions in the derived section ⑫ can be traced on the sketch pages shown in Example 77. They begin the stave system just below the final, mediated version. (Note that these fragments are recast, here, in Ex. 77, at MM 54.)

Example 75
A "note list" produced by the SPLITZ algorithm.

Examples 75 and 76 give a parallel basic picture of how the SPLITZ process is applied to the Linear core theme to produce the derived section ②, which follows the core theme in the Linear stratum. Since the derived music in this case is written at MM 54, the durations in seconds must be converted to rhythmic values at this tempo. This is accomplished in the leftmost column: 2.189" ⇒ 1.97 beats, 4.861" ⇒ 4.38 beats, etc.[26]

Example 76
The Linear core theme from *Variation*, with superimposed rhythmic values showing its proportional subdivision.

The Linear element is shown proportionally subdivided into 37 fragments. These can be found, renotated at MM 54, in the stave system just above the mediated final result, towards the end of the manuscript page reproduced as Example 77a.

Example 77 (a–e)
Five successive pages from the sketch for *Variation*, showing the mediation from raw fragments to finished continuity.

Example 77 shows the sketch for the composite of elements highlighted in Example 72. The mediation process can be followed by comparing the final version with the materials available (above and below the large middle stave system) at every moment.[27]

While the SPLITZ application to the Linear element (shown above the larger central stave system) involves singular occurrences of each derived fragment, the treatment of Figurative (shown on the lower stave system) involves three "passes" of the algorithmic process and, hence, three occurrences of each extracted fragment. In Examples 77c and 77d, for instance, one can find 21_3, 21_2, and 21. In this case, only the first two find their way directly into the mediated result, whereas 21 contributes just four pitches, the third and fourth (C and B) of which sound octava. Opportunity beckons in a specific way but is not reliably heeded. There is something very attractive to me about such quasi-rigorous interactions: a principled proposal, accepted or rejected as the musical moment dictates.

Just before the ② materials (beginning in Ex. 77a on the three stave systems above the larger central pair) start, there are two small annotations:

"pre-emphasis on odd ① – ⑲",
"post-emphasis on even ⑳ – ㊲".

This practice is borrowed from the fashion in which the SPLITZ algorithm operates in the digital domain (that is, when the computer algorithm is processing a particular recorded sound directly). There, all odd fragments in the output are given an amplitude envelope that includes a sharp initial transient, whereas the even segments have a parallel spike on their trailing edges. The result is that all even segments appear with accented releases. In this "by-hand" use of SPLITZ, I substituted pitch repetition as a form of emphasis. Just below the beginning of odd segment ①, it is clear that the F/F♯ dyad that follows the initial D♮ in the source occurs a second time in the mediated continuity as a "pre-echo".

The same is true of segment ⑮ in Example 77d. Just before the moment at which a portion of ㉑ from the lower system occurs, the ⑮ motive appears, but its terminal G/E dyad now occurs as a pre-echo in retrograde. In the last measure of Example 77d, the even segment ㉛ receives "post-emphasis" when the penultimate F is repeated after the original F/F♯ sequence.

There are, of course, numerous examples of approximation as regards rhythmic placement. These "irregularities" should serve to reemphasize the often-stated fact that the palette of potential generated by the algorithmic processes specified by the overall plan is *only an invitation* meant to stimulate the composer's sense of a viable, derived musical continuity.

Example 78

A table comparing the SPLITZ and SPIRLZ algorithms.

The chart in Example 78 shows a categorical comparison between the two editorial algorithms; their complementarity is clear. Although a more detailed discussion of these procedures is inappropriate here, it should be noted that they provide an impressive wealth of potential, both in straightforward applications (where widely varying choices can be made for the several influential variables that guide each autonomous process) and in more radically rethinking their potential applications. The complementarity evident in this comparison resulted from considerable tinkering with the basic concepts in order to achieve the most comprehensive and powerful operations.

A considerable amount of time has been spent on a brief survey of these two algorithms and their actual application. Naturally, this is not done with the expectation that these processes will or even could be adopted by others. My purpose is rather to give instances of principled procedures and the ways in which their characteristics can be used by molding the literal into a more integral flexibility.

As examples of novel applications, one can mention the possibility of using the SPIRLZ output to achieve polyphonic results by parsing the output stream into two or more complementary lists, or to suppress odd or even segments of a SPLITZ output so that a derived section primarily asserted by a fully displayed first pass could be subtly shadowed by odd- or even-only successions from nested second and third passes.

Though the process of using these algorithms in their present form is certainly arduous, there is a characteristic pleasure in the mediating process — what to keep, what to omit, considering which subtle modifications of register, and so on, would improve the result?

The attractiveness of these algorithmic procedures also resides in the way that they directly and powerfully serve the goal I identified earlier for method: to make a compelling and coherent link between materials and large form. It is important to recognize that neither material (too fundamental) nor form (too idiosyncratic) are algorithmically addressed in these essays, only the extrapolation of the essences of one towards the dimensionality of the other. This is my current conviction about the appropriate place of autonomous procedures in composition.

Symphony[Myths] (1990) for orchestra.

The series used for *Symphony[Myths]* is non-symmetric, as is that for *Variation*, but it does have one nearly complementary relationship, that between the original form and the mirror a major second above. Because of the particular importance of harmonic design in this work, the row was chosen for its attractions when taken three or four at a time, as a generator of useful harmonic successions.

Example 79
The chart of row forms used in *Symphony[Myths]*.

Although the pitch, proportional, and rhythmic materials were interactively derived (as is my normal procedure) and are therefore integrally dependent upon one another, they are presented independently here for the sake of clarity.

The composer finds pitch materials of differing sorts useful while nevertheless requiring that they remain coherently related. (One thinks of the distinctions between melodic invention and passage-work in traditional music.) Examples 80 and 81 show this. The intermediate resources illustrated here are not precisely *material* since they already represent constructs based on other, formalized aspects of the work (pitch series, proportional number series, harmonic, melodic, and figurative requirements, etc.), but they are also not yet at the stage of actual, composed music that will appear directly in the work. They have a status intermediate between the raw materials themselves and the realm of method — similar to, perhaps, but not exactly parallel with the place of "core themes".

Example 80
Derivation from basic row forms of 91-note secondary pitch resource for *Symphony[Myths]*.

Example 81
Full secondary pitch resource with 29-, 91-, and 180-note sequences from *Symphony[Myths]*.

In *Symphony[Myths]*, a second level of pitch organization superseded the basic charts of transpositionally related rows. A three-strata pitch resource was designed. The center stave of the three-stave grouping was developed first (Ex. 80). It resulted from arranging various forms and transpositions of the row, including overlappings (where, for example, the last 2 notes of BO are also the first 2 of F♯MR). Overlapping was used both to increase the heterogeneity of this "derived row", and to target the number 91. 91 (13×7) had been, at an earlier stage of basic work, the number posited as the uppermost extension on one of the *Symphony[Myths]* integer sets: 1, 3, 5, 9, 16, 29, 52, **91**. (Later, however, the 91 term was adjusted to 94 as a result of other considerations.)

From the central 91-tone sequence, a 29-tone subset was devised, consistent with, although not systematically derived from, the central series. (The number 29 derives from the height of one of the rocks in the formation that served as the original impetus for this work, cf. below, Ex. 86.) In addition, as can be followed in Example 80, further forms of the basic row were woven into the original 91-tone succession (examine the lower five staves in this regard) to bring the resultant "derived row" to a total of 180 (the largest number in the overall proportional series that controlled the formal design of the entire work).

At the most fundamental and idiosyncratic level, there is now a 29-pitch succession.

Central to the design, as a kind of norm, is a 91-pitch succession, which has embedded in it the more elemental 29-note series.

At the most general and elaborate level is a 180-pitch sequence which is extrapolated from the central series (and also contains it).

I used the 29-note series for the fundamental harmonic design of materials, the 91-note series for normal melodic functions, and the 180-note sequence for elaboration and virtuoso figuration, where needed. These categories, then, fulfill functions not unlike those provided for in traditional contexts by scales, arpeggios, and a melodic design that follows the weighting of scale degrees by harmonic implication within a particular key.

The central, 91-note sequence was devised first, as shown. While, originally, register was treated as a routine matter, in the final second level pitch resource, attention was given to what might be termed a melodic (and harmonic) bias. Contour, that is, became a weighted influence on my later invention. The 29-pitch series is treated at all times as normative; it is an influential, though not a dictatorial force.

Examples 82–84
Three stages in the derivation of temporal control for *Symphony[Myths]*.

As with pitch, there was also a 3-tiered *temporal* consistency for *Symphony[Myths]*. The impetus for the first movement of this work (and later, by extension, to the entire three movements) was a rock formation off the coast of Japan: *Futami ga ura*. This was discussed at some length in the first Essay. In my reading about the two large rocks that dominate this formation, it emerged that the larger was 29 feet in height, the smaller, or "female" rock, 13 feet. I decided to use these numbers as keys to the proportional and numerical character of the composition. (It is worth noting that, although this source may appear rather arbitrary, the proportion has attractive features. If, for example, their relative height had been 30 : 15, I would have bypassed this datum.)

Because there were two primary rocks in the guiding impetus, both for the first movement and the last, I decided to define two rhythmic collections by means of which it would be possible, for example, to differently characterize the periodicities of the two primary layers of the third movement (cf. Exs. 103–106).

Experimenting with straight lines drawn on semi-log graph paper, I settled upon a third smaller number to complete a basic triad: 29 : 13 : 9. Next, I looked for two related but distinct number collections that featured these small integers, collections that were logarithmically spaced out and also distinct from one another:

1, 2, 4, 7, 13 and
1, 3, 5, 9, (cf. Ex. 85)

Knowing that the largest "rock" in Movement I could probably not be sustained for more than three minutes because of the insistently ostinatic nature I had planned for it, I began then to extrapolate these basic collections to see whether a relatively large (perhaps even 29?) collection of approximately logarithmic integers could be found. Beginning with 13, taking 26 equally spaced readings on semi-log graph paper, and terminating with the value 180, I obtained the sequence shown in Example 83. An extended search (for example, cf. left of primary column in Ex. 83, factoring by 13) did not produce a plausible set of integers, so I settled on the numbers outlined by a vertical box:

13, 14.3, 15.9, 17.7,…

By repeating three of these 26 numbers, I could get a total collection of 29, and this seemed acceptable (involving a further play with the centrality of "3", the three rock elements in the central impetus, the *Futami ga ura* formation).

Coincidentally, the process of settling upon the two rhythmic collections (1, 2, 4, 7 and 1, 3, 5, 9, 16) was informed by the fact that they could be seen — in approximation, to be sure — to be embedded within the 26-member collection which now became the arbiter of sectional proportion as I began to plan the overall form of the work.

The three tiers of temporal influence were now:

29 : 13 : 9 for large-scale design (e.g., numbers of pitches, numbers controlling ostinatic strata, etc.) and, not incidentally, the fact that there are three terms to this most basic set;

a 26-member series of numbers, logarithmically related, that range in consistent steps from 13 to 180 seconds (since three of the 26 are repeated, the total of proportional elements arrayed into the form of the whole is 29, cf. column at right margin of Ex. 87);

two small-integer collections which guide, in a characteristic way, the temporal detail of the music. It was later decided that the 4- and 5-number collections (= 9) were, in fact, too confining, and so they were extended upwards (logarithmically) to create a greater range of flexibility in applications (cf. Ex. 85):

1, 2, 4, 7, 13, 24, 45
1, 3, 5, 9, 16, 29, 52, 94

Example 85
Semi-log graph paper showing the *Symphony[Myths]* rhythmic sets.

Example 85 illustrates how straight lines were used on semi-log graph paper to identify sets of numbers that have orderly relationships to one another. Naturally, in many cases — including these — some rounding off is required. The plausibility of such relationships as experienced in time is not, I believe, seriously disturbed by these approximations. The familiar Fibonacci series is one such integer set which does not require any "adjustments".

As in the case of pitch, the categorization of resource in relation to anticipated function is the underlying issue here. And it is not claimed that the particular way in which I estimate, shape, and apply objective resource to the complexly intuitive art of composing is definitive. What I do believe is that the control of time needs to be hierarchically considered in the sense that some appropriate attention is given to shaping both the large-scale form, the middle level sectional and phrase structure, and also the local rhythms. The way in which, or the degree to which, the control of these levels is coordinated seems to me still a matter of investigation.

Example 86
A very early sketch of the possible application of the 26 + 3 proportional number series to the formal design of *Symphony[Myths]*.

It was now possible to return to the schematic early sketch and to begin tracing its elaboration, seeking in the process a way of accommodating the 29-term series and the durations of the structural blocks that it posits. This fitting of resource to function involved, of course, a process of trial and error. The critical thing is that I first accepted the "necessity" (entirely self-directed) of using 29 "blocks" and then set about trying to devise a way of utilizing exactly this number, and in their prescribed proportions. Note, for example, that three of the larger blocks — ⑦, ⑪, and ③ — were eventually used to position the *kami* or "spirit rock" within the architecture of the first movement. The placement of some blocks was straightforward: the longest (180 sec.) serving for the overall dimension of the largest rock in the first movement, while other large ones were used for the "female" rock, for the central intermezzo, and for the first major division of the third movement. The placement of others followed as this formal "puzzle" was resolved.

Example 86 shows the early efforts to find appropriate use of the 29 durations, and, in Example 87, they have been neatly drawn up in the proper proportions. One might wonder whether the extra effort involved in reframing, in the latter Example, information already objectively present in the former, was worthwhile. My experience has been that when information is indistinctly or inaccurately characterized, and one consults it continuously, undesirable distortions do indeed slip into the process. Cleaning up and accurately portraying anything that serves as a source, as a continuing reference, pays dividends in removing vagueness where it is not a welcome factor.

Example 87
Final overall plan for the sectional design of *Symphony[Myths]*.

The *Futami ga ura* formation contains not only the two massive, framing rocks but also a small *kami ishi* (or "spirit rock") just at the water's surface and between them. When it was decided to use this formation as a model not only for the first large movement, but for the structure of the whole work, some way of tying the central intermezzo to both the first and last large movements was needed. This need was resolved by using an ostinatic framework with nine levels operating both in sections ⑪ and ④ of the plan in Example 87. Section ④ echoes an essential formal device of the first large movement, but is expanded and placed in a different context. The two lyrical elements (section numbers ⑧ and ⑳) occur as virtually literal repeats, soloistically in the intermezzo and orchestrated appropriately in the last large Movement III. Thus there are various direct links between the central intermezzo and the framing movements.

Though it would be difficult to detail after the fact, part of the strength of the general procedure traced here is the fact that there is a constant interplay between one's rational and intuitive faculties. Thus, at the stage of the work reflected in these two Examples, there was first an interplay between the general image of the characteristic rock formation and the specific ways in which it might be converted into a musical form, manifested in sound. Next, the emerging specifics were considered against a repertoire of musical "blocks" of graded size. (Keep in mind that these blocks were still no more than regions of distinctive potential opportunity.) A conflict arises because — for numerical reasons already indicated — there is a collection of 29 such blocks of given size, and their necessary incorporation involved more than a straightforward modeling of the initial image of *Futami ga ura*.

I welcome the friction that arises when various criteria come into potential conflict, for it is often as a result of some mismatch (here, too many potential sections for the apparent need) that gives rise to significant opportunities for invention. In any case, at every level of the compositional process there is an interaction between constraints (or obligations) accepted and the musical needs at hand. As in *Variation*, a mediation between algorithmically derived materials was necessary; here it was required between intuitively general (or urgent) goals and objective, rational strategies: once the magnitude 29 was accepted, and therefore a substantial range of sectional blocks was mandated, there was, at every appropriate point, a strong pull towards 29 rather than some other, similar number. (But, for example, the notion of a 29-layered ostinatic structure would have been musically absurd.) In turn, once 29 block dimensions were established, I took it as my obligation to find a place (and thus a function) for each, to find a plausible fit between *resource* and *function achieved*.

Because I intended to manifest not only the massive stability of the two framing rocks but also their spiritual vibrancy, it was necessary to devise a fitting texture. The approach taken was to compose two parallel but distinct, 13-layered ostinati. They were informed by several considerations:

timbric design,
phase or element design,
harmonic design (aggregate harmony and ostinatic succession),
gestural type,
internal rhythms.

The initial rock mass was to parallel the male god, Izanagi, so that a very wide-range, assertive *timbric design* was required: piccolo and piano at the top, contrabassoon, tuba, and piano defining the bottom. The choice of instrumentation for this section and the registrally narrower, smaller-scaled, and more covert sonority of its female counterpart is shown in Example 88. This was not determined summarily but rather in stages: a proposal, then adjustments for categorical balance, another adjustment for articulative fluency (in response to *gestural type*), a further proposal, perhaps, and again other adjustments, this time as a function of the specifics of pitch design and, for example, the passagework necessary to accomplish an initial flourish (while such a gesture might be inappropriate to the tuba or contrabassoon, it could be entirely idiomatic for the viola, trumpet, or marimba). The basic task was the creation of two meaningful complements and a related, linking subset of soloists.

Example 88
The timbric design of the three "rock" elements for *Symphony[Myths]*, Movement I.

The 9-layered ostinatic structure of the accompanimental framework for the intermezzo (as well as for the subtle presence of the central spirit rock during the first movement's lyrical middle section) was conceived soloistically, as befits the more personal quality of the "spirit". Its instrumentation is closer to that of the female rock — with lower-register, reedy, and muted sonorities. The entire orchestral resource is implicated in serving the composite need of the three, layered sections, but each draws upon it distinctively.

Example 89
The 13-layered structure of superimposed ostinati for element ① of *Symphony[Myths]*,
Movement I.

Each of the three "rock" structures implied a *phase or element design*, and this involved the idiosyncratic assignment of characteristic periodicities to each layer. Example 89 shows the basic layout for the male rock in Movement I. Thirteen individual durations were selected. They came from among those values generated in the search for a collection of logarithmically related block lengths out of which to devise the work's formal character. That is to say, the 13 values used in the male rock — they result in durations ranging from 30" to 7.8" in length — have a numerical relationship to one another that is an extension of the lower end of the series of 26 values (180 – 13) that underlie the proportions of the large form (cf. left side of Ex. 87 and also Ex. 83). Those selected, however, are not placed in contiguous strata according to adjacent magnitudes, and some of these values are much smaller than those selected to establish the block lengths of the overall form (13 is the smallest of these, but 7.8" is the shortest internal period). The subdivisional grain of the various strata is varied from bottom to top in order to ensure aural cohesion of the whole.

Note that each periodicity, from the shortest (7.8") to the longest (41") has a unique number of iterations. These are listed at the right margin of Example 89. Note also that there is an offset time for the beginning of each layer except the first, a factor that influences both the overall character of this large section (here the mass grows rather gradually and ends rather suddenly, with seven of the thirteen layers stopping at the same moment) and the desire to minimize the number of internal seams shared between strata (e.g., five layers have a seam in the vicinity of 85 seconds, but none actually coincide).

The design features a heterogeneity of periodicities as one scans upwards from the lowest stratum, which at 30 seconds, has the third longest; to the next, which is of a slightly shorter periodicity; but then, on what is still one of the lowest registral layers, the shortest period of all occurs (7.8"). The careful balancing of register and period length enhanced the perceptual vitality of the result beyond a more conventionally regular progression from low register-long to high register-short.

A parallel process of detailed framing was followed for the other large rock, and for the 9-layered version. It was then possible to write out a precise temporal design for the entire movement.

Example 90
Detailed temporal design for Movement I, *Symphony[Myths]*.

It is important to note that, while the overall nature of this formal plan should be and is, of course, perceptible to the listener, its major function is in coherently guiding the moment-to-moment exercise of intuition as it takes responsibility for the emergence of a specific realization, for a form which at this stage still exists only as a structure of potential. It is misleading to consider such a detailed (even, seemingly, over-detailed) scheme without recognizing as well the process of consideration and adjustment that was required to achieve it. Its purpose, of course, remains the creation of what is, in effect, an invented conventionality, a persuasive normalization against which to work.

Though such objective, middle-ground definition is rather uncommon, it is clear that the emergence of any complex scheme involves the resolution of myriad details. The question is: How is this best achieved? Note that the central, three-part strand of the movement involves six contiguous sections, with five more (one is a repeat) below. The latter blocks (㉓ – ㉖) define and correspond to the tassels that can be seen in Examples 13 and 86, and are here manifested by rapid, descending figuration in the piano, harp, and percussion.

Example 91
The pitch content of the 13-layered, ostinatic strata of element ①, Movement I,
Symphony[Myths].

Because the large masses that frame the first movement must be both stable (their harmonic essence, after it is achieved at approximately 60″, displays no tendency whatever to migrate, though it thickens and thins) and yet complex enough to be constantly in renewal, an overall *harmonic design* involving 29 pitches with assigned register was chosen and then parsed so as to allow 13 distinct "ostinatic" alternations. The lowest has three associated pitches, the next lowest stratum only two, the next two as well, and so on. In addition to one instance of a shared pitch (A between layers 7 and 8), there are several overlaps between strata (the G♯ in layer 3 occurs within the D/A 5th of layer 4), so that a harmonic/melodic interlocking occurs which helps to bind the overall structure together. The pitch consistency of the gestural figuration to be discussed in Example 93 refers back to the basic row forms.

The overall, bottom-to-top distribution of pitches parallels that 29-note succession found at the most elemental level of the three-part pitch resource mapped out in Example 81. The small, intermediate ostinatic structure, in comparison, utilized only nine pitches, and the female rock thirteen. These two collections were derived from the original 29-note structure.

Example 92
The extrapolation of element ①'s 29-note structure into the 13- and 9-tone forms
(*Symphony[Myths]*).

Two transpositional levels were used. The 9-tone collection involving a minor 6th rise and the 13-tone one a major 2nd rise. These intervallic spacings of the transpositional design mimics the placement of the first three pitches of the 29-note series (B, G, C♯). In both derivations, a subset of the original with more restricted range was chosen. (And, thus, the more vertically compact image of section ⑤ in Ex. 90 was realized.) In the whole-step transposition, the selected subset is retained intact. For the minor 6th transposition, some revoicing was done. All decisions regarding harmonic identity were also colored by testing for appropriate 2- and 3-note ostinatic subdivisions, so that the horizontal, quasi-melodic aspect of the layered textures was cared for.

Example 93
A schematic plan for the structure of the female rock in Movement I of *Symphony[Myths]*.

A schematic plan of the female rock is shown in Example 93 and one can trace the use of three basic *gestural types* which embellish the repetitive texture. As regards the animating flourishes that occur in each of the 82 individual blocks of this section, there are:

initial flurries followed by ostinatic alternations in strata 6 and 8,

ostinatic successions interrupted by asymmetric staccato bursts, in strata 1, 2, 3, 4, 10, 12, 13,

ostinatic alternations ending with repeated-note gestures, in strata 5, 7, 9, 11.

It is worth mentioning that the desire to end the whole movement with the mournful iterations of the exposed oboe line (cf. layer 9) was in my mind already here. Thus, the details of temporal placement in planning can already carry expressive weight even at such an early stage. The process of pre-forming that I am describing may appear to separate quite categorically the objective preparation from the subjective act of composing itself. In practice, of course, each is constantly invaded by the other. The preliminary setting up of opportunity is a *primary* concern at the early stages, but does not exclude consideration of expressive matters. On the other hand, in the midst of composing, it may occasionally be necessary to stop and, as it were, reengineer some framing perspective because it is not functioning well expressively.

Example 94
A detail of the female rock textural design from Example 93.

The three gestural types — an initial, continuous flourish, a central, disjunct diversion, and a closing flourish of rising repeated notes — are distributed throughout the 13 strata so as to activate effectively the overall design of this large closing formation in Movement I.

A more varied textural flux — distinct from that in the opening block ① — is assured by the suppression of the central blocks in the 5th through 11th strata of this element (⑤). It becomes less monolithic, more chameleonic in its effect, as seemed fitting. The closing flourish characteristic of the 9th stratum (cf. Ex. 93) is heard alone at the end of the movement, as was mentioned above. Thus, a figure that has been present as an unexceptional part of a complex texture is allowed to emerge unexpectedly as thematic and to mark in mood the meaning of the close.

Example 94 shows in detail the way in which individual blocks, identical in their duration and component potential are, nevertheless, individually realized: the ordering of pitches, the temporal subdivision, and the placement of the flourish vary from block to block within a stratum. For example, in stratum 8, an initial flourish leads to equal 2-second G, B, and F♯'s, then to an identical pitch sequence that is temporally uneven, and next to an also irregular sequence in which the three ostinatic pitches are rearranged: B, F♯, G, B, F♯.

It is the fluid and variegated relationship between the categorical consistency of the overall design and the flexibility of actual detail that lends to the whole the desired equipoise between macro-stability and micro-level mobility.

Example 95

The rhythmic structure of 13 ostinatic layers in element ① of Movement I, *Symphony[Myths]*.

Example 96

A detail of the 13-layered rhythmic structure from Example 95.

The *internal rhythms* controlling the ostinatic alternations within each stratum block are derived by multiplying a basic rhythmic unit (here it is the ♪) by a series of integer values taken from one of the rhythmic series in Example 84. Some appropriate combination of the following units is fit to each block:

$3 \times$ ♪ $= 0.375$ seconds at MM 60,
$5 \times$ ♪ $= 0.625,$
$9 \times$ ♪ $= 1.125,$
$16 \times$ ♪ $= 2.0,$
$29 \times$ ♪ $= 3.625,$
$52 \times$ ♪ $= 6.5,$
$94 \times$ ♪ $= 11.75.$

Some approximations are required in order that each block contain an appropriate sum. These "non-conforming" durations (e.g., 1.75 in stratum 9, Ex. 96) define the extent of the flourishes, and thus a conflict between adopted constraints and expressive need is resolved. (The rhythmic design of both large rocks in Movement I was based on the same 1, 3, 5, 9, 16, 29, 52, 94 integer collection, since it allowed for a wider durational variety than the 1, 2, 4, 7,... collection would have.)

In Examples 95 and 96, what had been a schematic and numerical level of planning (cf. Exs. 93 and 94) is converted into precise rhythms at the prevailing tempo. (Note that the design shown here is for the initial, male rock ①.)

Although the rhythms for the 13 strata are all plotted out on a 4/4 metrical basis, the resultant, composite rhythm was then examined and rebarred for optimum performance, as can be seen above layer 13 in Example 96.

Example 97

The derivation of the 3-stranded central section of Movement I of *Symphony[Myths]* begins with a subdivision of the 3-level pitch resource first shown in Examples 80 and 81.

The process of deriving the three-part counterpoint that supports the middle section of Movement I is shown in Examples 97–101. The central section (blocks ㉒, ⑲, ⑱, ⑰, ⑯, and ⑮, cf. Ex. 87) is a three-part contrapuntal strand, lyrically falling from the highest register (the top of the Izanagi rock) downwards towards its female counterpart (Izanami) (cf. Exs. 86 and 90). In keeping with the principles of pitch design discussed in Examples 79–81, this passage depends upon the central or "melodic" level pitch series (91 tones). The procedure was one of successive approximation, just as arriving at the detail of the rhythmic design for blocks ①, ⑤, and ⑪ was.

The first stage established a roughly aligned linear succession, block by block (from ㉒ to ⑲ to ⑱, etc.). This was done by distributing the pitches from the 91-note succession between three adjacent lines, maintaining correct succession in each (cf. Ex. 98). The sequences 4, 7, 8, 11; 2, 3, 6, 9, 12; and 1, 5, 10 are in chronological order. In Example 99, the ordering of the sequences was refined so that the relative voice-leading and hence the harmonic motion was determined. Finally, as can be seen in Examples 100 and 101, the voice-leading criterion (which pitches are to combine and in which orderings) was concretized rhythmically, with values derived by multiplying the 1, 3, 5, 9,... number collection by the basic note value ♪. The upper line combines $52 + 16 + 16 + 16 = 100$, the middle one $9 + 9 + 16 + 9 + 29 + 5 + 16 + 7$ ($+ 9$ when transferred to the lower line $= 16$) $= 100$, the lower one is $16 + 9 + 16 + 29 + 29 + 1 = 100$. This rhythmic design was finalized in conjunction with a dynamic and articulative level of consideration that helped to optimize the harmonic and melodic flow of the whole passage. As with parallel discussions regarding *Variation*, rhythm here involves an intuitive fitting of a resource with set content but flexible application within a given framework of conditions.

Example 98
Rough counterpoint is established in *Symphony[Myths]*, using a 3-part distribution of the 91-note central row composite.

Example 99
Increasing precision of harmonic positioning (L = longer value and S = shorter), *Symphony[Myths]*.

Example 100
A detail of the specific rhythmic values from *Symphony[Myths]* as they refine the relative temporal placement, drawing upon the rhythmic collection of integers.

Example 101
The completed voice-leading of elements ㉒ and ⑲, Movement I, *Symphony[Myths]*.

Example 102
The preliminary design for the overall structure of *Symphony[Myths]* suggests the design of Movement III.

Let us now turn to the second large movement of *Symphony[Myths]*. Returning to a preliminary version of the overall design (Ex. 102), it is possible to observe how the general idea of an introductory passage followed by two cycles of contraction and expansion, and then a coda-like close was formalized, allowing for two strata of independently converging and diverging successions of subblock sections (Ex. 103). These function in a parallel way to the regular subsections of each stratum of the Movement I masses ①and ⑤: to support at the local level the overall nature of the larger blocks and the structural divisions of the whole movement that they, in turn, serve.

The expanding or contracting trends of subunit durations in the two rhythmic strata are drawn, as one might expect, from the original large-scale extension of the logarithmic series shown in Examples 82 and 83, in effect they are the same values used to define phase differences in the design of the first movement composite strata: regularly repeated there, constantly changing here in a trending fashion.

Example 103
The developed plan for Movement III of *Symphony[Myths]*.

The final plan for Movement III in Example 103 is clearly shaped, but it provides for, rather than specifies (yet), the details that will directly support a realization. Provision is made for introductory and closing functions (㉑, ⑭, and ⑩) and the remainder of the movement is devoted to the clashing arrivals at 185 and 368 seconds. The upper (the "5") layer is consistently more fine-grained than is the lower (the "4") layer.

Example 104
Symphony[Myths], Movement III, detailed plan for the first cycle of convergence.

The converging or expanding segments of the upper and lower strata now are given further momentum by an iterative pattern within each block subsection, whereby the same harmonic structure recurs as chords of identical duration. The number of such repetitions in the upper stratum is 2, 4, or 7 (from the 1, 2, 4, 7, 13,... collection in Ex. 84) while those for the lower stratum, are repeated 3, 5, or 9 times (from the 1, 3, 5, 9,... collection).

The variance of duration in the length of block subsections and thus of their equal subdivisions (into 4 or 5, for example) mitigates against points of coincidence between these coexistent but non-synchronous processes. Only at the center (between the upper stratum subsections ㉑ and ㉓ and the lower stratum subsections ⑳ and ㉒ as seen in Ex. 104) do they meet. (There is a lone exception around 213 seconds, on the lower half of this diagram.)

In order to further energize the perceived effect of the two rhythmic strata, every fifth swell of the upper level and every seventh in the lower level is activated by the addition of iterative detail including trills and repeated notes. The waxing and then later the waning of the number of elements occurring during a unit time (combined with the reduction and then expansion of block size) confers a palpable sense of arrival upon the center of each of the two large cycles. This experience of dynamic change is further enhanced by the irregular, disruptive energies of the textured swells.

Example 105
The secondary pitch resource for *Symphony[Myths]* (as in Exs. 80 and 81), showing the chord sources for Movement III strata.

Example 106
The chordal structure for upper and lower strata, first convergence, Movement III, of *Symphony[Myths]*.

The evolution of pitch design for the two cyclical strata can be followed in Examples 105 and 106. Examining Example 106, it can be seen that the density of chords in the two layers has a numerical aspect just as their repetition patterns do. The 1, 2, 4, 7, 13,... number collection guides the upper layer while the 1, 3, 5, 9,... collection constrains the lower. Utilizing the most detailed level pitch series (with 180 notes), harmonic choices are made according to the following sequence of steps:

Begin the lower layer's first chord with the initial pitch (B♮) of the basic 29-note pitch series, introduced in Example 81.

Take, in order, the number of pitches from the 180-note series necessary to meet the immediate density specification (here, for the initial chord of the bottom layer, 3).

Begin the next selection — now for the upper rhythmic stratum — with the next available pitch from the 29-tone series (G♮), and again count off the number of pitches required (here, 4).

Continue this alternating process (with occasional overlaps).

The interaction of aspects of this procedure for establishing the harmonic interplay between strata causes several circumstances that, again, involve a mediating adjustment:

In some cases, the result of moving on to the next available pitch from the 29-note series (as happens between the first trichord, B, C, E, and the second beginning on G), would produce a logistically unacceptable situation. Thus, for example, here, the third pitch of the 29-note series is included in the second tetrachord (G, C♯, G♯, C), and thus the next "available" pitch from the basic series would be F♯.

I chose to begin instead with C♯, creating a 3-tone overlap in the content of the third and fourth chords, but preserving, thereby, the ongoing criterion of beginning each chordal aggregate with one of the 29-level pitches, in series.

The unpredictable gaps or congestion that come about in proceeding this way inevitably leaves groups of notes from the 180-note series unused. These become a "free" resource that is employed in various ways to harmonically inflect the basic progressions in the two layers. They are (cf. Ex. 106) identified as "pre" or "free", indicating that they will be used as rapid, anacrustic chords leading to the primary, repeated harmonies, or in some other idiosyncratic fashion.

As was the case in the design of the center section of the first movement, the intermediate stage shown in Example 106 allowed me to synchronize the interaction and evolution of the two harmonic strata as they were worked out. There were numerous adjustments of registration and iterative numbers in order to maximize desirable harmonic superimpositions and to minimize those that were undesirable.

Whispers Out of Time (1988) for string orchestra.

Example 107
The subsection proportionality for *Whispers Out of Time*.

In the string orchestra work *Whispers Out of Time*, a comparable external image led to a characteristic treatment of phrase lengths. Instead of two mythic centers involving rock pairs,

I used a poem. In *Self-Portrait in a Convex Mirror*, John Ashbery repeatedly employs images involving a back and forth movement in space, and in time, from our contemporary existence to the 16th-century world of Mannerist painter Parmigianino. For example, "In a movement, supporting the face, which swims / Toward and away…"; "Lively and intact in a recurring wave / Of arrival…"; "But how far can it swim out through the eyes / And still return safely…"; "… as you fall back at a speed / Faster than that of light to flatten ultimately…" This aperiodic fluctuation of perspective, felt in different ways, seemed to me so fundamental a matter in the affective impact of the poem that I decided that the form of my musical response must be infused with this same phenomenon. Example 107 shows the way a favorite basic series of logarithmically spaced numerical proportions (3.5, 5.5, 9, 14.5, 23.5, 38) was used to create a continuous flow of contiguously related proportional values.

Although the larger sections of the six movements are not in strict accord with extensions of the above proportional sequence, their component subsections never stray from a conjunct succession (although, in Movement V, there are occasional repetitions of a durational value). There is no question in my mind that the fluid continuity of related proportionality in the sectional structure of *Whispers* is an important factor in projecting the desired poetic elasticity.

Personae (1990) for solo violin, chamber ensemble, stereophonic or quadraphonic computer processed sound.

Example 108
The overall plan for *Personae*.

It is now appropriate to examine in more detail than was useful in the first Essay how the proportional aspects of *Personae*'s form were derived, and, in turn, how their small integer set, rhythmic counterparts were arrived at and used. Example 109 shows a piece of semi-log graph paper on which various proportional relationships were tentatively considered (even the notion of non-linear curves). In Example 110, a variety of related number successions are arranged in a table as they were considered. At the lower right of Example 109, a straight line establishes a logarithmic relationship between 29, 48, and 80, as the relative durations of the initial sections of the three strata of the plan: Tape, 29; Ensemble, 48; Solo, 80.

Example 109
A semi-logarithmic grid allows a set of straight lines at different slopes to establish the related numerical series necessary to shape the overall form of *Personae*.

Example 110
Data from a page of the sketchbook for *Personae*, showing the derivation of proportional series relationships and of a set of integers for controlling rhythm.

Examining the bottom two rows of the primary table in Example 110, the following picture emerges: the first of these lays out a logarithmically related series that can be found in Example 109: 29, 54, 102, 192, 356, 668, and 1252. These numbers can be thought of as establishing points along a line that delimit proportional durations. The first element duration is 29 seconds. If 29 is subtracted from the next proportional point (54), the result is 25, and this will be the time intervening until the next occupied duration which is $102 - 54 = 48''$ long, etc. Four different series beginning with 48 were examined as possible determinants of the Ensemble series (48, 146,...; 48, 200,...; 48, 213,...; 48, 166,...). The Solo series (the top row in the table) was the first settled on and was the basis for the Solo layer durations of 80, 78, 200, and 530 seconds, and also for an overall length for the whole composition of 1380 seconds, or 23 minutes.

The numerical processes I am describing here establish a basic nature for the structure of the work and help to spur, as well as guide, invention. Still, it is often the case that adjustments are made in later stages of composition or in rehearsals. I am not troubled by the notion that a regularity that serves as a scaffolding, that forms part of the basis for the working out of a musical composition, might then require modification as it gains actual physicality in rehearsal. It would, on the other hand, never occur to me to argue that numerical precision or proportional exactness will necessarily confer upon this or any composition, special merit. The function of proportionality is to establish local normalcy, or conventionality, a coherence that is generally adhered to but not slavishly followed.

As a part of the process by means of which three parallel, 7-term logarithmic series were chosen (each resulting in four sections, appropriately spaced out in time), offset times for their beginnings in the overall plan were factored in: in the case of the Tape layer, a delay of 128 seconds added to the overall duration of 1252'' (last box on the second row from the bottom of the table in Ex.110) results in the correct total duration of 1380. A further proportional subdivision of the last, very large Solo layer duration (530'') was also made in precise parallel to the way that the full-scale subdivisions were. The Ensemble stratum was subject to two requirements: that it must have a duration with an 80'' offset — so as to begin immediately after the opening violin Solo — and that its length total be $2 \times 1380 - 80 = 2680$. There were other considerations as well, however. The arrangement of elements in the three layers was not, of course, a matter of chance:

The first Ensemble section (its response to Solo I) was to enter precisely as the first Solo ended.

The second Solo was to begin, with the first Tape response, just as the first Ensemble response ended. (Thus, the very first sequence of layer entrances is optimally clear to the listener.)

I wanted, also, the blocks related to Solo II to occur in close proximity, but in a new temporal relationship: Solo, Tape, Ensemble.

The related Solo III elements were to be more widely distributed and to be already interpenetrated by Solo IV forms.

Thus, it will be clear, even when the first two requirements were met, there was still considerable adjustment necessary. As a result, the non-linear curves on Example 109 were also considered.

The derivation of the small integer series that controls rhythm can also be traced in Example 110. Taking as a starting point the scheme of proportional subdivisions associated with the Ensemble layer (48, 160, 422, 1000), a sequence of factorings and roundings-off brought about a related series of small integers:

48,   98,   160,   282,   422,   670,   1000

divided by 2 =

24,   49,   80,   141,   211,   335,   500

rounded off to the nearest number divisible by 5 and then divided by 5:

5,   10,   16,   28,   42,   67,   100

rounded off again to the nearest number divisible by 5, and divided by 5:

1,   2,   3,   6,   9,   13,   20

In effect, the original series is rounded off to the nearest multiple of 50, and then divided by that factor, but as one follows a less economical path, it is sometimes the case that more unexpected possibilities emerge. Dispatch may mislead. This collection became the source of basic rhythmic definition for all *composed* (as contrasted with algorithmically extrapolated) materials.

Example 111
Comparison of the absolute durations of rhythmic values at the four tempos used in *Personae*.

Characterization of the four basic solo sections (discussed in the first Essay) required movement at distinctive rates. Again, as was the case with *Variation*, a structure of related tempos was evolved, one that would allow for reasonably precise renotation of material written originally at one tempo and then recast at a different one for simultaneous presentation, as the overall plan sometimes requires.

Looking at the plan in Example 108, one can see that the very slow Meditator material (330–530 seconds), conceived at a MM 44 speed, overlaps with the last of the Ensemble Dancer element. The Dancer material is conceived at MM 132 (cf. Ex. 111); if it maintains its natural perceptual speed, a choice will be necessary between conveying the composite of soloist and ensemble in MM 132 or 44. In general, since the four Solo elements move, respectively, at MM 66, 132, 44, and 88, the plan shown in Example 108 involves several such speed intersections.

The chart in Example 111 shows that, although the four tempi used in *Personae* are simply related, when smaller, irregular beat subdivisions come into play, approximate equivalences are still required. The chart shows the various alternative approximations so that optional choices can be made in each renotation, and, hence, although interacting through superimposition, each musical character can maintain, more or less, its temporal individuality. At the left is a column giving the absolute duration in seconds of each unit specified in the next four columns in the $2:3:4:6$ proportionality of speeds.

Example 112
The row chart for *Personae*.

Personae's series is, for me, uncharacteristically conjunct, confined to only three intervals. It ensures the possibility of a direct transfer of row forms into figurative usage, and *Personae* did not, therefore, require the intermediate, conjunct linear pitch structures employed in *Symphony[Myths]* (cf. Exs. 80 and 81). There is a more reductive world of pitch relationships in this work when compared with the *Symphony* or *Variation*, for example, and there is a reason for this. My image for *Personae* was very concentrated from the outset. I wanted the Ensemble materials to be directly derived from those of the soloist (cf. Exs. 120–122), while the Tape materials were *literally* dependent upon the Solo writing as performed. This closeness suggested to me a less highly flavored and more malleable pitch resource.

Example 113
The first page of the sketch for Solo I of *Personae.*

The first page of the sketch for The Conjuror (Solo I) appears in Example 113. Above the two staves containing the primary line is a time line showing the subsectional structure by beats at MM 66. The inner proportions were derived from the basic logarithmic relationship mentioned above (80, 48, 29, 18, 11) as defining the size of the opening section in each layer. Since the total duration of Solo I is 80", 80 − 48 = 32; 48 − 29 = 19; 29 − 18 = 11; and 18 gave an appropriate total. They were arranged in a 19, 11, 32, 18 order to support a later culmination. Each section was then subdivided according to a similarly shaped but reordered proportionality, so that 19 seconds became, in beats, 11, 5.25, 2.5, 2.25; 11 seconds became 6.5, 3.25, 1.25, 1 beats; etc. This change in the durational contour of sectional non-linearity came about in an effort to create the effect of a "cresting" of intensity at the close of each of the four subsections.

For the first two parts of the "19" subdivision, the basic rhythmic unit is ♪.

11 beats contain 44 ♪'s.

The rhythmic integer collection for *Personae* is 1, 2, 3, 6, 9, 13, 20 (cf. Ex. 110).

A sequence of values drawn freely from this collection is found that serves the musical intent and also sums to 44:

13, 1, 9, 1, 2, 6, 1, 1, 1, 9 = 44

The same process provides:

9, 1, 3, 1, 1, 2, 1, 1, 1, 1 = 21 x 's for 5.25 beats. (Some flexibility is added rhythmically within the first 9 and in the later quintuplet that bridges the 3, 1, 1, 2,... sequence.)

At the next subdivision, 2.5 seconds, the basic unit changes to ♪⁶ from ♪ and the resulting 15 units are distributed approximately:

1, 6, 1, 1, 1, 3, 1, 1 = 15 (this as in the music, not as above the stave).

Note the approximation that occurs here. The collection beginning at the top right of Example 113 (in the music 1, 6, 1, 1, 1, 3, 1, 1) and associated with this 2.5-beat unit was, of necessity, shifted forward slightly. The actual beginning should have been (according to the preceding 5.25-beat second subsection) on the second ♪ (or 0.25) of the beat. But it actually occurs at ♪³ (or 0.33) of the beat, and there is, thus, an "error" of 0.08 seconds. The musical continuity is not strained by this adjustment, in part because the components of the rhythmic gestures here are fairly anonymous (in their relativity of large versus small).

After an unarticulated 2.25" subsection, another 6.5-second subsection follows, also with a ♪⁶ basic unit (the notation above the second staff system regarding these 39 ♪⁶ beats is incomplete):

13, 3, 3, 6, 1, 1, 1, 1, 3, 1, 3, 1, 2 = 39

and then the temporal grain returns to the ♪. What happens, in effect, is that there are small adjustments in perceived tempo while the basic collection of numerical components out of which rhythms can be devised, proportionally, remains constant. Of course, the integer collection for *Personae* (1, 2, 3, 6, 9, 13, 20) is rather characterless — one might charitably say "flexible" — at its low end, taking on profile only with the larger values 9, 13, and 20.

A further temporal element is overlaid on the design just described in the form of a relentlessly rising series of *sffz* events, which I thought of as a "clock" function, occurring regularly every 5.5 beats. Although the disruptive influence of this sequence is small at the outset, it grows slightly more so as more than one pitch is included — always *ff* — in the interjection.

The pitch design of the clock layer is very straightforward (particularly as this is the opening passage of the work), beginning with a sequential presentation of the AO (original) form of the row. A braiding effect occurs, however, because this sequence is interspersed with a basic line already formed out of a different sequence of rows: the A♭ Mirror, followed by DO, where the 12th tone of the first row is shared as the first of the second form. The sketch was initially begun in a straightforward 4/4 scheme and then rebarred as the development of the music required.

As has been indicated earlier, the process of composition itself becomes an intuitive interplay of categories of choice to be made against and within a preexistent framework of shaping constraint. In the case of the Solo sections of this concerto, the constraints are comparatively slight, since there is a particular requirement to achieve an effective projection of the characteristics of the four basic personae. In other words, the particular *inflections* in the writing may be of basic importance, here, to project the intended personae, and thus a looser framework was adopted, one that would better accommodate whimsy.

Example 114
Diagrams showing the internal proportional structure of Solos III and IV *(Personae)*.

Example 115
Details of the inner structure of Solo III, including the distribution of harmonic content *(Personae)*.

The plan for Solo III (The Meditator) is shown in Example 114, and is marked by its symmetry. In an effort to underscore this nascent tendency (the fact that the beat equivalents of the time proportions given [7 + 13.25 + 24.25 = approximately 44, and 10.25 = approximately 11] suggested structures within cycles of 11 beats). As has been the case with Solo I, a two-level approach was also taken to the rhythmic organization of the material for this Solo.

An alternating pattern of two subdivisions of 11-beat units was used, as can be seen in Example 115:

4 + 7, 3 + 3 + 5, 4 + 7, 3 + 3 + 5, etc.

Superimposed on this modulated regularity is another pattern which closely approximates the basic proportions of the Solo III subsections:

7, 13, 24, 11, 11, 24, 13, 7

The basic sequence (made up of 4 + 7 and 3 + 3 + 5-beat groupings) establishes a tranquil, chorale-like harmonic process, repetitive, but nevertheless asymmetrical. The overlayed 7, 13, 24, etc., establish the contour of a tendency towards elaborate embellishment that is metaphorically associated with "enlightenment". There is, then, a kind of expansive chant that occasionally gives way to flight, this in the service of the Meditator persona.

Meter is normally only an organizational device for me, facilitating performance by its grouping and coordinating capacities. Loosening the tie between harmonic function and meter has diminished the latter's importance. Incessant metrical shifts in more complex contemporary music further disrupt its middle level temporal function: that which establishes a framework of regularity above the level of individual beats, a reference that can function powerfully in relation to flexible phrase structure. I have not been attracted by the tendency of some composers to slow tempi radically, employing minute beat subdivision in a virtual substitution of beat for bar. My approach to the level of musical discourse that the measure has traditionally addressed can be found in the refined lower limits of proportional, sectional subdivisions such as those in Solo I, discussed in relation to Example 113. Sometimes, nevertheless, metric units come into play for me particularly when repetitive patterns are involved, as they are, appropriately, here.

Each sub-element of the 11-beat segments is assigned a harmonic substance identified by a Roman numeral and a letter. The derivation of these harmonic identities can be seen in Examples 116 and 117.

Example 116

The initial derivation of the harmonic resource for Solo III *(Personae)*.

Example 117

A more advanced stage of categorization for the dyad content of Solo III *(Personae)*.

Three overlapping row forms (ER, FM, BM) provide a linear resource from which consecutive groups of 3, 6, 4, 7, 5, and 8 pitches are taken (= 33, relating this process to the local conventionality of "11"). These pitch collections are voiced as vertical chords within the range of the violin, and with due consideration of its physical structure (the four strings, their tuning, etc.) as well as performance problems. Categorically labeled chords corresponding to the above densities were worked out:

    3 — I
    6 — II
    4 — III
    7 — IV
    5 — V
    8 — VI

The density range (3 to 8) in its unordered state came about because the same bar-defined sequence (4, 7/3, 3, 5/4, 7/3, 3, 5/4, 7) occurs twice as a result of Solo III's symmetry, and hence there was an aggregate need for 24 dyadic resources. The basic pattern of 4 Solos suggested four cycles of six chords ($\Rightarrow 4 \times 6 = 24$). The six, non-repeating integers that sum to 33 are 3, 4, 5, 6, 7, 8, and they were permuted by interleaving two rising groups of three: odds, 3, 4, 5, and evens, 6, 7, 8.

An optimal chord spacing was designed, including a high percentage of open strings and natural harmonics to nourish a clean, predictably uninflected sonority. Smooth dyadic transitions from one aspect to another were searched out and categorized as Ia, Ib, Ic, and so on (cf. bottom and top three staves associated with central chords I, II, III,…, Ex. 116). In the first set, Ia, the open A-string is joined first by an A♯ on the E-string and then this is smoothly crossed over to F♯ on the D-string.

Naturally, the harmonically denser chords (such as the 8-tone one) generate the largest number of options (8 in this case), and this helps to lend variability and dimension to the resulting passages that traverse these chords in changing but harmonically redundant ways. All of these derived materials were then gathered together and categorized (reading across): IA, IB, IH, IIA, IIB, IIC, IIH,… in the chart in Example 117. Below, the distribution of actual densities is surveyed: 3-element phrases occur twice; 5, 6, 7, and 8-element phrases one time each in the A column, for example. The A-H columns came about as a result of the desire to categorize conveniently. It might appear that they lend some differentiation to harmonic resource, fluctuating as they do from the use of all six chord densities (in categories A, B, and H) to only one (in category G). But this is a circumstantial envelope, and was not put into play in the actual choice of dyad resources assigned in the metric scheme of Example 115.

Example 118

The dyadic successions specified in Ex. 115 are realized as actual progressions.

In Example 118, the design schematically presented in Example 115 is written out on a stave, sequentially. Now all aspects of the dyadic subphrases must be considered so that fluidity of line and technical feasibility are given due weight. It is worth emphasizing that even with such careful preparation and an expansiveness of tempo, such dyadic successions are extremely perilous in performance. I had to decide whether or not a certain instability or hesitancy (inherent in the effort to combine harmonics and stopped notes in double stops, for example) fit with the musical character envisioned.

Example 119

The sketch from the beginning of Solo III (The Meditator) in *Personae* showing the harmonic successions of Example 118 combined with the temporal proportions indicated in Example 115.

In Example 119, the rhythmic dimension is added. Note that, while the distribution of harmonies over time does conform to the slower pace of the irregular metric periodicity (4/4, 7/4, 3/4, 3/4, 5/4,…), each metric unit has associated with it a characteristic "inner temporal grain". This grain, whether based on the unit ♪^{5} (as in the 4/4), ♪ (in 7/4), ♪^{6} (in 3/4), or ♩'s (in 5/4), is activated flexibly as a function of the number of events in the designated harmonic traversal (namely, 7 in the VI$_E$ assigned to the first 7/4 in Example 119, and 6 to the VI$_C$ assigned to the second 7/4). Thus, as mentioned above, the bar is acting, here, in a way that is directly analogous to the subsections of 11, 5.25, 2.5, 2.25, 6.5, etc., beats in Example 113. (Note also that, in the actual realization of V$_C$ in the first bar of Ex. 119, as compared with the categories in Ex. 117, the A^b was changed to A.)

Further rhythmic flexibility is necessarily introduced as the second structural aspect of this Solo (embellishment) begins to appear: first around the 7th beat (during the first 7/4 bar), with an accelerating and decelerating trill activity, and then around the 20th beat (at the third beat of the first 5/4) and the 44th (7 + 13 + 24, cf. Ex. 115) at the 5th beat of the second 5/4, with more trill activity. The embellishment here is comparable in concept, though not in effect, to the intrusive *sffz* clock that invades Solo I. There is such a character-deepening addition that illuminates each persona in some germane fashion.

The feeling of this passage should remain tranquil, spaciously paced, but irregular enough to suggest an uncommon physical (and mental) respiration that is tenuously maintained, one that occasionally trembles.

Example 120
A derived harmonic structure for use in the Ensemble response to Solo III (*Personae*).

In Example 120, the same collection of chords derived for Solo III (Ex. 116) now becomes the basis for the instrumental harmony in the Ensemble III response beginning at rehearsal letter H [page 35 in the C. F. Peters edition of the score]. The spacing of these basic harmonies, however, is greatly broadened not only to take advantage of the greater registral and timbral resource of the Ensemble as a whole (as compared to the compass of a violin), but also to reflect the much slower harmonic rhythm (the first Ensemble chord is held almost nine beats at MM 44), for the factor 2.2 now multiplies the numerical sequence 4, 7, 3, 3, etc., mirroring the metric structure of the Meditator Solo, so that the succession is now:

8.8 beats, 15.4, 6.6, 6.6 beats, etc.

Utilizing only the six basic pitch collections from which the dyads used for Solo III were generated, a viable succession of ten harmonic regions (Ex. 120) was arrived at, filling out the basic sonority for letter H. The density-8 chord (VI) is divided into two tetrachords which oscillate in order to maintain a relative harmonic clarity and to reinforce the meditative tranquillity of this persona.

Example 121
A sketch page for the Ensemble response to Solo III corresponding to Example 120.

Example 122
The printed score page from *Personae* corresponding to the Example 121 sketch.

The spaciousness of the Ensemble harmonies here is used as a foil against which fluid cadenzas in the bass clarinet (cf. Ex. 121), viola, and then piano occur, while a lyrical obligato unfolds in the high register for the solo violin. The violin line is not yet present in the sketch shown, but can be seen in its final form in Example 122. The pitch material of the superimposed solos is taken directly from the row chart shown in Example 112, and thus various forms and rates of evolution of the basic series are simultaneously projected as is normally the case in my music.

This example indicates the ways in which ensemble material reflecting each of the first three solo personae could be derived from their organizational underpinnings, both from the pitch and also rhythmic or textural design. Evidently, this process is very straightforward in this instance. In others, such as the playing out of the three-level ostinatic structure underlying Solo II, it was much more involved. The fourth persona, The Advocate, is less easily characterized so far as derivation is concerned because it has a heavier functional burden: a far greater length, the requirement of summation and restatement of earlier solos, as well as rhetorical completion.

Solo IV is reflective of the persona The Advocate. The purpose of this music is to summarize what has come before while adding — to the Advocate's closing argument, as it were — a new sense of urgency. The distinctive moderation of the original Solo III (The Meditator) had to be overcome, and this was done by using the SPLITZ algorithm. A 97-term proportional series was applied to an original phrase 200 seconds in length in order to achieve an "output" of 285 seconds. This length, in turn, was required in order to span the duration between 945 and 1230 seconds in the overall plan (cf. Ex. 108), bridging inclusively the two III subsections of IV: IV_{III} and $IV_{II/III}$. These two subsections come at the beginning: IV_{III} $945 - 1019 = 74$ seconds, and end: $IV_{IV/III}$ $1197 - 1230 = 33$ seconds of the 285-second "output" section of algorithmically derived material.

A basic unit of $\flat^7$ at MM 44 provided an appropriate rate of motion, and this required, then, a sum for the proportional series such that:

60 / 44 = 1.3636 (the duration of a beat at MM 44)

1.3636 / 7 = approximately 0.1948

or, at MM 44 = approximately 0.1948 seconds per $\flat^7$

The desire here was, then, to have an output with units of time that were factors of 0.1948-second subunits (0.1948×2, 0.1948×3,...).

Because the materials here were from Solo III, the proportions of its Ensemble sections were taken as the terms of the proportional series for the SPLITZ algorithm: 20, 38, 70, 29 (cf. Ex. 108 from 668–1090 seconds of the overall plan). A proportional series was found where the total sum of a 97-term collection of 20's, 38's, 70's, and 29's would = 17746. The total number of terms for a SPLITZ series must be odd (as previously discussed in regard to Ex. 71), but the term magnitude of 97 — as contrasted, say, with 79 or 63 — came about as a function of the need for an output subunit of $\flat^7$ length (0.1948).

Example 123
Basic exploration of "proportional series" characteristics in preparation for applying the SPLITZ algorithm to Solo III material from *Personae*.

The 200-second Solo III original statement divided into 17746 parts gives 0.01127-seconds/part, and

$20 \times 0.01127 = 0.2254$

$29 \times 0.01127 = 0.3268$

$38 \times 0.01127 = 0.4283$

$70 \times 0.01127 = 0.7889$

These durations match acceptably with multiples of the basic $\flat^7$ unit:

$0.2254 \Rightarrow 0.1948$

$0.3268 \Rightarrow 0.3896$

$0.4283 \Rightarrow 0.5844$

$0.7889 \Rightarrow 0.7792$

Example 124

The results from a computer run of the SPLITZ algorithm used to generate material for Solo IV
from *Personae*.

The computer print-out in Example 124 shows the points in the original 200-second span from which segments are extracted (Columns 5 and 7 indicate time in sample numbers), how long the extracted segment is (Column 4) and where the segment is to be situated in the resulting 285-second output passage (Column 2). On the far right, the time in seconds (Column 2) has been converted to beats at MM 44.

The relevant segment numbers are given in column 6 (①, ③,..., ④⑨ for the odd half-pass, ⑤⓪, ⑤①,..., ⑨⑦ for the even). Because higher sample numbers indicate later clock times in the original source, it will be evident that odd segments are cut out of the source in chronological order, from beginning to end, and that they are similarly mapped out in the derived output. The even segments, also extracted from beginning to end, however, are resituated in reverse order in the derived output passage, as was discussed in relation to Examples 71–78. Thus, not only is the rhythmic grain (at MM 88) further refined to ♪^{7} units continually articulated in the derived passage (♪^{6} at MM 44 was the smallest value in the source passage, and only in the 3/4 bars), but the order in time of the original materials is shuffled. There is a heterogeneous mix of early and late materials (referring here to the original source passages from Solo III) at the beginning and end of the newly derived music, but its central portions (were they to have been used) would have been more or less in their original surroundings, as is characteristic of the SPLITZ process.

Example 125

A detail from the beginning of the sketch for Solo III from *Personae*, showing the rhythmic points
at which segments were extracted by the SPLITZ algorithm.

The original beginning of Solo III is shown, in sketch, in Example 125. Below it the segments designated by the algorithm are indicated by successive rhythmic values that are multiples of the ♪^{7} unit. Rising (①, ②, ③,... odd segments) numbers alternate with falling (⑨⑦, ⑨⑥,... even segments) values. Towards the end of the 7/4 bar, the larger numbers in the proportional series (304, 232,..., cf. Ex. 119 as well) begin to have their effect, and recognizable subsegments of Meditator materials are allowed to enter the Advocate's agitated discourse. Naturally, the initial, tiny fragments, only ♪^{7} long, would be very difficult to recognize independently of the larger, derived context. Because only the beginning 74-second and the last 33-second portions of the derived materials are used (cf. the earlier discussion under Exs. 108 and 124), there was no need to determine the identity of finely divided segments for the central portions of the derived passage, for they would not have been used in any case.

The combination of relatively slow harmonic evolution and extraction of small segments ensures that the resulting material from this application of the algorithm will have a repetitive, urgent, intensely rhetorical character as it reappears in Solo IV.

Example 126

The beginning of the sketch for Solo IV from *Personae*, showing the laying out in a new continuity
of the small segments of Solo III that have been algorithmically identified and repositioned.

Example 127
Detail of Example 126.

Examining the sketches in Examples 125–127 shows just how radically the influence of the algorithm has altered the Solo III. The detail also makes clear that a further level of rhetorical recursiveness (not at all inappropriate to an advocate's ways) was introduced by the second algorithmic pass of SPLITZ: extracts, ①, ②, ③,..., with which this passage begins, recur again starting at the second beat of the second bar here, but they are now interspersed not only with the occasional even segment (from late in the Solo III passage which was used as a source: ㊿, (51)), but also by more advanced elements from the same odd series (⑪, ⑫,...). As this passage unfolds (cf. pages 46–47 in the C. F. Peters published score, Exs. 128 and 129), it continues to grow more diverse and discontinuous, suggesting the rising agitation of the Advocate's argument.

Example 128
Page 46 from the published score of *Personae.*

Example 129
Page 47 from the published score of *Personae.*

Example 130
The original sketch for a particular spatialization effect included in the computer part of *Personae.*

One aspect of the design and realization of the whole composition has not yet been broached: the spatial distribution and differentiation of information in the computer processed layer. Because of the inevitable and desirable close spectral parallels between the solo violin and the computer processed responses presented during a performance (the computer contributions, it will be recalled, are all derived from actual recordings of the solo violin materials), particular attention was paid to the spatial characterization of the electroacoustic element: the contrast between the stationary and proximate soloist and the mobile and often spacious quality of its computer-processed reflections was highlighted. Two examples will indicate the range of spatial strategies used in differentiating the several manifestations of violin spectra from one another.

A complex and idiosyncratic design was used for the Solo II (The Dancer) computer response. During a winter drive just before beginning work on *Personae,* I had a visual experience that was spatially suggestive and I decided to attempt to incorporate it into the new composition. The pattern of blowing snowflakes apparently rushing towards and then around the windshield of the car in which I was riding provoked the thought that something of the sort might be done with a quadraphonic disposition of tiny sonic fragments. Example 130 shows a preliminary notebook sketch of the idea. In realizing this idea, an 11-pass (that is, 11 identical odd and even sets of segments contrapuntally superimposed) SPLITZ processing produced 22 streams comprising hundreds of individual sound fragments that were used to define an identical (22) number of spatial paths with bilateral symmetry. The rough design appears at the bottom right of Example 131 and the final design in Example 132.

Example 131
Notebook sketches of spatialization strategies for *Personae.*

Example 132
The final design of the spatialization image sketched in Example 130.

Example 133 (a-b)
A portion of the detailed plan for the final section of the last Solo (The Advocate) of *Personae.*

For the Tape IV drone — some nine minutes in length — two pairs of path segments were designed, one of closed and the other of open loops (cf. Exs. 27 and 28 from the first Essay). The extended computer section corresponding to Solo IV consists of phase vocoder stretchings of relatively long tones from earlier solos (e.g., the sequence F♯, A, A♯,... appearing in Ex. 131). The resynthesis of these tones in their extended form was done so as to separate the odd from the even frequency components of each spectrum. These complementary continuities were then placed on similarly complementary spatial paths. The sketches in Example 131 show how the effects of each modular path segment were examined, and then an appropriate pair assigned to the pitches of the given sequence. (Each path sequence indicated was accompanied by another symmetrical one to establish complementing pairs.) Attention was paid not only to motion, but to the ways in which fusion and loudness would be affected by the interaction of path pairs.

The beginning of the Tape IV computer section is shown in the detailed plan of Example 133. Here, among other things, it is possible to see the sequence of paths applied to pitch in filling out the work's overall design. A canonic drone relationship between the Ensemble and computer layers can also be seen as a part of the concern, here, with tonal connectivity. But the primary effort in this passage was given to maintaining the independent integrity of several aspects of the work as a whole.

I argued earlier that the formal persuasiveness of this composition required the clear characterization and differentiation of the Solo sections one from the other. Further, the responsorial paradigm embedded in this work — that the Ensemble and the Tape both respond in their ways to each Solo statement of the violin — requires that these layers also remain perceptually separable. Lastly, since the spirit of Solo IV (The Advocate) involves summation, and this section of the piece is also the area in which the tendency for hierarchical nesting is greatest, there is, even more than elsewhere, a need to maintain clarity in the face of a convergence of material. For all of these reasons, the careful planning of a spatial signature to be impressed on the extended drones of the tape is critical. One understands the importance of this issue clearly in performance, as the solo violin is surrounded by its own emanations yet remains singular.

CONCLUDING REMARKS

It is worth restating one last time that the detailed framework of shaping methods that is presented here was not developed in the context of one compositional project, with the goal of creating a complex and comprehensive technical design. It is rather a flexible network of methods, strategies, habits that might qualify as an *ethic* of sorts (of how, when, whether to proceed). This network has come about through trial and error over more than thirty years of working as a composer. No part of it was arrived at for reasons other than those rooted in the creative requirements of particular compositions and the subsequent satisfaction or disappointment that I felt in their performances. Over time, one begins to understand what works for one and what doesn't. I have never thought of what I do as constituting a "theory", though it is certainly true that I have quite particular ways of dealing with the different needs that arise as I compose. For me, this is a critical distinction: I have a practice rather than a theory. It will be evident to the reader that the different needs (pitch, temporal design, formal shaping and so on) are also differently served from one work to the next. Each engagement, flowing more than likely from an idiosyncratic impetus, will arouse not only its own expressive envelope but, also, particularly suitable methods with which to address the factors to be brought into play. For me, technique involves a personal tool kit of sorts that can be rummaged about in, and that will reliably contain useful items to be applied in each project. It is also not unusual, though, to find oneself devising some new extension of a known way or some alternative that is required by the previously unencountered landscape of a new work. If a fresh "wholeness" such as I mentioned in the first Essay as the *sine qua non* of musical art is to be achieved in our time, it will not come about through any "natural" or wholly intuitive process. The welter of materials and contexts with which we must contend cannot be absorbed and intuitively shaped by a composer except by recourse to well-established conventionalities. To do something more responsive to our own time requires a consciousness of scaffolding and choice that must be personally forged. Disciplined ways are, of course, essential to the pro-jection of *any* intent, whatever its stylistic cloak.

The way that I try to integrate material with the larger imperatives of form is at root meant to summon a level of consistency and coherence that would have been a given for composers in a common practice period. It is an emergent characteristic of our century that a number of "local consistencies", or delimited "traditions", have been achieved. In these instances, an individual composer's sense of aesthetic consistency has been so strong that it was able to achieve its goals *in spite of* the extraordinary inconsistency of the procedures and styles that we all now face.

Varèse is an example who vehemently rejected and apparently remained purposefully uninvolved with methodologies of any sort, whereas, on the other hand, Webern built a mature language that is virtually inseparable from the methods it manifested.

As the century closes, I do not find the composer's situation to be more straightforward. To the contrary, I feel that the difficulty in and therefore the importance of achieving coherence in individual works — perhaps, if one is fortunate, even across a body of work — are absolutely fundamental. I offer the foregoing as examples for consideration and response, not, certainly, as prescriptions. There has been, in the past several decades, an almost complete silence regarding the ways in which recognized figures actually go about their work. While interviews and profiles have their place, they do not allow the necessary connections to be made between a captivating musical experience with the music in concert or on recordings and knowledge about the organizational ways that fostered it. There is, of course, more than a little "music theory" available, but this has in most cases little to do with what seems to me to be the deeper wellsprings of musical art. Description and prescription are by no means reciprocal. I am not advocating a specifically structured approach to composing. It is not clear enough at this time what direction, what new *conventionality* might emerge (and I use that word with respect). I do believe, however, that each composer needs to be conscious of evolving over his or her creative life, **a way**. This way may vary widely, but it is practiced, dimensional, flexible and nourishing, in the ideal — calling upon the full range of resource the composer has to offer to his or her work. These Essays may serve as a beginning by insisting as they mean to that one may be variously disciplined without being formally theoretical or doctrinaire. If such matters are not discussed more, we will remain in the kind of alchemical and anecdotal haze that has enveloped us in recent decades.

Notes

23.   Forward progressing samples, as with e, g, i, k in the second cycle in Ex. 65, can be contiguous as they are here or could also be overlapping (if this factor were, say, sample size/2), or non-contiguously spaced out (if this factor were sample size × 2). Note that, in the last case, some of the subject material would be omitted in the initial cycle, though it might be partially recovered in a later one.

24.   In this case, each new cycle begins later in the subject material, and therefore contributes to the convergence effect. But this effect could be reversed so that the content of the SPIRLZ output converged towards the material at the beginning of the subject, or it could remain fixed so that the traversal of the subject alters only in terms of rapidity, and one moves towards a kind of summary experience of the whole.

25.   It should be noted in passing that one could, of course, bypass the matter of samples, and deal directly in seconds, but I sometimes use the computer to make rough "sketches", applying the algorithm in differing ways until I get a result that is musically appealing. Since the computer needs to process information in particular ways, the print-out shown in Ex. 68 reflects its requirements rather than the more direct needs of the composer working "by hand" in the world of instrumental music.

26.   The prior column makes a parallel conversion for MM 81; this is required for derived sections ④ and ⑤. Also indicated above are the durations at MM 81 to be associated with certain segment lengths (as shown in column 4): 1.710 ⇒ ♩♪, 0.950 ⇒ ♩♪, etc.

27.   The second odd fragment in derived section ② was misplaced in time by one beat and then corrected.

BIBLIOGRAPHY/DISCOGRAPHY

COMPOSITIONS

Works not issued in formal, printed editions by C. F. Peters Corporation, New York, are made available, on request, in various formats as is standard practice in the music publication business. C. F. Peters is copyright owner of all works except for a few listings,* which are in the Reynolds Trust. Dates listed below are the year of composition. Manuscripts and related sketches in the Reynolds Trust are maintained in The Library of Congress, Music Division, Washington, DC.

Epigram and Evolution (piano), 1960; C. F. Peters, withdrawn.*

Situations (cello, piano), 1960.*

Acquaintances (flute, piano, contrabass), 1960; C. F. Peters, withdrawn.*

Continuum (viola, cello), 1960.*

Four Etudes (flute quartet), 1961; C. F. Peters, withdrawn.*

Consequent (alto flute, violin, bassoon, piano), 1961.*

Wedge (chamber ensemble), 1961; C. F. Peters, withdrawn.*

Dervish (piano, percussion, contrabass, stereophonic electroacoustic sound), 1962.*

Sky (soprano, alto flute, bassoon, harp), 1961.*

Mosaic (flute, piano; 12 minutes), 1962; C. F. Peters.

String Quartet (13 minutes), 1961; C.F. Peters.

The Emperor of Ice Cream (8 voices, piano, contrabass, percussion; 15.5 minutes), 1961–62; C. F. Peters; revised 1974, second edition C. F. Peters.

A Portrait of Vanzetti (instruments, narrator, stereophonic electroacoustic sound; 17 minutes), 1962–63.*

Fantasy for Pianist (solo piano; 19 minutes), 1964; C. F. Peters.

Graffiti (orchestra; 9 minutes), 1965; C. F. Peters.

Quick Are the Mouths of Earth (chamber ensemble; 19 minutes), 1964–65; C. F. Peters.

Gathering (woodwind quintet; 10 minutes), 1965; C. F. Peters.

Ambages (flute; 9.5 minutes), 1964; C. F. Peters.

Masks (orchestra, chorus; 25 minutes), 1965; C. F. Peters.

Blind Men (brass, piano, percussion, mixed chorus; 16 minutes), 1966; C. F. Peters.

Threshold (orchestra; 18 minutes), 1968; C. F. Peters.

…between… (chamber orchestra, live electronic processing; 17 minutes), 1968; C. F. Peters.

Ping (piano, flute, percussion, 35mm slide projections, film, live electronic processing, quadraphonic electroacoustic sound; 22 minutes), 1968; (originally in SOURCE Magazine, No. 6, 1969); C. F. Peters.

Traces (piano, flute, violoncello, multichannel electroacoustic sound, live electronic processing; 23.5 minutes), 1968; C. F. Peters.

I/O (9 female vocalists, 9 male mimes, 2 flutes, clarinet, 35mm slide projections, live electronic processing; 35–70 minutes), 1970; C. F. Peters.

Again (2 sopranos, 2 flutes, 2 trombones, 2 percussion, 2 contrabasses, quadraphonic electroacoustic sound, amplification, optional lighting; 30 minutes), 1970, revised 1971–74; C. F. Peters.

Compass (tenor, bass, violoncello, contrabass, 35mm slide projections, quadraphonic electroacoustic sound; 30 minutes) 1972–73; C. F. Peters.

…from behind the unreasoning mask (trombone, percussion, quadraphonic electroacoustic sound; 17 minutes), 1974–75; C. F. Peters.

Still [VOICESPACE I] (quadraphonic electroacoustic sound; 21:35), 1975; C.F. Peters.

A Merciful Coincidence [VOICESPACE II] (music theater for three vocalists, with quadraphonic electroacoustic sound; 36 minutes), 1976; C. F. Peters.

A Merciful Coincidence [VOICESPACE II] (quadraphonic electroacoustic sound; 35:47), 1976; C. F. Peters.

The Promises of Darkness (chamber ensemble; 22 minutes), 1975; C. F. Peters.

Only Now, and Again (23 winds, piano, 3 percussion; 11 minutes), 1977; C. F. Peters.

Fiery Wind (orchestra; 17.5 minutes), 1977; C. F. Peters.

…the serpent-snapping eye (trumpet, percussion, piano, quadraphonic computer generated sound; 20 minutes), 1978; C. F. Peters.

Less than Two (2 pianos, 2 percussion, quadraphonic computer generated sound; 22 minutes), 1978; C. F. Peters.

Eclipse (media version, quadraphonic computer generated sound and electronically processed voices; 16.5 minutes), visuals (film, video, 35mm slide projections) by Ed Emshwiller, 1979; C. F. Peters.

Eclipse [VOICESPACE III] (quadraphonic computer generated sound and electronically processed voices; 16:10), 1979; C. F. Peters.

The Palace [VOICESPACE IV] (bass-baritone, quadraphonic computer processed sound, modest staging, lighting; 16 minutes), 1978–80; C. F. Peters.

The Tempest (Incidental music for Shakespeare & Company's production of *The Tempest*) (quadraphonic electroacoustic sound; 40 minutes), 1980.*

Shadowed Narrative (chamber quartet; 30 minutes) 1977–82; C. F. Peters.

Archipelago (chamber orchestra, quadraphonic computer generated sound; 32.5 minutes), 1982–83; C. F. Peters.

Transfigured Wind I (solo flute; 9 minutes), 1984; C. F. Peters.

Transfigured Wind II (solo flute, orchestra, quadraphonic computer processed sound; 35.5 minutes), 1984; C. F. Peters.

Transfigured Wind III (solo flute, chamber ensemble, quadraphonic computer processed sound; 35.5 minutes), 1984.

Aether (violin and piano; 22 minutes), 1983; C. F. Peters.

Mistral (6 brass, 6 strings, amplified harpsichord; 21 minutes), 1985; C. F. Peters.

Summer Island (Islands from *Archipelago*: I) (solo oboe, quadraphonic computer generated tape; 13.5 minutes), 1984; C. F. Peters.

Transfigured Wind IV (solo flute, quadraphonic computer processed sound; 18 minutes), 1984; C. F. Peters.

Sketchbook (for *The Unbearable Lightness of Being*) (alto, piano, live electronic processing; 30 minutes), text by Milan Kundera, 1985; C. F. Peters.

Coconino…a shattered landscape (string quartet; 16.5 minutes), 1985, revised 1993; C. F. Peters.

The Behavior of Mirrors (guitar; 6.5 minutes), 1986; C. F. Peters.

Vertigo (quadraphonic computer processed sound; 16:50 or 19:30), 1985; C. F. Peters.

Vertigo (media version, quadraphonic computer processed sound, video by Ed Emshwiller; 16:50), 1985. C. F. Peters.

Autumn Island (Islands from *Archipelago*: II) (solo marimba; 14 minutes), 1986; C. F. Peters.

The Vanity of Words [VOICESPACE V] (stereophonic computer processed sound; 20:12), text by Milan Kundera, 1986; C. F. Peters.

The Dream of the Infinite Rooms (solo cello, orchestra, quadraphonic computer processed sound, 24 minutes), 1986; C. F. Peters.

Symphony[Vertigo] (orchestra, quadraphonic computer processed sound; 23 minutes), 1987; C. F. Peters.

Not Only Night (soprano, flute [picc], E♭ clarinet [B-cl], violin, cello, piano, stereophonic computer processed sound; 10 minutes), 1988; C. F. Peters.

Versions/Stages I-V (quadraphonic computer processed sound; 25 minutes), 1988–91; C. F. Peters.

Whispers Out of Time (solo violin, viola, violoncello, contrabass; string orchestra; 26.5 minutes), 1988; C. F. Peters.

Variation (solo piano; 22 minutes), 1988; C. F. Peters.

Focus a beam, emptied of thinking, outward... (solo cello; 12.5 minutes), 1989; C. F. Peters.

Personae (solo violin, chamber ensemble, stereophonic or quadraphonic computer processed sound; 26 minutes), 1990; C. F. Peters.

Dionysus (flute [picc], clarinet [B-cl], trumpet, horn, bass trombone, percussion, piano, contrabass; 14.5 minutes), 1990; C. F. Peters.

Symphony[Myths] (orchestra; 21 minutes), 1990; C. F. Peters.

Visions (string quartet; 32 minutes), 1991; C. F. Peters.

Kokoro (solo violin; 18 minutes), 1992; C. F. Peters.

Dreaming (orchestra; 24.5 minutes), 1992; C. F. Peters.

Symphony[The Stages of Life] (orchestra; 28 minutes), 1991–92; C. F. Peters.

Odyssey (8 channels of computer processed sound, 16 instruments, mezzo-soprano, bass-baritone, lighting; on a text by Samuel Beckett; 77 minutes), 1989–93; C. F. Peters.

Ivanov (Incidental music for Tadashi Suzuki's production of Chekhov's *Ivanov*) (8-channel computer processed sound; 50 minutes), 1991.*

The Ivanov Suite (quadraphonic computer processed sound; 32:20), 1991; C. F. Peters.

last things, I think, to think about (bass baritone, piano, stereophonic computer processed sound, optional 35mm slide projections; text by John Ashbery; 66 minutes), 1994; C. F. Peters.

Ariadne's Thread (string quartet, stereophonic or quadraphonic computer generated sound; 16 minutes), 1994; C. F. Peters.

Watershed I (solo percussion; 27.5 minutes), 1995; C. F. Peters.

Watershed III (solo percussion, chamber ensemble, optional real-time computer sound spatialization; 31 minutes), 1995; C. F. Peters.

Watershed IV (solo percussion, real-time computer sound spatialization; 28 minutes), 1995; C. F. Peters.

The Red Act Arias (orchestra, chorus, narrator, computer processed and spatialized vocal, instrumental, and environmental sound; 47 minutes), 1997; C. F. Peters.

Elegy — for Toru Takemitsu (solo flute, solo percussion, string orchestra; 7 minutes), 1996; C. F. Peters.

Two Voices — an allegory (orchestra, stereophonic computer processed sound; 16 minutes), 1996; C. F. Peters.

On the Balance of Things (solo oboe, flute [picc], clarinet [B-cl], trumpet, percussion, violin, cello, stereophonic computer processed sound, optional dance component; 24 minutes), 1996; C. F. Peters.

The Red Act Arias Suite (8-channel computer processed sound; 15.5 minutes), 1997.*

Will you answer if I call? (solo harpsichord, flute, clarinet, bass clarinet, bassoon, horn, 2 violins, viola, cello, contrabass; 8 minutes), 1998; C. F. Peters.

JUSTICE (soprano, actress, percussionist, real-time computer sound spatialization, and 6 channels of computer processed sound, staged; 48 minutes), 1999; C. F. Peters.

A Crimson Path (solo cello, piano; 22 minutes), 2000; C. F. Peters.

"…brain ablaze…she howled aloud" (one, two, or three piccolos, real-time computer sound spatialization, 5 channels of computer processed sound; 22 minutes), 2000; C. F. Peters.

Work-in-progress *The Angel of Death* (solo piano, chamber ensemble, quadraphonic computer processed sound; 27 minutes), 2001.

COMMERCIAL RECORDINGS (LP)

** = all-Reynolds recording

Ambages, R. Noguchi, flute, Japan Victor SJV-1513.

Quick Are the Mouths of Earth, The Contemporary Chamber Ensemble, A. Weisberg, Nonesuch, M-71219.

** *Traces*, Y. Takahashi, K. Reynolds, L. Barron, CRI SD 285.

** *Ping*, K. Reynolds, R. Reynolds, P. Chihara, A. Johnson, CRI SD 285.

Blind Men, The Peabody Concert Singers and Chamber Ensemble, G. Smith, CRI SD 241.

Ambages, H. Sollberger, flute, Nonesuch HB-73028, ℗© 1975.

The Emperor of Ice Cream, The Gregg Smith Singers, G. Smith, conductor, Turnabout TV 34759, ℗© 1980 The Moss Music Group, Inc.

Fantasy for Pianist, Y. Takahashi, Mainstream MS/5000.

… from behind the unreasoning mask, M. Anderson, T. Rainey, R. Reynolds, New World Records, NW 237, ℗© 1977 Recorded Anthology of American Music, Inc.

** Electronic/Instrumental Music: *Ping* and *Traces*, CRI SD 285, reissue on cassette, CRI CAS 285/384, ℗ 1976 Composers Recordings, Inc.

** VOICESPACE I-IV, (2 discs), P. Larson, C. Plantamura, EVTE, Lovely Records VR 1801, 1802, © 1982 Vital Records, Inc., ℗ 1982 Roger Reynolds.

Record of Computer Music, excerpt of *…the serpent-snapping eye*, accompanying a book, *Computer-Musik*, text by Heinz Josef Herbort, IBM Deutschland GmbH 1984.

IRCAM: un portrait (research examples related to the evolution of *Archipelago*), IRCAM 0001, © 1983.

…the serpent-snapping eye, E. Harkins, D. Pratt, C. Lytle, CRI SD 495, ℗© 1984 Composers Recordings, Inc.

** *Aether*, J. Négyesy, violin; C. Lytle, piano, Lovely Music VR 1803, © 1987.

** *Less than Two*, Sonor Ensemble: J.-C. François and D. Stevens, pianos; D. Pratt and D. Dunbar, percussion, Lovely Music VR 1803, © 1987 Lovely Music, ℗ 1987 Roger Reynolds.

COMMERCIAL RECORDINGS (CD/DVD)

** = all-Reynolds recording

Autumn Island, G. Stout, marimba, Neuma 450–72, ℗ © 1988.

The Vanity of Words [VOICESPACE V] (computer processed sound), Wergo WER 2024–50, ℗© 1989 WERGO Schallplatten GmbH.

Coconino...a shattered landscape, Arditti String Quartet, Gramavision R2 79440, ℗© 1989 Gramavision Inc.

Transfigured Wind IV, H. Sollberger, flute, Neuma 450–74, ℗ © 1990.

** *Transfigured Wind II*, San Diego Symphony Ensemble, J. Fonville, flute, H. Sollberger, conductor, New World 80401–2, ℗© 1990 Recorded Anthology of American Music, Inc.

** *Whispers Out of Time*, San Diego Symphony Ensemble, Sonor Ensemble soloists: J. Négyesy, Y.-J. Lu, P. Farrell, B. Turetzky; H. Sollberger, conductor, New World 80401–2, ℗© 1990 Recorded Anthology of American Music, Inc.

Four Etudes, P. Bacchus, G. Pusch, R. Schmidt, W. Stern, flutes, CRI CD 581, ℗ © 1990 Composers Recordings, Inc.

Archipelago (extract), Music Composed at IRCAM: The Eighties, MPO/France CD 0002 A, ℗ 1990.

** *Still* [VOICESPACE I] (electroacoustic sound), Lovely Music LCD 1801, ℗© 1992 Lovely Music, Ltd.

** *Eclipse* [VOICESPACE III] (computer generated sound), Lovely Music LCD 1801, ℗© 1992 Lovely Music, Ltd.

** *The Palace* [VOICESPACE IV] (computer processed sound), P. Larson, bass-baritone, Lovely Music LCD 1801, ℗© 1992 Lovely Music, Ltd.

** *Personae*, Sonor Ensemble, J. Négyesy, violin, R. Steiger, conductor, Neuma 450–78, ℗© 1992.

** *The Vanity of Words* [VOICESPACE V] (computer processed sound), Neuma 450–78, ℗© 1992.

** *Variation*, A. Karis, piano, Neuma 450–78, ℗© 1992.

The Dream of the Infinite Rooms, Cleveland Chamber Symphony, R. Mushabac, cello, E. London, conductor, GM2039CD, ℗ © 1993 GM Recordings, Inc.

The Behavior of Mirrors, T. Seelye, guitar, Bridge BCD 9042, ℗© 1993.

** *The Ivanov Suite* (computer processed sound), New World 80431–2, ℗© 1993 Recorded Anthology of American Music, Inc.

** *Versions/Stages I-V* (computer processed sound), New World 80431–2, ℗© 1993 Recorded Anthology of American Music, Inc.

Not Only Night, Sonor Ensemble, C. Plantamura, soprano, H. Sollberger, conductor, CRI CD 652, ℗© 1993 Composers Recordings, Inc.

** *Summer Island*, J. Leclair, oboe, Neuma 450–91, ℗© 1996.

** *Autumn Island*, S. Schick, marimba, Neuma 450–91, ℗© 1996.

** *Fantasy for Pianist*, S. Dunn, piano, Neuma 450–91, ℗© 1996.

** *Odyssey*, Ensemble Intercontemporain, D. Robertson, conductor, M. Kobayashi, mezzo-soprano, P. Larson, bass-baritone, Neuma 450–91, ℗© 1996.

** *Archipelago*, Ensemble Intercontemporain, P. Eötvös, conductor, Neuma 450–91, ℗© 1996.

Watershed I, S. Schick, percussion, Neuma 450–100, forthcoming.

Odyssey [excerpt], Ircam — Les années 90, Ircam 008, © 1998.

… from behind the unreasoning mask, M. Anderson, trombone, T. Rainey, percussion, R. Reynolds, assistant percussion, New World 80237-2, ℗ 1977 © 1998.

** *Watershed IV* (DVD), Stephen Schick, percussion, P. Otto, spatialization, Mode 70, ℗© 1998.

** *Eclipse* (DVD), multimedia version, Mode 70, ℗© 1998.

** *The Red Act Arias* [excerpt] (DVD), Mode 70, ℗© 1998.

** *Coconino…a shattered landscape*, Arditti String Quartet, Auvidis/Naïve MO 782083, ℗1994/1996/2000 © 2000.

** *Visions*, Arditti String Quartet, Auvidis/Naïve MO 782083, ℗ 1994/1996/2000 © 2000.

** *Kokoro*, I. Arditti, violin, Auvidis/Naïve MO 782083, ℗ 1994/1996/2000 © 2000.

** *Ariadne's Thread*, Arditti String Quartet, computer generated sound, Auvidis/Naïve MO 782083, ℗ 1994/1996/2000 © 2000.

** *Focus a beam, emptied of thinking, outward…*, R. de Saram, cello, Auvidis/Naïve MO 782083, ℗ 1994/1996/2000 © 2000.

** *last things, I think, to think about*, P. Larson, bass baritone, A. Karis, piano, Mode, forthcoming.

** *Traces*, Y. Takahashi, piano, K. Reynolds, flute, L. Barron, cello, A. Johnson, electronic processing, Pogus, forthcoming.

** *...the serpent-snapping eye*, E. Harkins, trumpet, J.-C. François, percussion, C. Lytle, piano, Pogus, forthcoming.

** *Ping*, R. Reynolds, piano, K. Reynolds, flute, P. Chihara, harmonium and percussion, A. Johnson, electronic processing, Pogus, forthcoming.

** *Symphony[Myths]*, Tokyo Philharmonic, K. Sato, conductor, Mode, forthcoming.

** *Whispers Out of Time*, Cleveland Chamber Symphony, E. London, conductor, Mode, forthcoming.

** *Dreaming*, San Diego Symphony, Y. Talmi, conductor, Mode, forthcoming.

** *JUSTICE*, L. Flanigan, soprano, E. Lauren, actress, S. Schick, percussion, P. Otto, real-time computer spatialization, Mode, forthcoming.

WRITINGS

BOOKS

MIND MODELS: New Forms of Musical Experience, Reynolds, Roger L., New York: Praeger Publishers, 1975. i–xxiv, 230.

A Searcher's Path: A Composer's Ways, Monograph, Institute for Studies in American Music, Brooklyn College of CUNY, 1987 © Roger Reynolds.

A Jostled Silence: Contemporary Japanese Musical Thought (edited and introduced by Roger Reynolds, serialized in 3 parts), *Perspectives of New Music*, Vol. 30, No. 1, Winter 1992: 22–80; Vol. 30, No. 2, Summer 1992: 60–100; Vol. 31, No.2, Summer 1993: 172–228.

ARTICLES

"Indeterminancy: Some Consideration", *Perspectives of New Music*, Vol. 4, No. 1, 1965: 136–140.

"Current Chronicle — Japan", *Musical Quarterly*, Vol. 53, No. 4, 1967: 563–571.

"Happenings in Japan and Elsewhere", *Arts in Society*, Vol. 5, No. 1, 1968: 90–101.

"It(')s Time", *Electronic Music Review*, No. 7, 1968: 12–17.

"Notes on the Control of Spatial Dimensions of Music", *Talea 2/3*, Universidad Naćional Autonoma de México, Mexico City, Spring 1976.

"Explorations in Sound/Space Manipulation, I. (1975)", *Reports from the Center for Music Experiment*, Vol. I, No. 1, UCSD, La Jolla, California, 1977.

"Inexorable Continuities: A Commentary on the Music of Conlon Nancarrow", *Soundings*, Book 4, Santa Fe, New Mexico, Spring/Summer, 1977: 26–39.

"Thoughts on Sound Movement and Meaning", *Perspectives of New Music*, Spring-Summer, 1978: 181–190.

"Rarely Sudden, Never Abrupt" (a study of two works of Toru Takemitsu), in *Takemitsu*, Tokyo: Shiseido, 1981.

"Modes, Not Media, Matter", in *Roger Reynolds: Profile of a Composer*, C. F. Peters, 1982.

"Notes on Musicians, Machines, and Tinkering with Time" (English version + French), *CNAC* magazine (Paris), 1983.

"Edgard Varèse's *Amériques*", San Francisco Symphony Program Note, April 1984.

"Hearing Further", article for commemorative book, *Horizons '84*, New York Philharmonic, 1984.

"Production at CARL and Related Issues", *Proceedings of ICMC*, The Hague, Fall 1986.

"Réaliser une expérience musicale", in *Quoi? Quand? Comment? La recherche musicale*, translated from English into French by D. Collins, edited by T. Machover; Christian Bourgois, Éditeur, Paris, 1985: 241–270.

"A Perspective on Form and Experience", *Contemporary Music Review*, Vol. 2, Part 1, 1987: 277–308.

"The Tenuous, Flickering Flip-Flop...", in *Complexity?*, Gaudeamus Foundation, Amsterdam, March 1990.

"... into the consciousness of the musical world" (published in Japanese), article, *Polyphone*, No. 8, Tokyo, 1991.

"L'ajustement de la sensibilité à un ensemble de contraintes", *Inharmoniques*, No. 8/9, Ircam, Paris, 1991: 173–177.

"The Shape of Ideas" (in Japanese), *Keiji Usami*, catalogue, December 1991.

"Across Unbridgeable Divides" (published in French), statement, *Utopies — Les Cahiers de l'IRCAM*, No. 4, Paris, 1993.

Notes for a Lecture: "Why are we *doing* what we are doing?", in *Sävellys ja musiikinteoria*, Sibelius Academy, No.1/95, Helsinki, Fall 1994; pp. 6–14.

Notes for a Lecture: *"Extending* Imagination's Reach", in *Sävellys ja musiikinteoria*, Sibelius Academy, No. 2/94, Helsinki, Fall 1994.

"Mirrors", by Toru Takemitsu, edited and annotated by Roger Reynolds; trans. with Sumi Adachi, in *Asian Art and Culture*, the Smithsonian Institution, Vol. VIII, Number 3, Oxford University Press, Fall 1995 (re-edited from an earlier *Perspectives of New Music* publication).

"...Taste, Boundaries, Relevance, Purpose, Risk... (about Salvatore Martirano)", In Memoriam Salvatore Martirano, *Perspectives of New Music*, Winter, 1996, Vol. 34, No. 1: 200–207.

Keynote Speech: "Connecting Dreams with Realities: a perspective on Technology from the (distant) domain of Art", proceedings of Open Classroom II Conference (School Education in the Information Society), Crete, Greece, 17–19 September 1997. Published: *http://openclass.lrf.gr:8080/keynote.htm*

"Principle and Accommodation: a Tribute to Roberto Gerhard", article in *Roberto Gerhard and His Music*, by Joaquim Homs, English edition by Meirion Bowen, Anglo-Catalan Society Occasional Publications in association with the Biblioteca de Catalunya, 2000.

"Roger Reynolds: 'I'm always interested in new experience': A Conversation with Paul Robinson" in *Music with Roots in the Aether*, by Robert Ashley, *MusikTexte*, Köln, 2000. Also, "Extending Instrumental Techniques", by Paul Robinson.

CHAPTERS

John Cage: "Interview with Roger Reynolds", *Contemporary Composers on Contemporary Music*, edited by Schwartz and Childs. New York: Holt, Rinehart & Winston, 1967: 335–348.

"Ives and Contemporary American Musical Thought", in *An Ives Celebration*, March, 1977, Urbana: University of Illinois Press. This presentation at the Charles Ives Centennial Festival-Conference was conceived and edited by Roger Reynolds, who also participated.

"The Edge of Imagination", chapter in *A Celebration of American Music: Words and Music in Honor of H. Wiley Hitchcock*, eds. R. Crawford, R. A. Lott, C. J. Oja, University of Michigan Press, Ann Arbor, 1990: 492–500.

"Par-delà les dimensions connues" ("Beyond the Edge of Known Orders"), chapter in *Le timbre, métaphore pour la composition*, ed. by Jean-Baptiste Barrière, Christian Bourgois, Ircam, 1991: 467–484.

"The Indifference of the Broiler to the Broiled", chapter in *Samuel Beckett and Music*, edited by Mary Bryden, Clarendon Press, Oxford, 1998: 195–211.

"Ross Lee Finney — *memorial words*", chapter in *Musically Incorrect: Conversations About Music at the End of the 20th Century*, edited by Hayes Biggs and Susan Orzel, C. F. Peters Corporation, New York, 1998.

REVIEWS

Review of *Twilight of the Gods* by Wilfred Mellers (New York: Viking Press), published in *The New York Times Book Review*, 22 September 1974.

"Warsaw Autumn: A Vigorous Festival Celebrates an Impressive Anniversary", *Musical America*, March, 1982.

"Some Remarks on a Stimulating Conference", letter to *The Computer Music Journal*, Summer, 1982.

Review of *Selected Letters of Virgil Thompson* for *The New York Times Book Review*, 28 August 1988.

"Seeking Centers", extended review article in *Perspectives of New Music* (Vol. 32, No. 2, Summer 1994) of *Music, Myth and Nature*, an explorative essay by F.-B. Mâche.

INTERVIEWS

"John Cage and Roger Reynolds: A Conversation" (1962), *The Musical Quarterly* (prepared and edited by R. Reynolds), October, 1979: 573–594.

"Conlon Nancarrow: Interviews in Mexico City and San Francisco" (in Mexico City, 12 July 1995), *American Music*, Vol. 2, No. 2, Summer 1984: 1–24.

"Wonderful Times" (commentary on Robert Erickson's thoughts), *Perspectives of New Music*, Vol. 26, No. 2, Summer 1988.

"Xenakis, Reynolds, Lansky, and Mâche Discuss Computer Music", moderated by Thanassis Rikakis, transcribed and edited by Karen Reynolds, read and approved by Iannis Xenakis. Computer Music Conference/Festival, 4 July 1992, Delphi. Published: *http://www.rogerreynolds.com/xenakis1.html* and *xenakis2.html*

"Das Aufeinanderprallen der Tempi trägt meine Musik", translated by Silke Hilger from the English version in *American Music*, *MusikTexte*, 73/74, Zeitschrift für Neue Musik, Köln, March 1998.

"Entretien avec Roger Reynolds", *Accents* Magazine of the Ensemble Intercontemporain, interviewer Véronique Brindeau, Paris, July 1997–January 1998.

Contact *http://www.rogerreynolds.com* for more information.

INDEX TO PART I

Form and Method: Composing Music

II

The Examples

EXAMPLES FOR ESSAY 1: FORM

ARCHIPELAGO (1982–83)

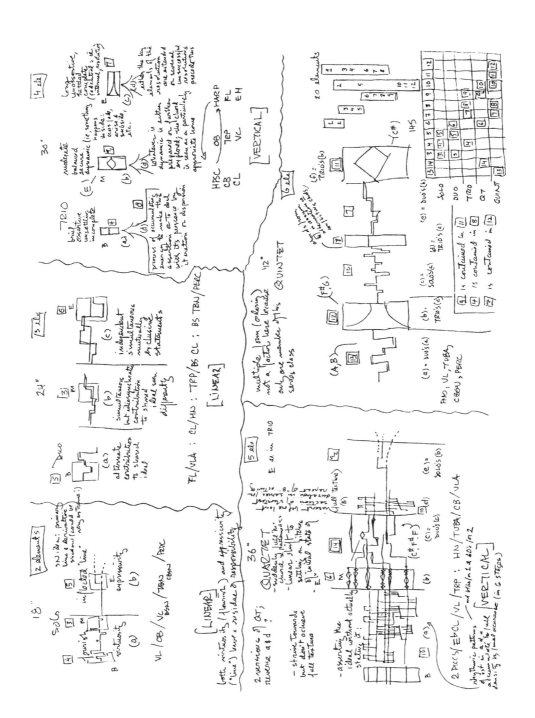

Example 1   Early consideration of theme types in *Archipelago*.

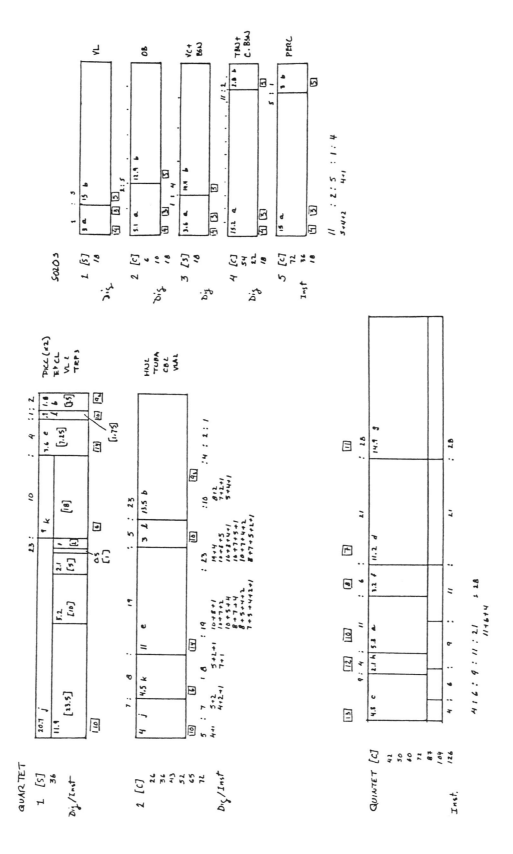

Example 2a   Formalizations of theme types in *Archipelago* (Solos, Quartets, Quintet).

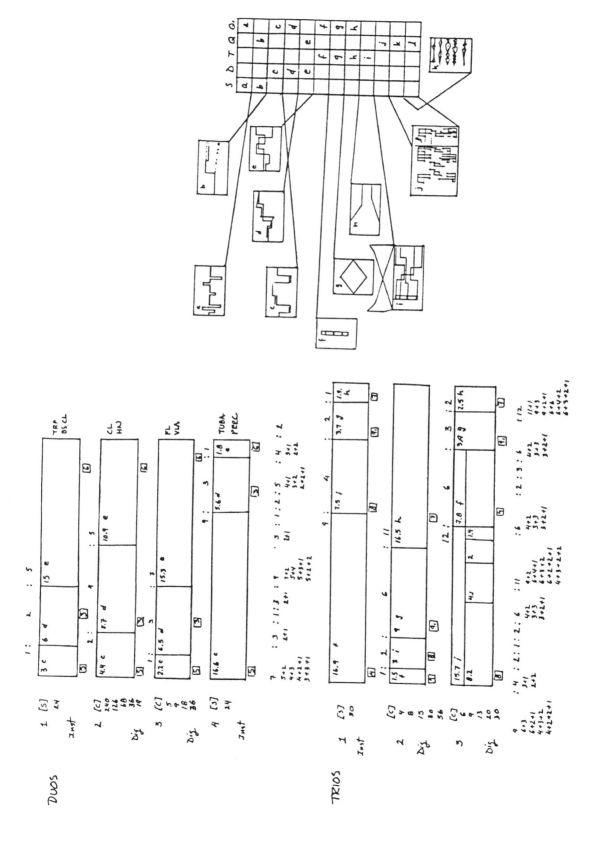

Example 2b   Formalizations of theme types in *Archipelago* (Duos, Trios).

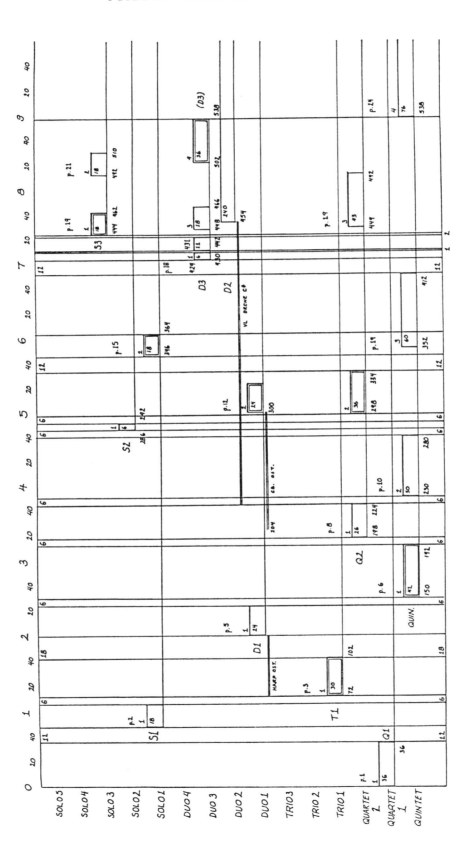

Example 3a   The overall plan for *Archipelago* (beginning).

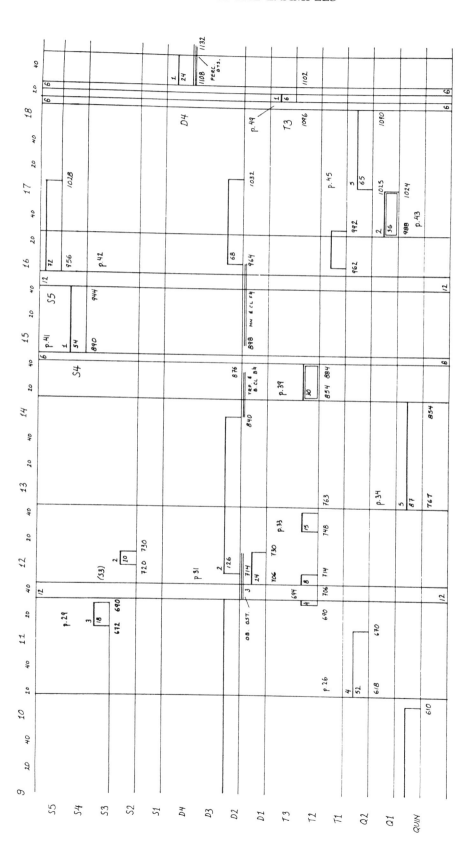

Example 3b   The overall plan for *Archipelago* (continued).

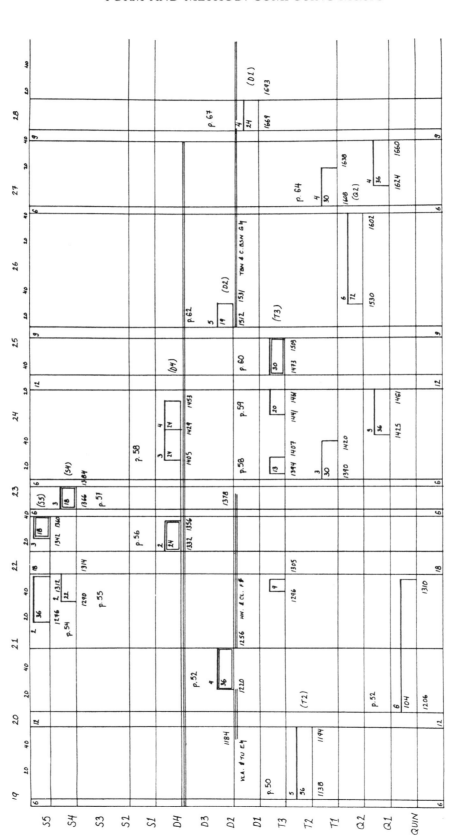

Example 3c   The overall plan for *Archipelago* (continued).

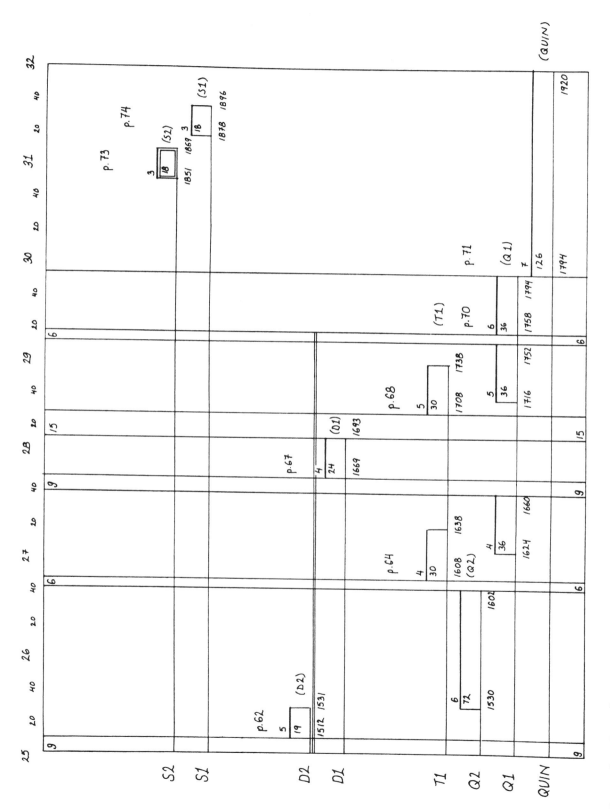

Example 3d   The overall plan for *Archipelago* (end).

THE BEHAVIOR OF MIRRORS (1986)

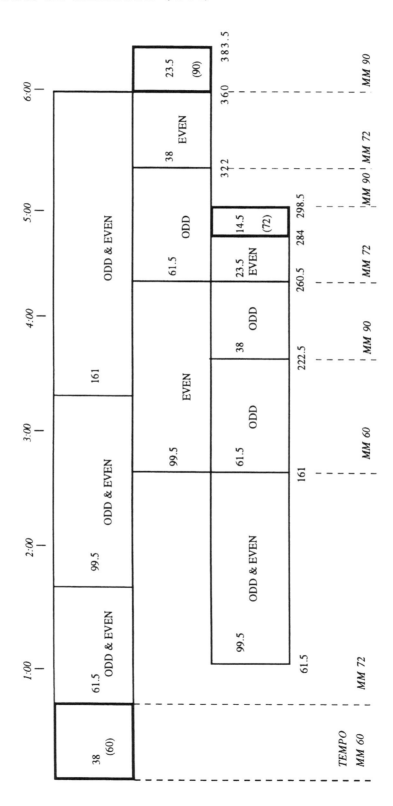

Example 4   The overall plan for *The Behavior of Mirrors*.

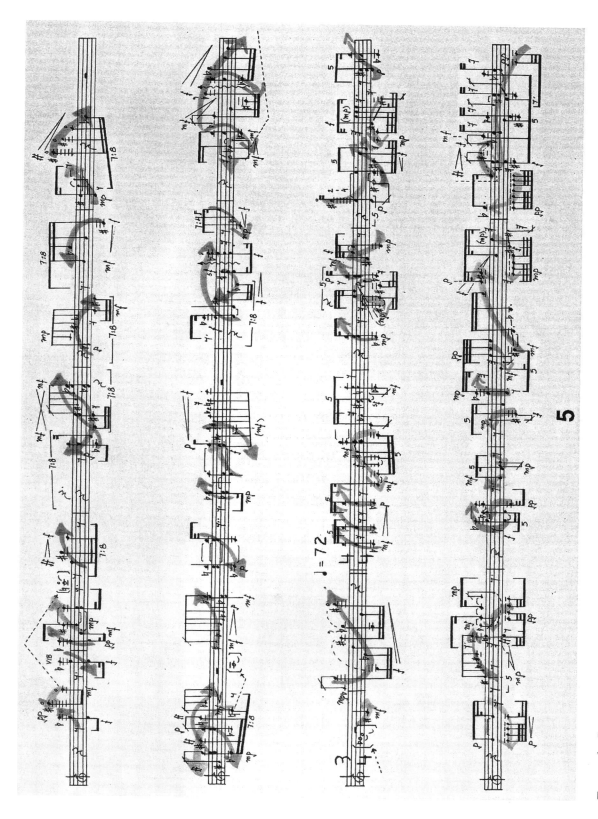

Example 5   A page from the score for *The Behavior of Mirrors* showing the interweaving of derived fragments from the three core themes. Colors correspond to the layers in Example 4 (green = top, blue = middle, orange = lower).

DIONYSUS (1990)

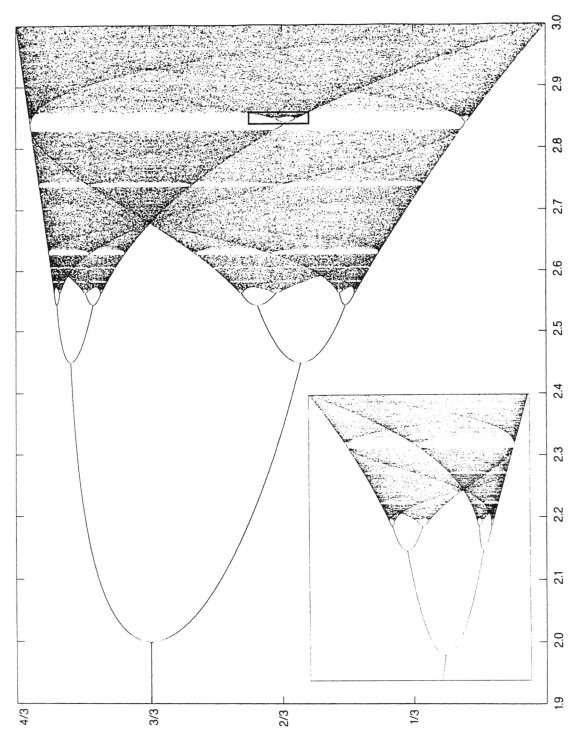

Example 6   A bifurcation diagram from the realm of chaos theory, showing the change in the value of a non-linear function over rising values of the critical variable (reproduced with the permission of Springer-Verlag).

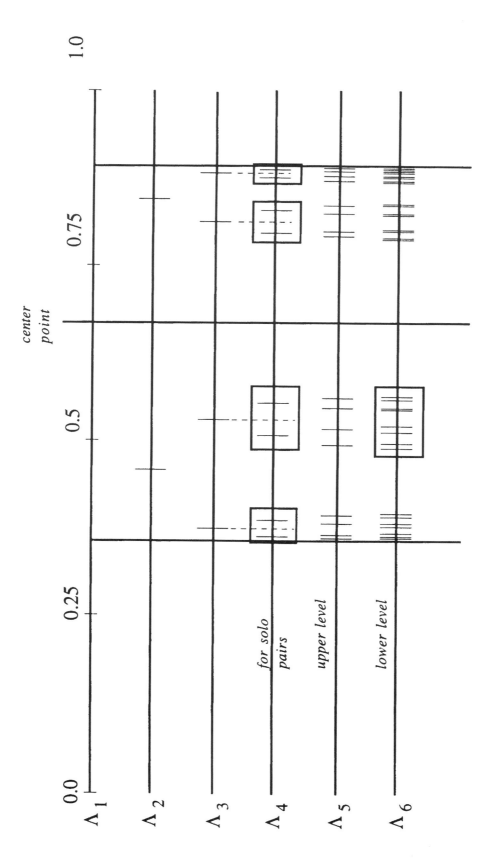

Example 7　　An alternative, cross-sectional representation of a bifurcation diagram.

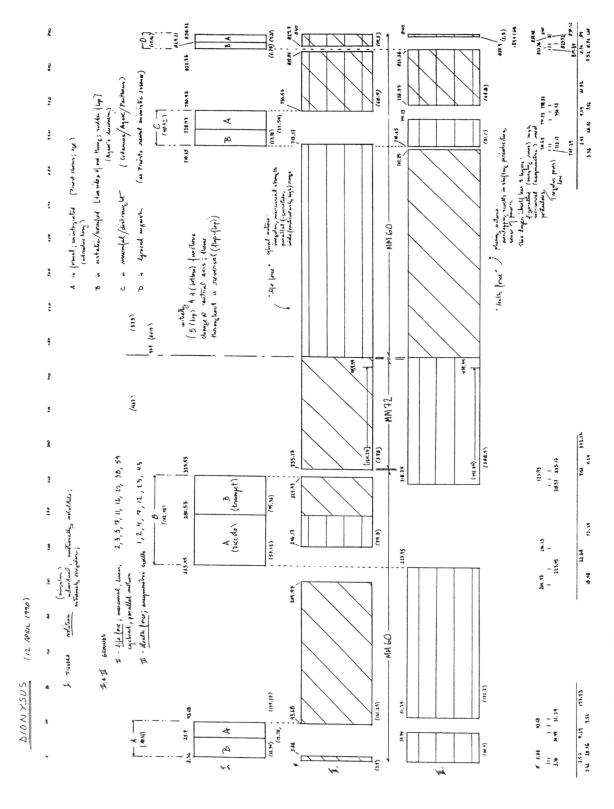

Example 8   The overall plan for *Dionysus*.

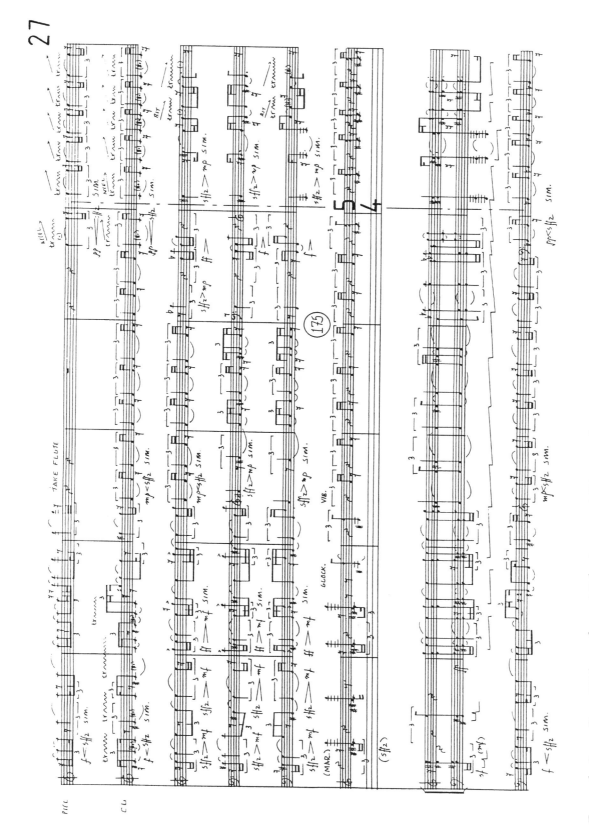

Example 9   Page 27 from the published score of *Dionysus* (reproduced with the permission of C. F. Peters Corporation, New York).

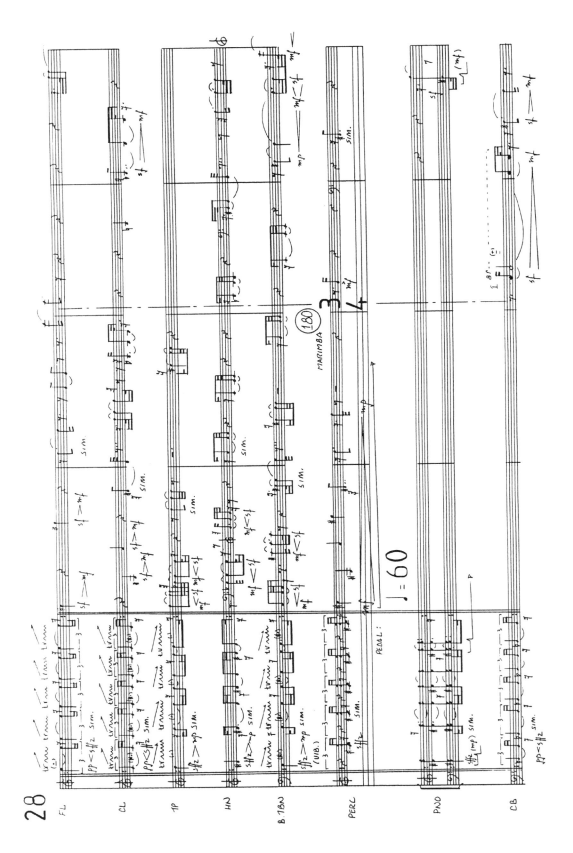

Example 10   Page 28 from the published score of *Dionysus* (reproduced with the permission of C. F. Peters Corporation, New York).

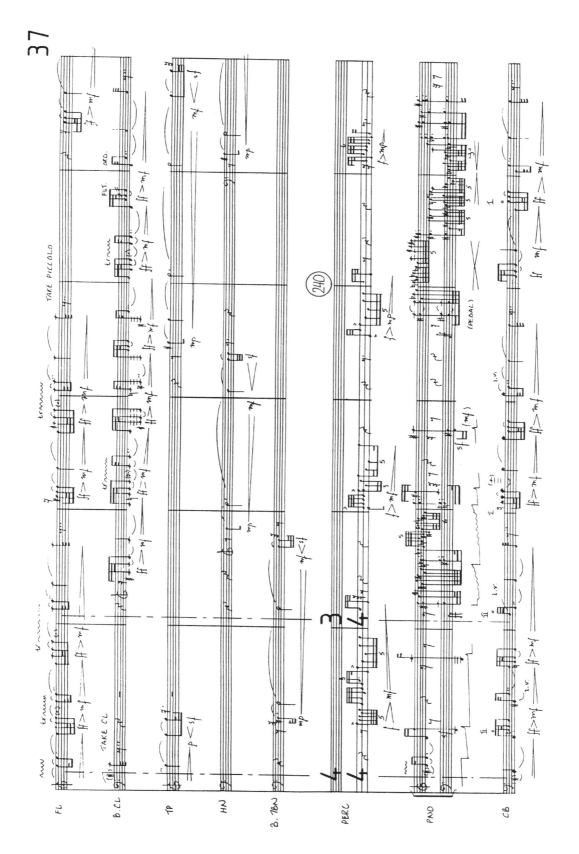

Example 11   Page 37 from the published score of *Dionysus* (reproduced with the permission of C. F. Peters Corporation, New York).

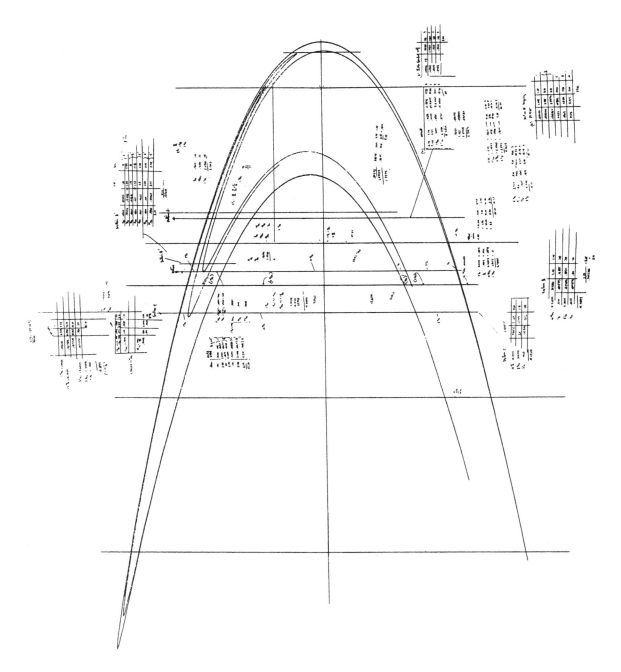

Example 12   The Hénon attractor shown with cross-sectional proportions.

SYMPHONY[MYTHS] (1990)

Example 13   A photograph of the Japanese rock formation *Futami ga ura* (reproduced with the permission of Kodansha International Ltd.).

Example 14   George Herriman's drawing of a rock formation, "a pair of Lithic mittens" (reproduced with the permission of Madison Square Press, Grosset & Dunlap).

Example 15   A Greek vase depicting rocks that define a narrow passage (reproduced with
the permission of Cambridge University Press).

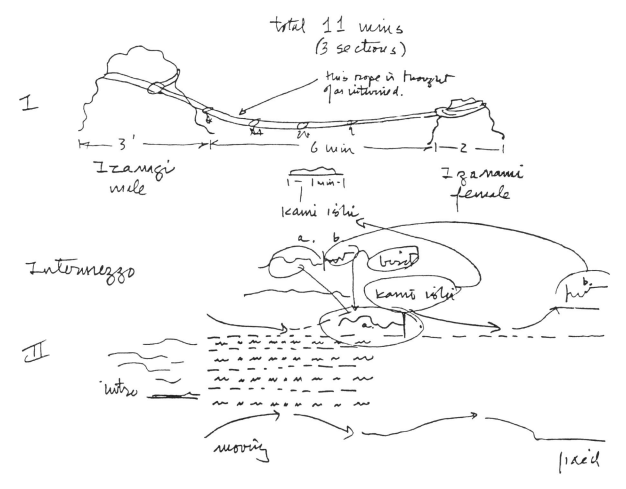

Example 16   The first sketch of the overall form of *Symphony[Myths]*.

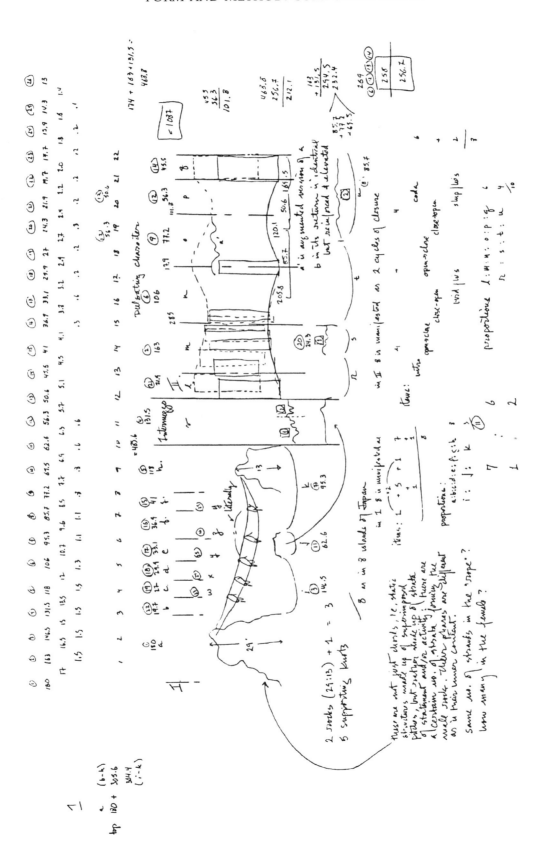

Example 17   A second more refined laying-out of the overall form of *Symphony[Myths]*.

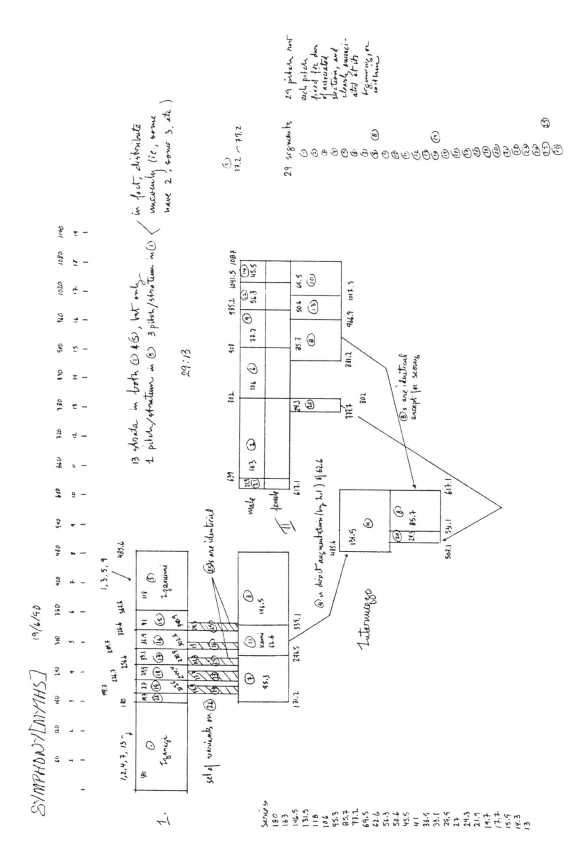

Example 18   The formalized plan for *Symphony[Myths]* with proportional specifics.

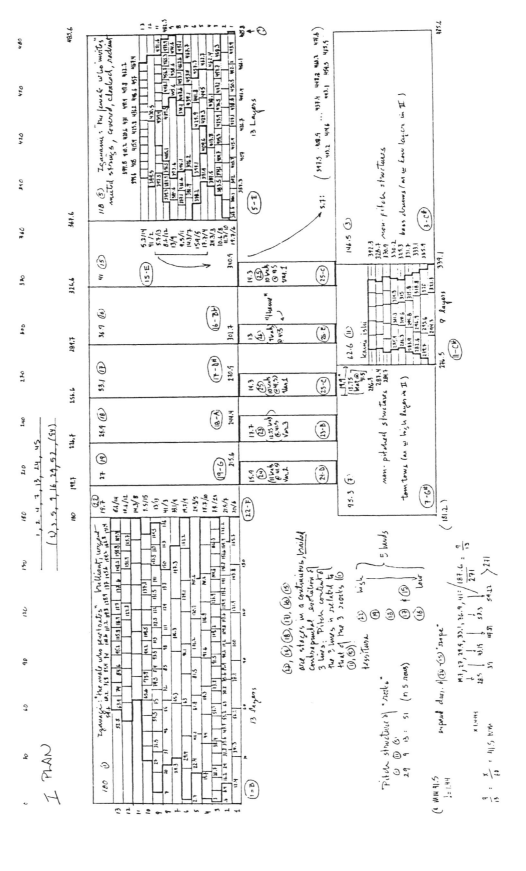

Example 19   First movement plan for *Symphony[Myths]*.

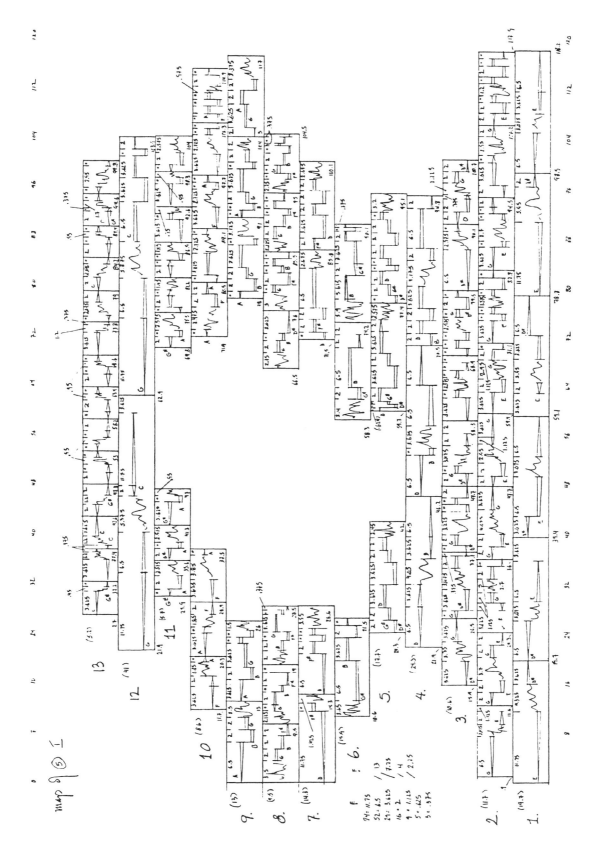

Example 20   The design of the "female" rock with 13 strata (*Symphony[Myths]*).

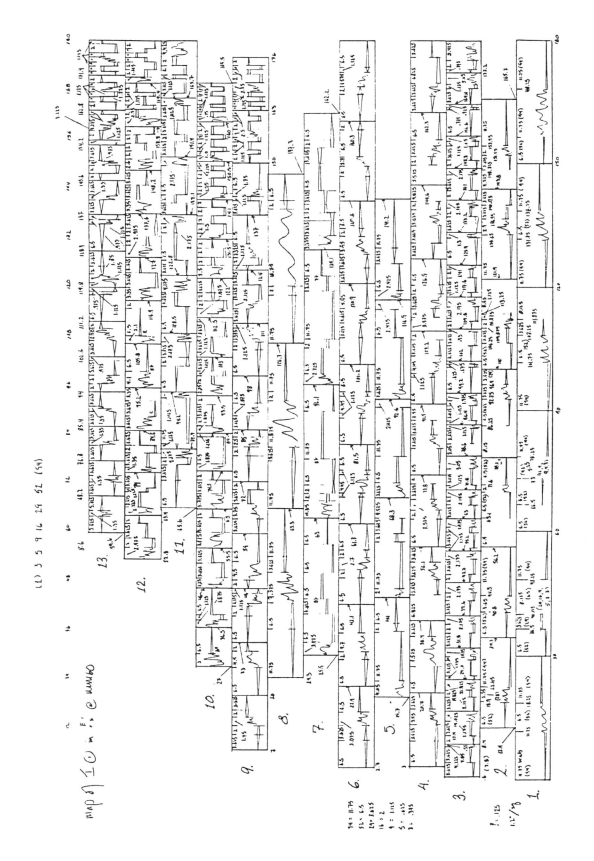

Example 21   The design of the "male" rock with 13 strata (*Symphony[Myths]*).

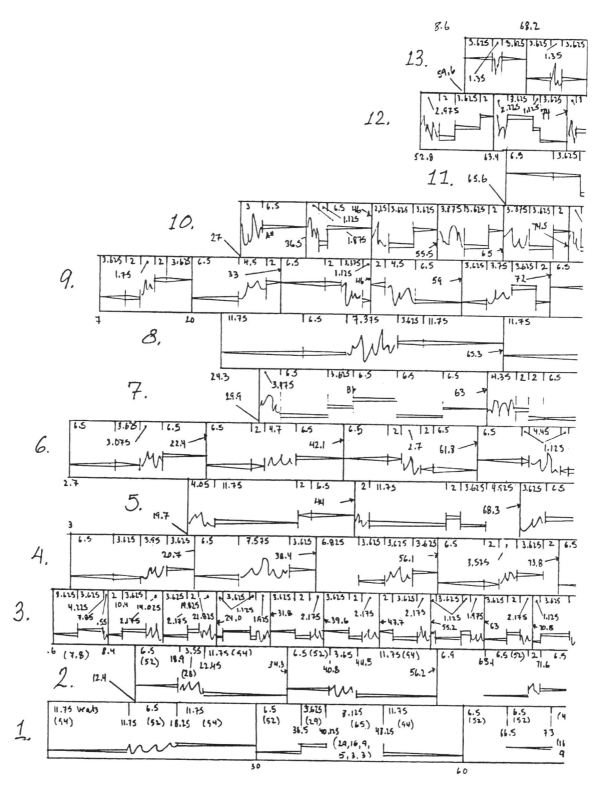

Example 22   A detail of the "male" rock design *(Symphony[Myths])*.

TRANSFIGURED WIND II (1984)

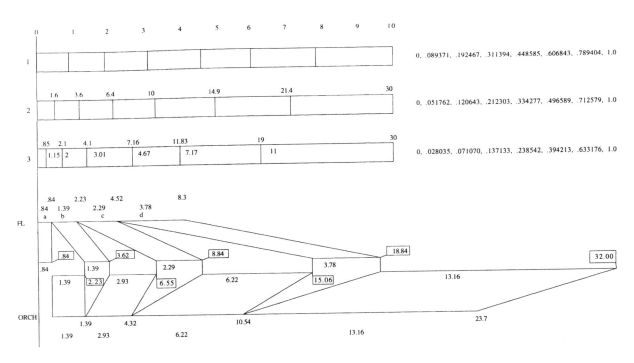

Example 23   The initial sketch for the overall plan, *Transfigured Wind II*.

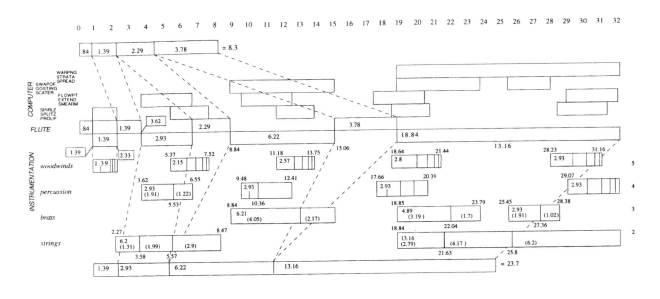

Example 24   Second sketch, overall plan for *Transfigured Wind II*.

PERSONAE (1990)

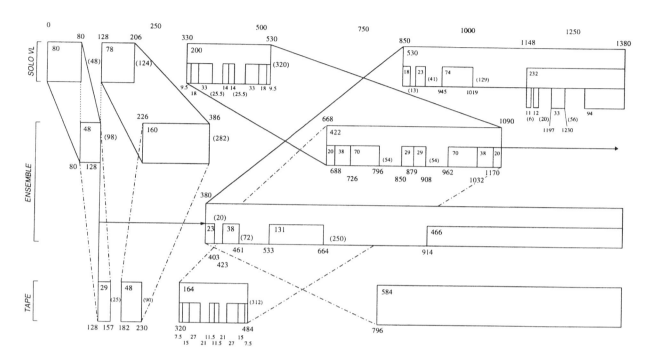

Example 25   Overall plan for *Personae*.

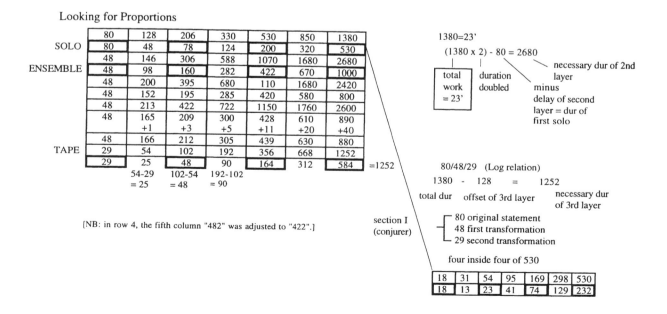

Example 26   Derivation of the proportional relationships between *Personae*'s three strata.

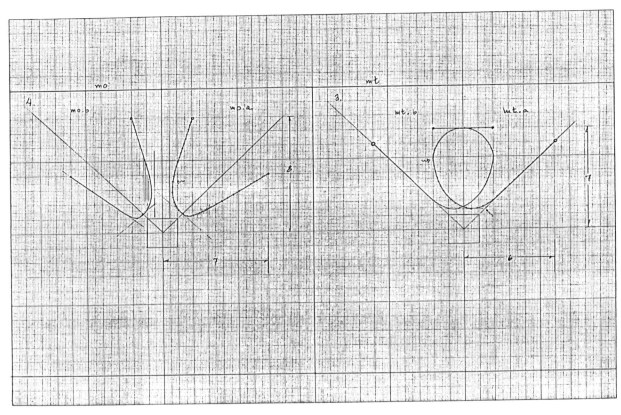

Example 27   The open path segments for spatialization from *Personae*.

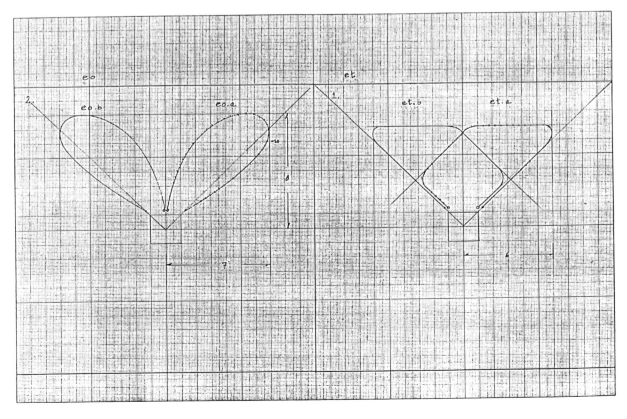

Example 28   The closed path segments from *Personae*.

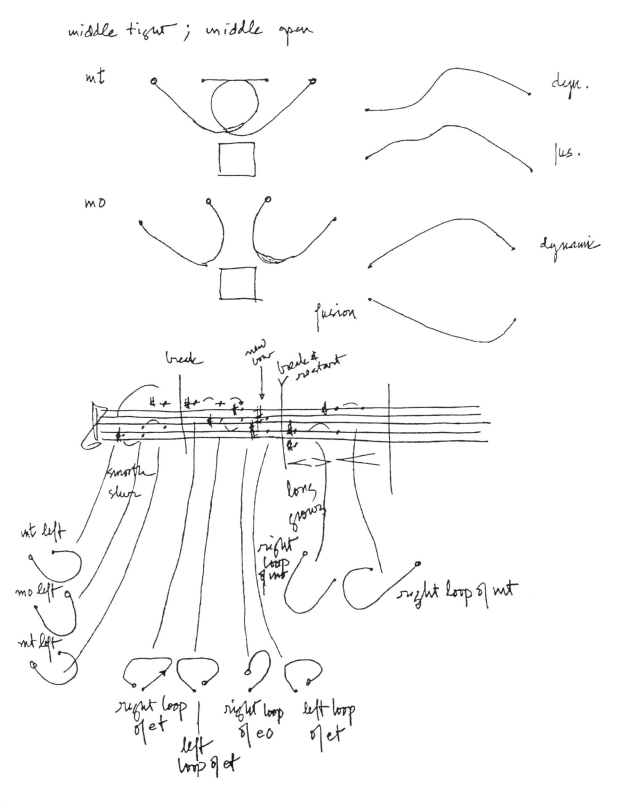

Example 29   The assignment of spatial paths to drone pitches from *Personae*.

consider relationship between line and other functions	LINE	INDICATION	REFERENCE

	(conjuring) CONJURER I.
	(♩ = 66) state of natural activity
	Nature
	INITIATOR
	    the artificer who
	    embroiders, unrealistically
	    embellishing or transforming nature
	    (alchemy)
		That which is referred to:
		
		something fairly broad (vast) in
		scale and moderate in motion;
		inertial constraint; perhaps
		cyclical like the "inevitability"
		diurnal cycles, etc. [Rothko;
		                 Johns]
		the way
			clock
			objective time

	(dancing) DANCER II.
	(♩ = 132) state of pattern as play
	Machine
	(Tinguely-type machines;
	inexplicable elements)
	RESPONDENT
	    one who recognizes –
	    and irrepressibly uses –
	    opportunity for play,
	    improvization, response to
	    a wondrous invitation
	    (summer daze in a sprinkler)
		That referred to:
		
		complex, though playful interaction between
		several pitch & several rhythmic cycles
		(all eccentric); this basis is permeated by
		negative cycles (of rests, accents, 8va
		dislocation, timbric norms, etc.) [Tinguely]
			fixed pitch grid(s)
			different fixity
			for each cycle

	(meditating) MEDITATOR III.
	(♩ = 44)
	      state of heightened awareness
	      resulting in visions, flashes
	Gods
	INITIATOR
	    one who may generate
	    or may seek to join [which?]
	    a particularly refined (probably
	    unreal) version or vision of
	    "ultimate" reality (not nature or
	    man but supernatural)
		That referred to:
		
		Vibrant (though quiescent) states which rather
		suddenly metamorphose into more expansive,
		revelatory, ecstatic states
		                [Rodin;
		                Matisse]
			temporal proportio
			favored interval(s)

	(exhorting) ADVOCATE IV.
	(♩ = 88) state of humanity's past
	(reference/dimension)
	RESPONDENT
	    the one who sees imprecisely,
	    yet better than most, all
	    of the above (Nature, mechanical, divine)
	    versions of reality, and also is a
	    part of a fourth (humanity's);
	    this one exhorts but not with
	    a decisive vision/view, i.e., he is
	    an actor (advocate) but the script is
	    unclear
	    (in the sense that it is not founded on
	    model)
		That referred to:
		
		A compound, a montage of the previous 3 +
		stately progression/procession (something
		suggestive of societies, rituals;
		formalized group behaviors, not individual
		expression or flexibility)
			polarities
			timbric/mood

Example 30   Exploration of the four basic personae.

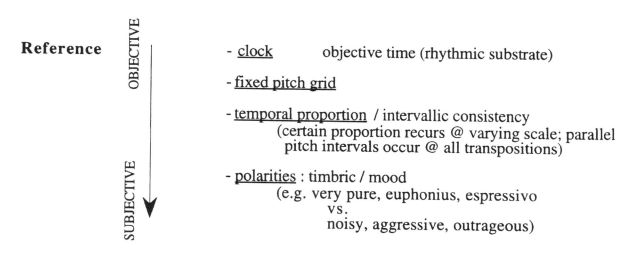

Reference

OBJECTIVE

- <u>clock</u>   objective time (rhythmic substrate)

- <u>fixed pitch grid</u>

- <u>temporal proportion</u> / intervallic consistency
        (certain proportion recurs @ varying scale; parallel
          pitch intervals occur @ all transpositions)

- <u>polarities</u> : timbric / mood
        (e.g. very pure, euphonius, espressivo
                vs.
            noisy, aggressive, outrageous)

SUBJECTIVE

Interesting to have <u>reference against which</u>
<u>a role</u> (imitating/responding) <u>is played</u>
<u>out, becoming increasingly less objective</u>

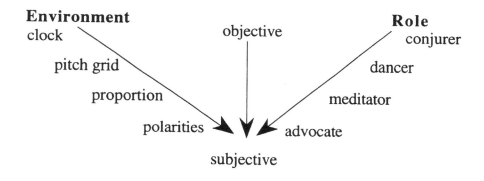

Environment
clock

pitch grid

proportion

polarities

objective

subjective

Role
conjurer

dancer

meditator

advocate

Example 31   Categorizing the personae.

ARIADNE'S THREAD (1994)

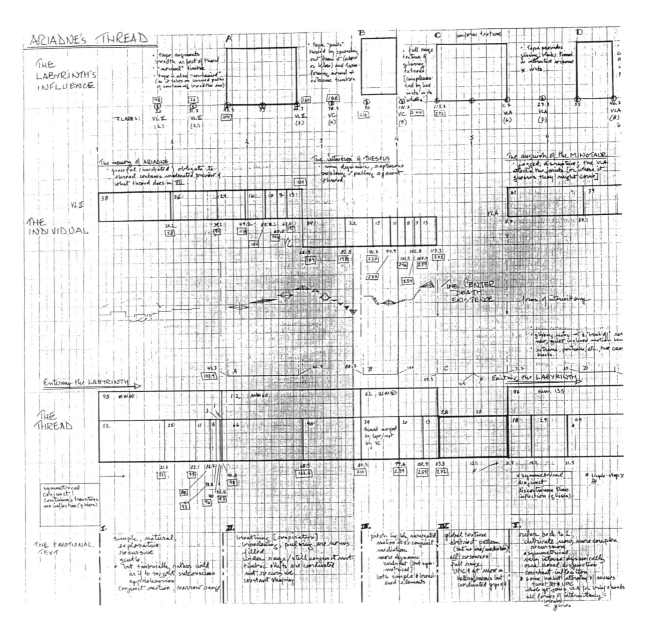

Example 32a The overall plan of *Ariadne's Thread* showing the structure of interaction between the thread, the characters, the labyrinth (beginning).

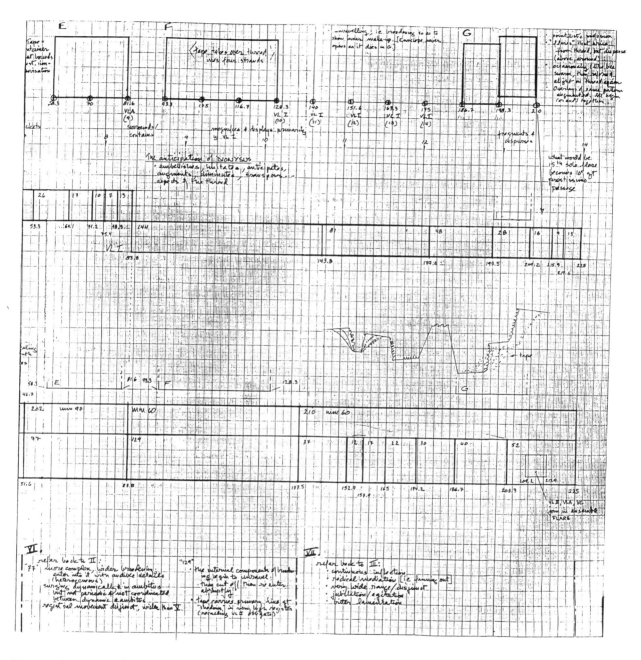

Example 32b   The overall plan of *Ariadne's Thread* showing the structure of interaction between the thread, the characters, the labyrinth (end).

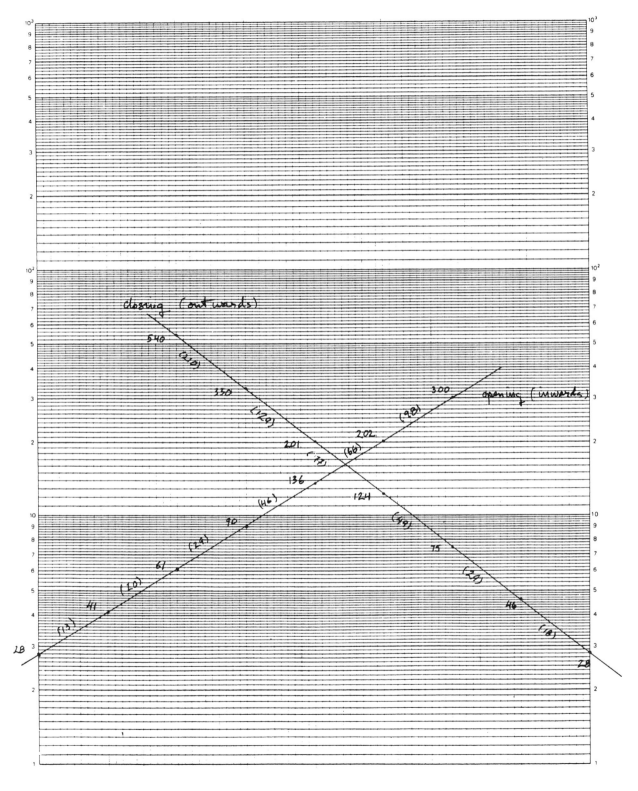

Example 33   The logarithmic proportions utilized in formalizing the overall plan of *Ariadne's Thread*.

Example 34   A drawing by Jasper Johns (© Jasper Johns/Licensed to VAGA, New York, NY; drawing in the collection of the artist; reproduced with permission).

Example 35   One graphic element from the Johns drawing; used as a notational stimulus in *Ariadne's Thread*.

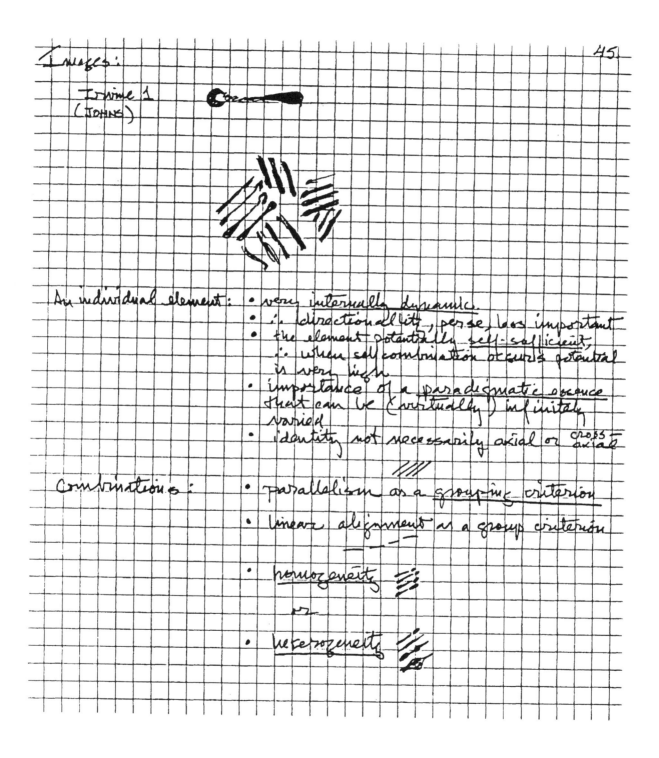

Example 36   An analysis of the element in Example 35 and its possible uses.

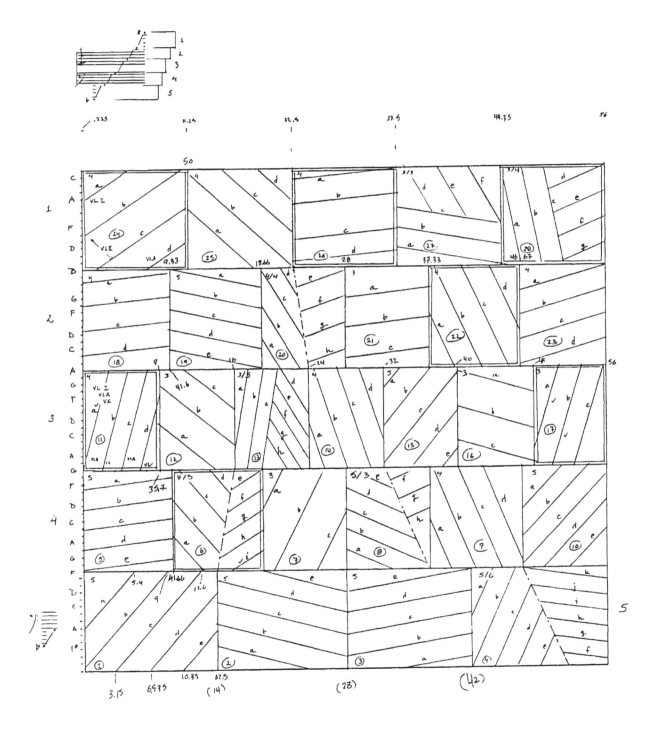

Example 37   Sketch for a textural parallel to the Johns drawing in Example 34.

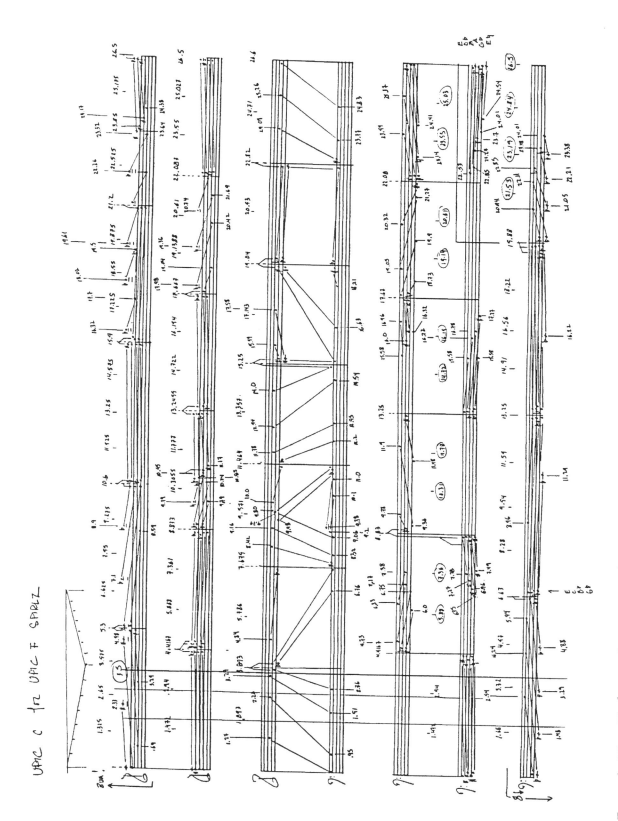

Example 38   Pitch specifications for the relative-pitch textural design in Example 37.

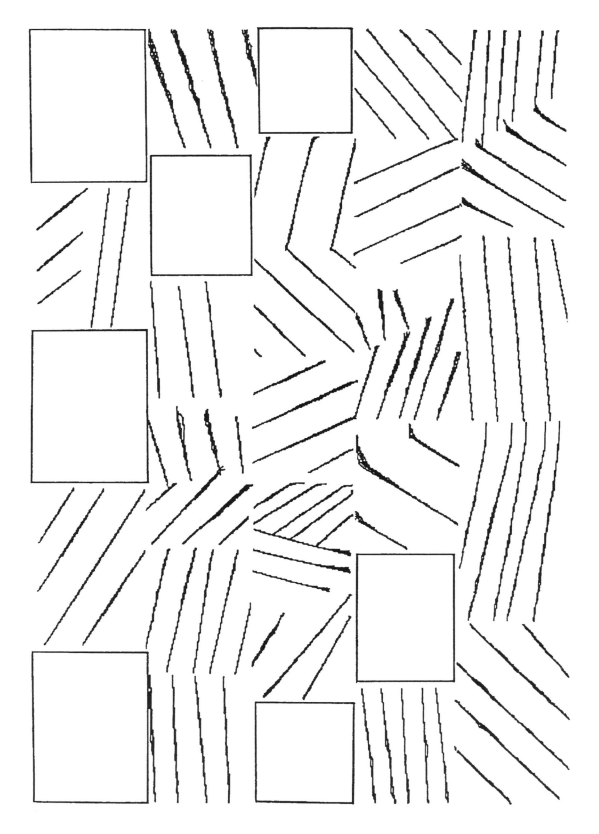

Example 39   The linear modeling of the Johns drawing represented as patterns of heavily retraced linear elements input to the UPIC System. (Note that the seven rectangles are "placeholders" for live quartet contributions.)

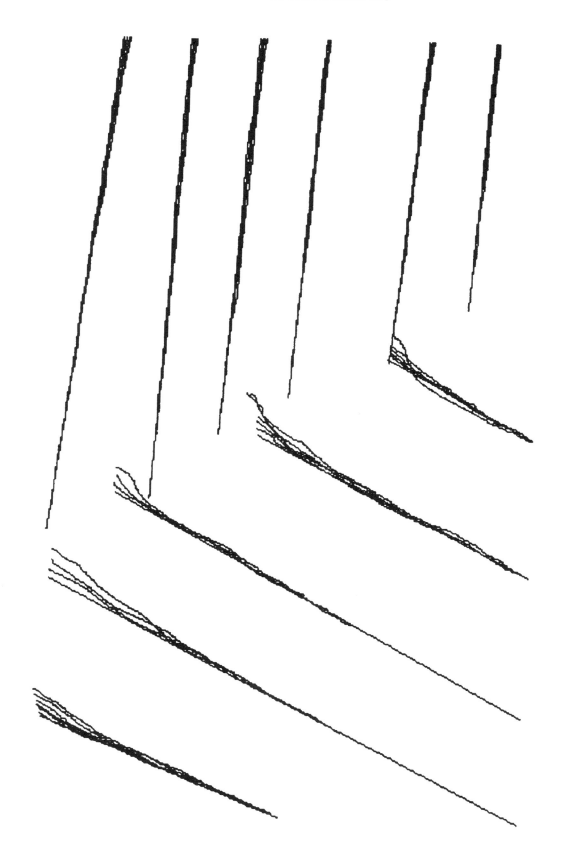

Example 40   A detail from the UPIC specification for *Ariadne's Thread*.

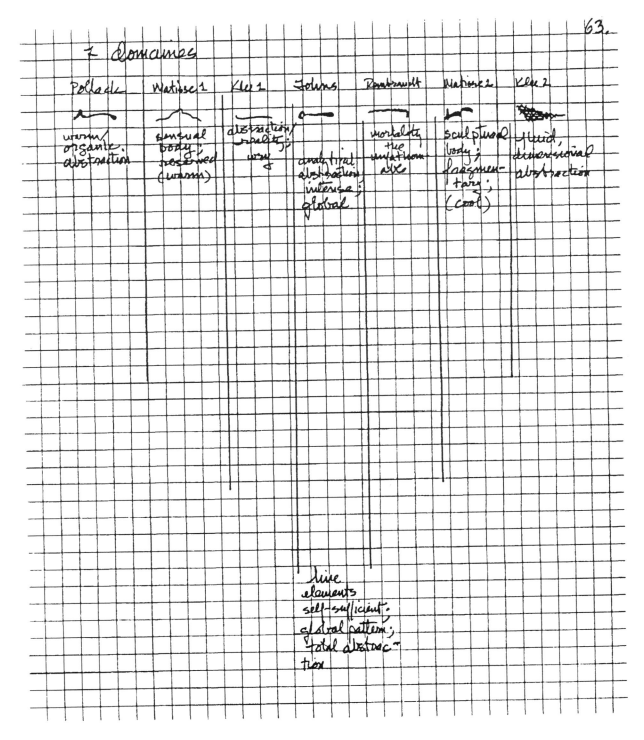

Example 41   A categorization of five artists' linear practice; from an early sketch for *Ariadne's Thread*.

OVERALL FORM

• Labyrinth and thread suggest symmetrical structure

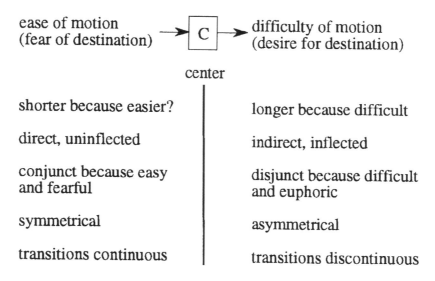

ease of motion
(fear of destination) → C → difficulty of motion
(desire for destination)

center

shorter because easier?	longer because difficult
direct, uninflected	indirect, inflected
conjunct because easy and fearful	disjunct because difficult and euphoric
symmetrical	asymmetrical
transitions continuous	transitions discontinuous

Example 42   A consideration of the overall form of *Ariadne's Thread* as it relates to the labyrinth; from early sketches.

VERSIONS/STAGES I–V (1986–91)

Example 43   *Rouen Cathedral, West Facade, Sunlight* (1894) by Claude Monet.

Example 44   *Western Portal of Rouen Cathedral – Harmony in Blue* (1894) by Claude Monet.

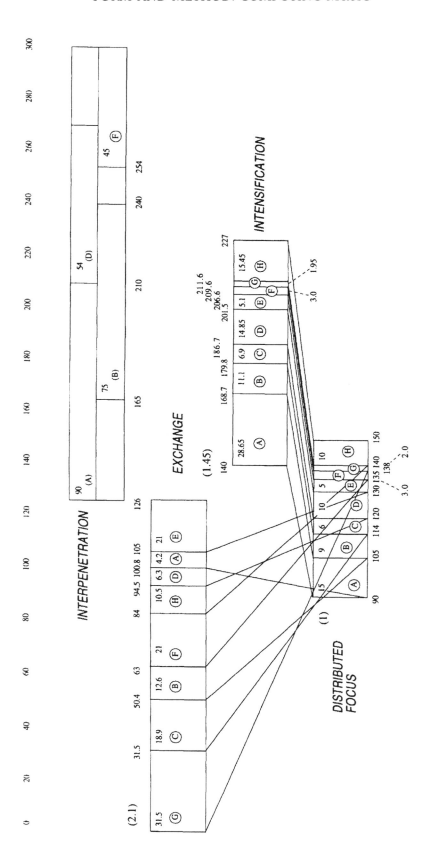

Example 45 The overall plan for *Versions/Stages I–V.*

EXAMPLES FOR ESSAY 2: METHOD

VARIATION (1988)

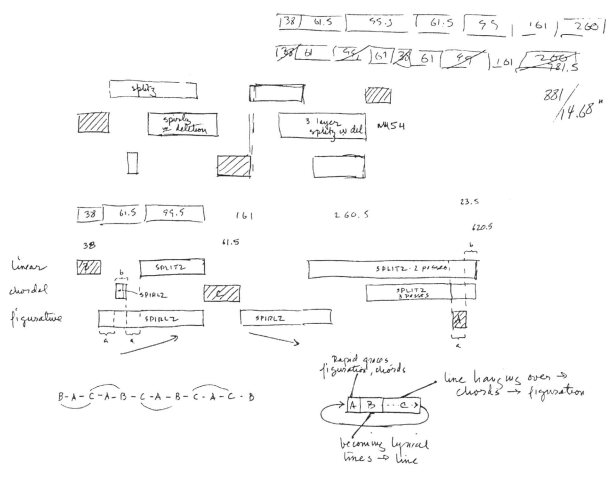

Example 46   Early sketch for *Variation*.

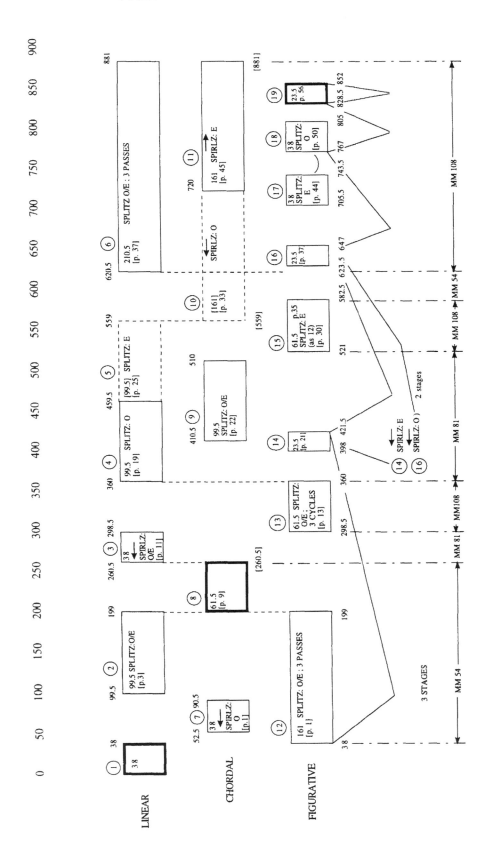

Example 47   Formal plan for *Variation*.

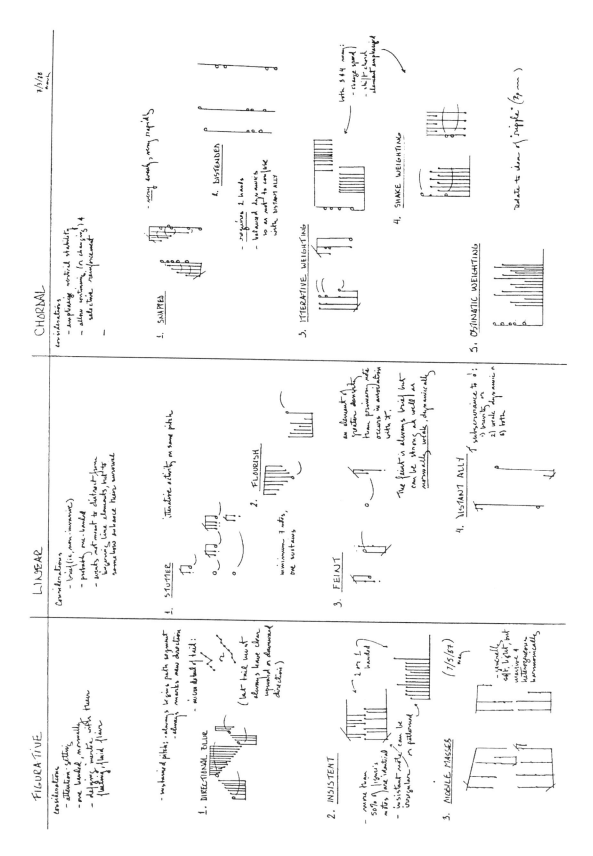

Example 48   Describing the "core" textures for *Variation*.

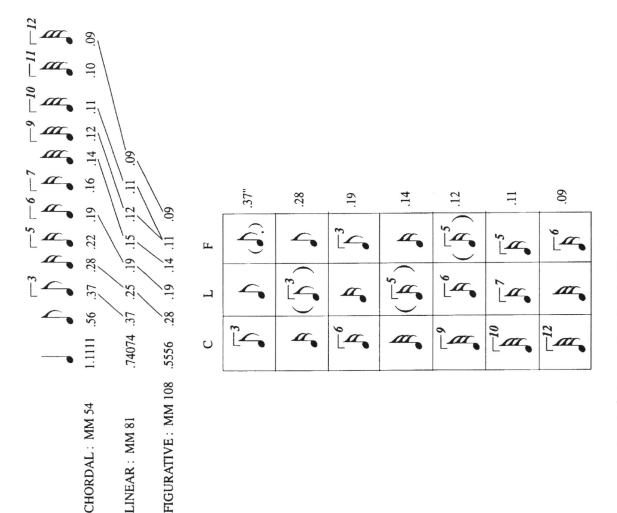

Example 49   Simultaneous tempi and their coordination in *Variation*.

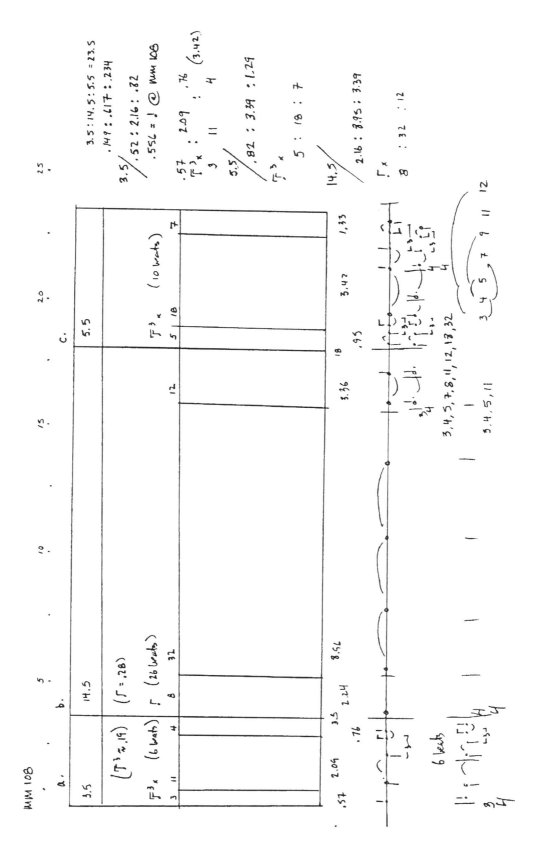

Example 50   The proportional structure of the Figurative "core" theme in *Variation*.

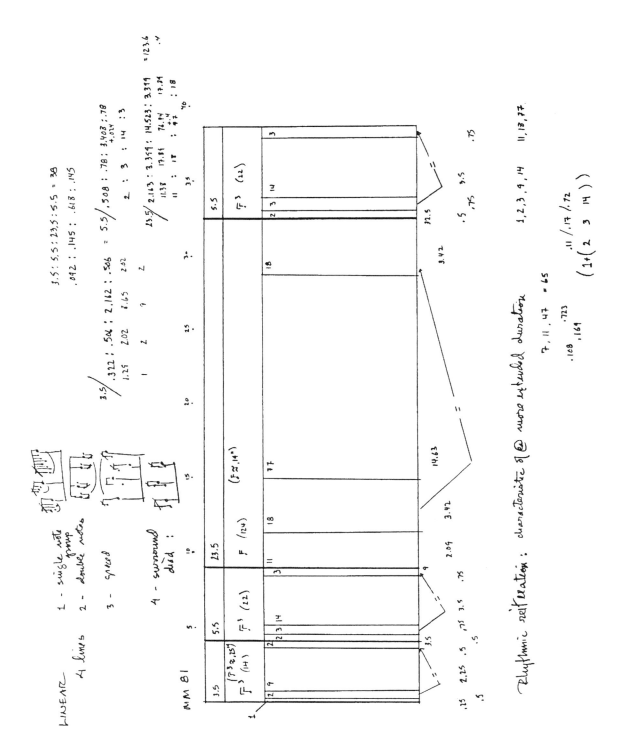

Example 51   The proportional structure of the Linear "core" theme in *Variation*.

Example 52   The proportional structure of the Chordal "core" theme in *Variation*.

Example 53   The row chart for *Variation*.

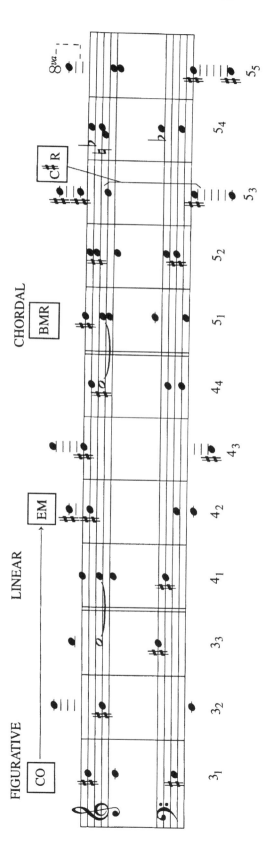

Example 54   Overall pitch emphasis in the core elements of *Variation* by section.

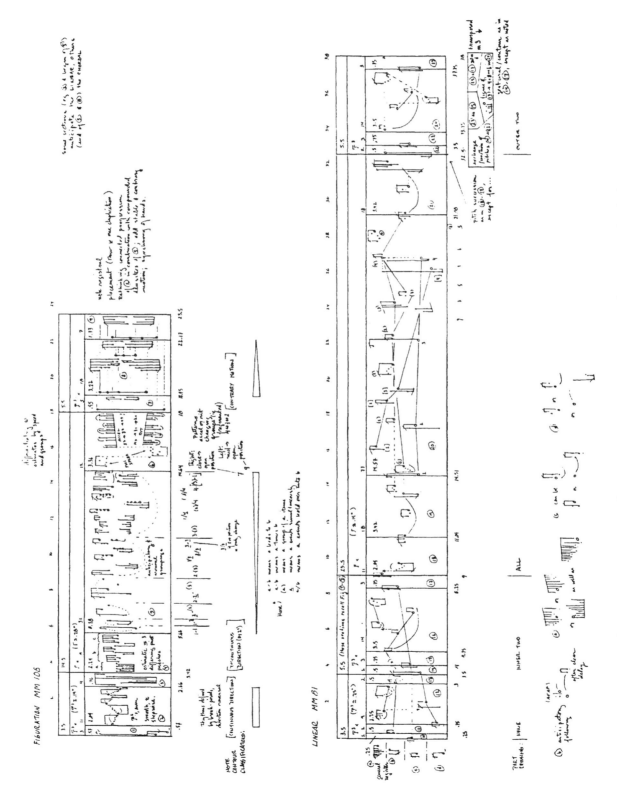

Example 55   Planning the textural detail of the Figurative and Linear core elements in *Variation*.

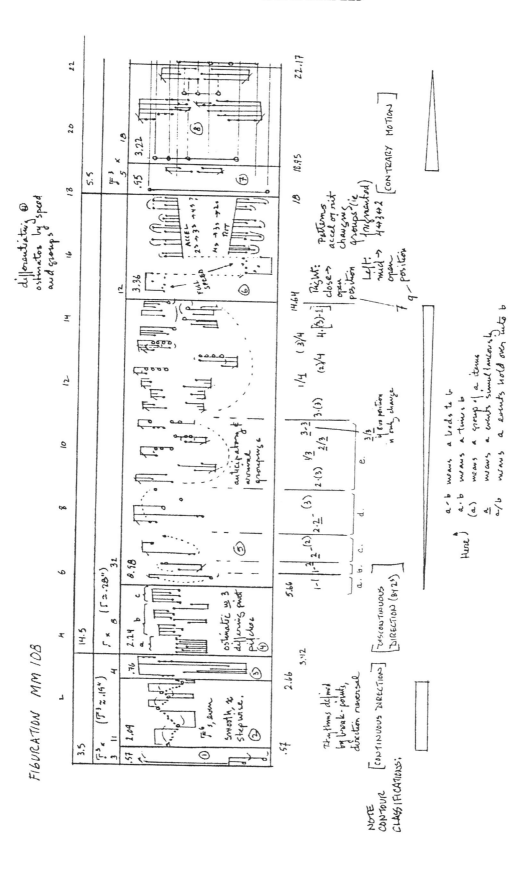

Example 56   Textural detail from Figurative in *Variation*.

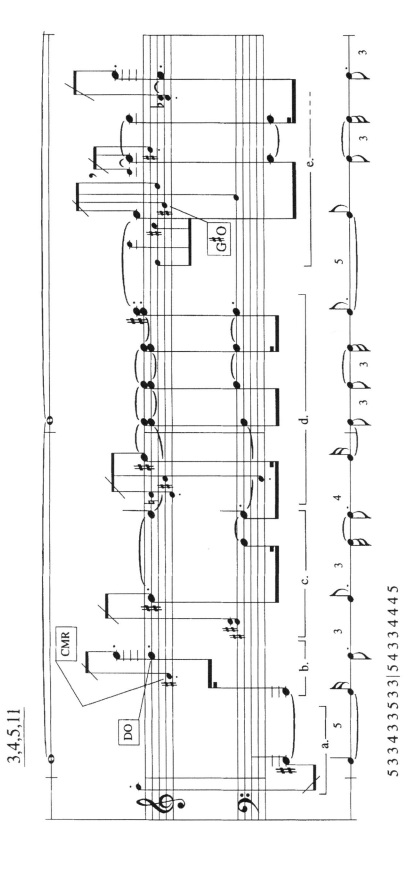

Example 57   The realization of the textural design from Example 56.

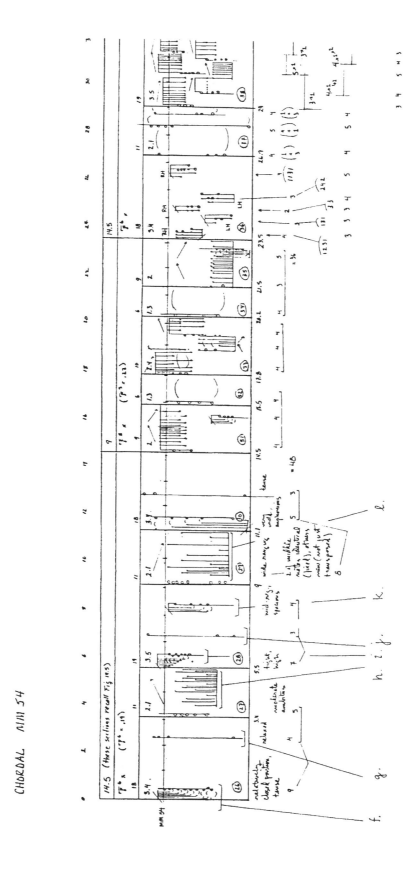

Example 58a   Textural design for the Chordal "core" element (beginning).

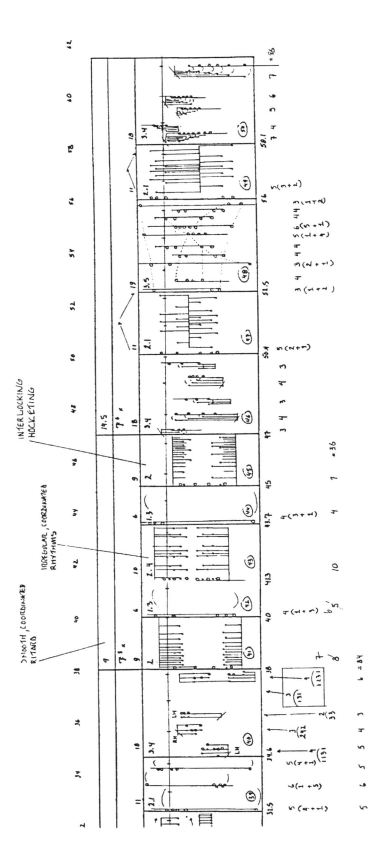

Example 58b   Textural design for the Chordal "core" element (end).

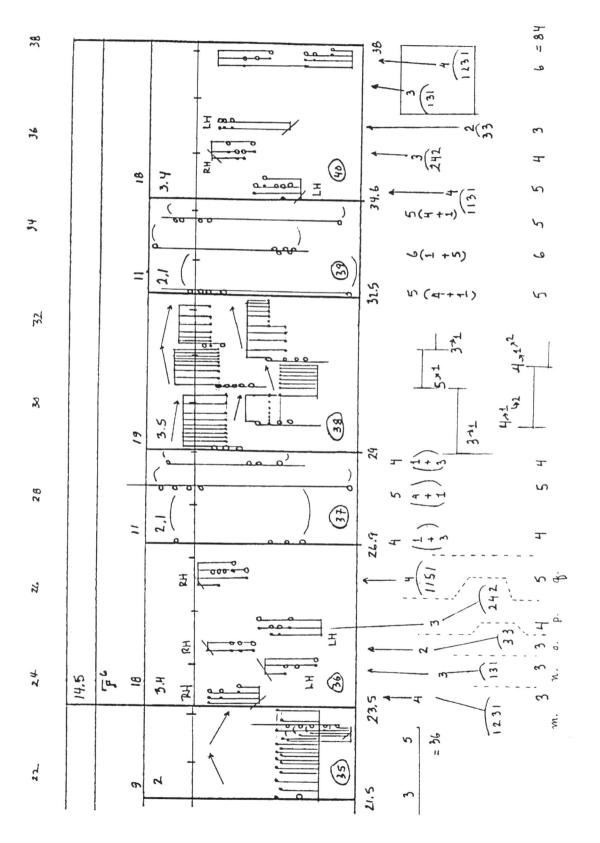

Example 59   A detail of the Chordal texture design, with iterative weighting (*Variation*).

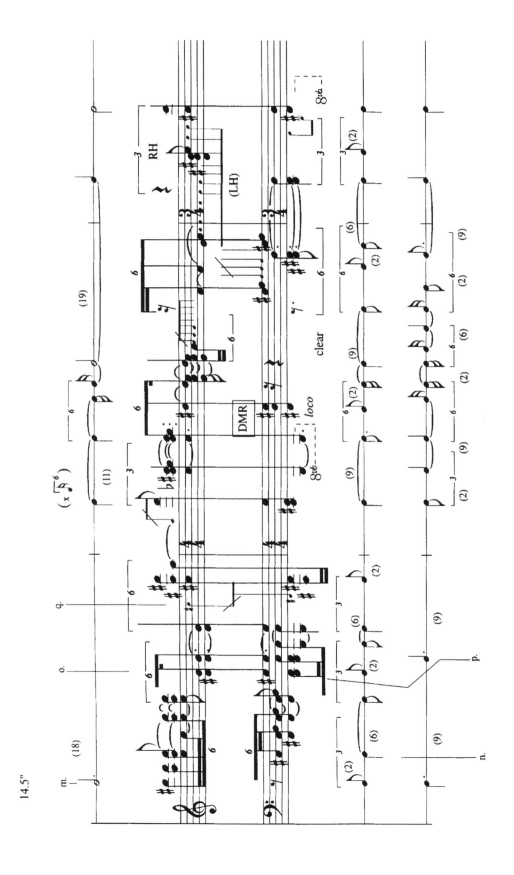

Example 60   The musical realization of the textural detail from Example 59.

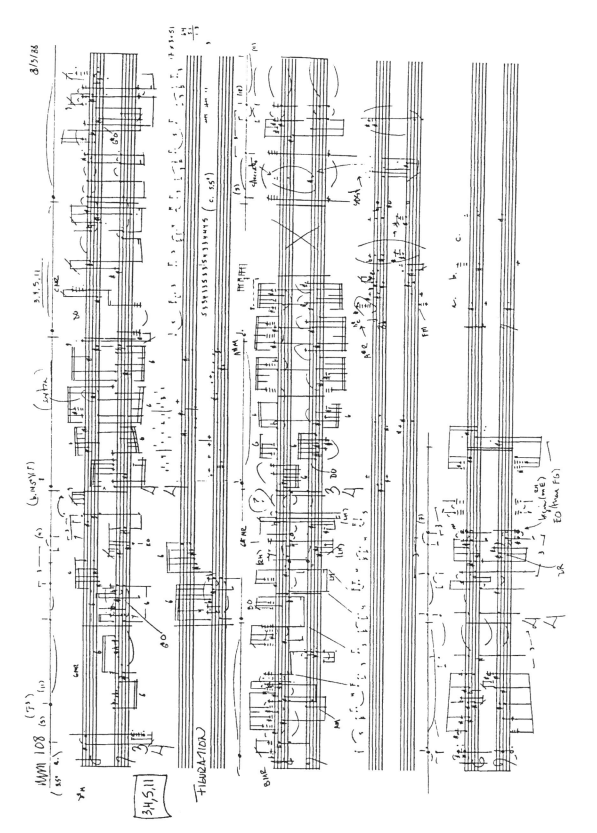

Example 61   The sketch of the Figurative core element from *Variation*.

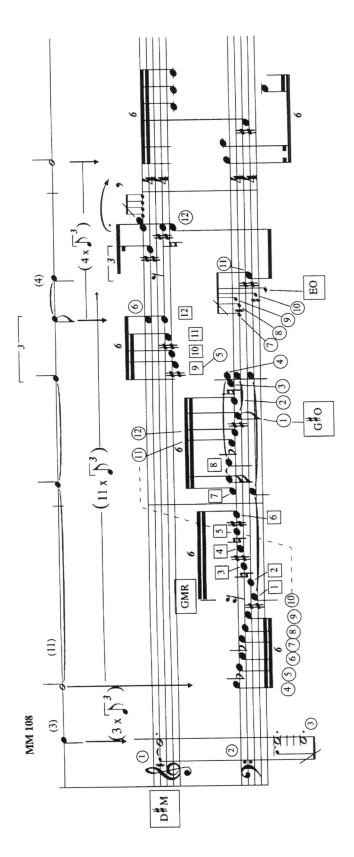

Example 62   A detail of the opening bars of the Figurative sketch (*Variation*).

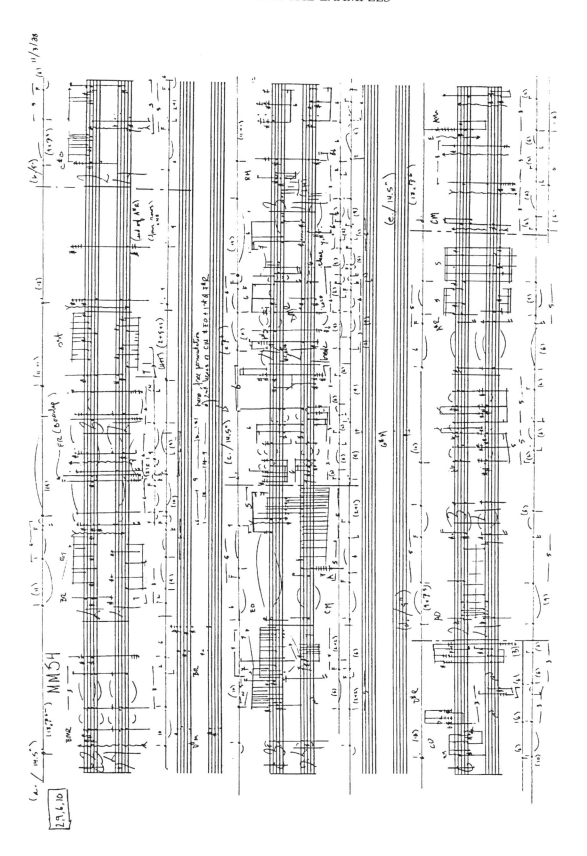

Example 63   A page of the Chordal core element sketch (*Variation*).

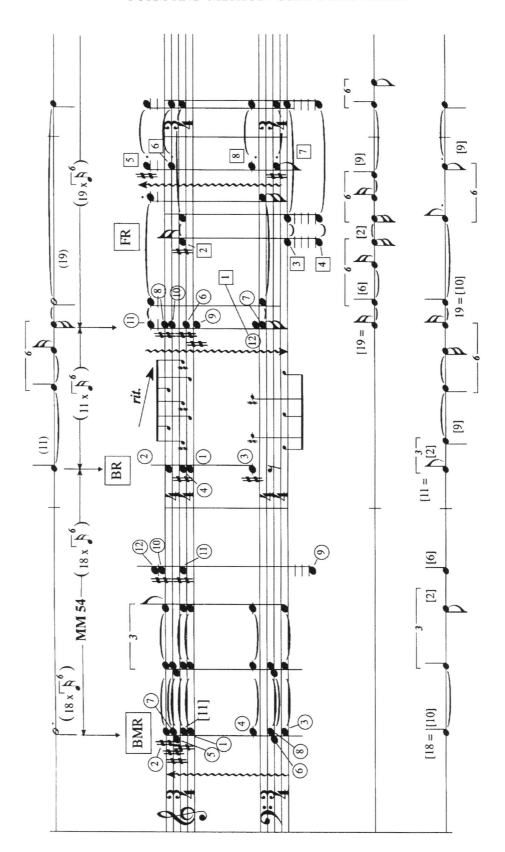

Example 64   A detail of the opening from the Chordal sketch (*Variation*).

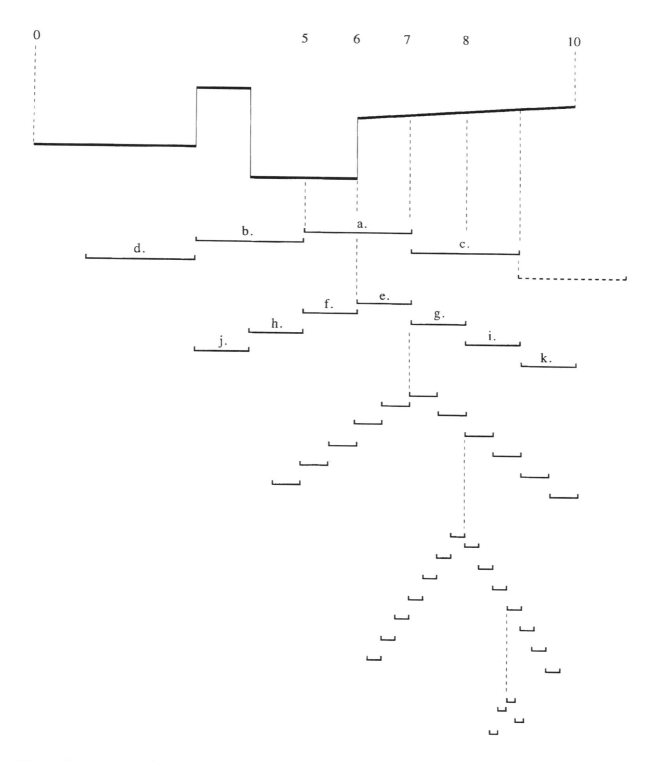

Example 65   A schematic view of the operation of the SPIRLZ algorithm.

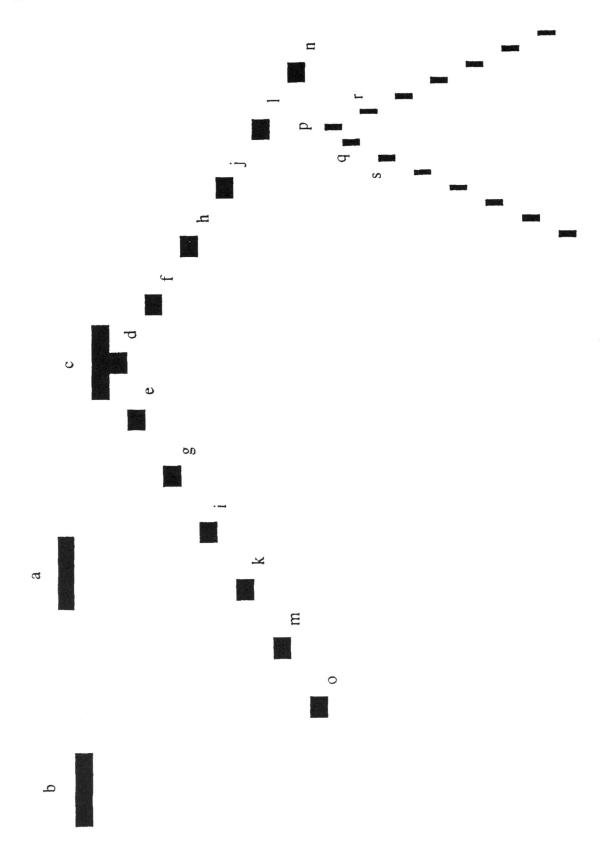

Example 66   The graphic output from a computer run of the SPIRLZ algorithm, displaying its product.

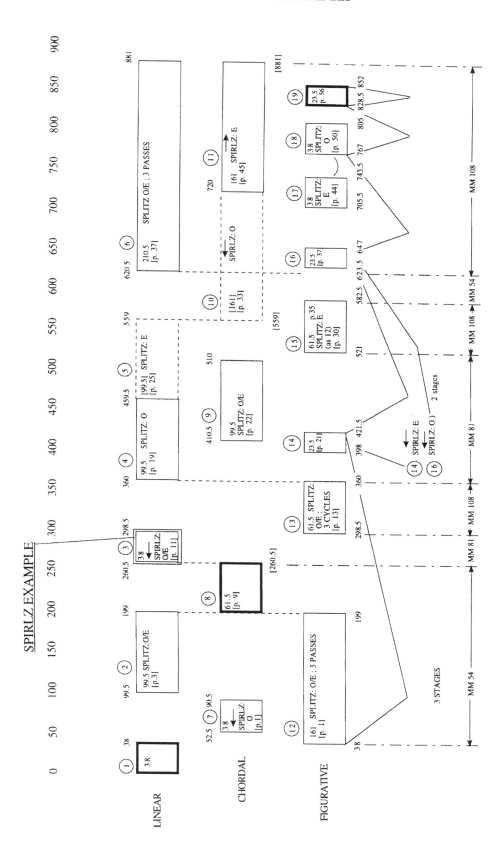

Example 67   Overall plan for *Variation* indicating SPIRLZ example.

segment dur.		begin sample	end sample			begin time in seconds of extracted segment
note 0 cut .76"	6225S	155648	161873	;	sec;	19.0
note 0 cut	6225S	144917	151142	;	sec;	17.7
note 0 cut	6225S	166379	172604	;	sec;	20.3
note 0 cut	6225S	134186	140411	;	sec;	16.38
note 0 cut	6225S	177110	183335	;	sec;	21.62
note 0 cut	6225S	123455	129680	;	sec;	15.1
note 0 cut	6225S	187841	194066	;	sec;	22.9
note 0 cut	6225S	112724	118949	;	sec;	13.8
note 0 cut	6225S	198572	204797	;	sec;	24.2
note 0 cut	6225S	101993	108218	;	sec;	12.5
note 0 cut	6225S	209303	215528	;	sec;	25.6
note 0 cut	6225S	91262	97487	;	sec;	11.1
note 0 cut	6225S	220034	226259	;	sec;	26.9
note 0 cut	6225S	80531	86756	;	sec;	9.8
note 0 cut	6225S	230765	236990	;	sec;	28.2
note 0 cut	6225S	69800	76025	;	sec;	8.5
note 0 cut	6225S	241496	247721	;	sec;	29.5
note 0 cut	6225S	59069	65294	;	sec;	7.2
note 0 cut	6225S	252227	258452	;	sec;	30.8
note 0 cut	6225S	48338	54563	;	sec;	5.9
note 0 cut	6225S	262958	269183	;	sec;	32.1
note 0 cut	6225S	37607	43832	;	sec;	4.6
note 0 cut	6225S	273689	279914	;	sec;	33.4
note 0 cut	6225S	26876	33101	;	sec;	3.3
note 0 cut	6225S	284420	290645	;	sec;	34.7
note 0 cut	6225S	16145	22370	;	sec;	2.0
note 0 cut	6225S	295151	301376	;	sec;	36.0
note 0 cut	6225S	5414	11639	;	sec;	.7
note 0 cut .38"	3112S	221184	224296	;	sec;	27.4
note 0 cut	3112S	215819	218931	;	sec;	26.3
note 0 cut	3112S	226549	229661	;	sec;	27.7
note 0 cut	3112S	210454	213566	;	sec;	25.7
note 0 cut	3112S	231914	235026	;	sec;	28.3
note 0 cut	3112S	205089	208201	;	sec;	25.0
note 0 cut	3112S	237279	240391	;	sec;	29.0
note 0 cut	3112S	199724	202836	;	sec;	24.4
note 0 cut	3112S	242644	245756	;	sec;	29.6
note 0 cut	3112S	194359	197471	;	sec;	23.7
note 0 cut	3112S	248009	251121	;	sec;	30.3
note 0 cut	3112S	188994	192106	;	sec;	23.1
note 0 cut	3112S	253374	256486	;	sec;	30.9
note 0 cut	3112S	183629	186741	;	sec;	22.4
note 0 cut	3112S	258739	261851	;	sec;	31.6
note 0 cut	3112S	178264	181376	;	sec;	21.8
note 0 cut	3112S	264104	267216	;	sec;	32.2
note 0 cut	3112S	172899	176011	;	sec;	21.1
note 0 cut	3112S	269469	272581	;	sec;	32.9
note 0 cut	3112S	167534	170646	;	sec;	20.5
note 0 cut	3112S	274834	277946	;	sec;	33.5
note 0 cut	3112S	162169	165281	;	sec;	19.8
note 0 cut	3112S	280199	283311	;	sec;	34.2
note 0 cut	3112S	156804	159916	;	sec;	19.1
note 0 cut	3112S	285564	288676	;	sec;	34.9
note 0 cut	3112S	151439	154551	;	sec;	18.5
note 0 cut	3112S	290929	294041	;	sec;	35.5
note 0 cut	3112S	146074	149186	;	sec;	17.8
note 0 cut	3112S	296294	299406	;	sec;	36.2
note 0 cut	3112S	140709	143821	;	sec;	17.2
note 0 cut	3112S	301659	304771	;	sec;	36.8
note 0 cut	3112S	135344	138456	;	sec;	16.5
note 0 cut	3112S	307024	310136	;	sec;	37.5
note 0 cut	3112S	129979	133091	;	sec;	15.9
note 0 cut .19"	1556S	286720	288276	;	sec;	35
note 0 cut	1556S	284038	285594	;	sec;	34.7
note 0 cut	1556S	289402	290958	;	sec;	35.3
note 0 cut	1556S	281356	282912	;	sec;	34.3
note 0 cut	1556S	292084	293640	;	sec;	35.7
note 0 cut	1556S	278674	280230	;	sec;	34.0
note 0 cut	1556S	294766	296322	;	sec;	36.0
note 0 cut	1556S	275992	277548	;	sec;	33.7
note 0 cut	1556S	297448	299004	;	sec;	36.3
note 0 cut	1556S	273310	274866	;	sec;	33.4
note 0 cut	1556S	300130	301686	;	sec;	36.6
note 0 cut	1556S	270628	272184	;	sec;	33.0
note 0 cut	1556S	302812	304368	;	sec;	37.0
note 0 cut	1556S	267946	269502	;	sec;	32.7
note 0 cut	1556S	305494	307050	;	sec;	37.3
note 0 cut	1556S	265264	266820	;	sec;	32.4
note 0 cut	1556S	308176	309732	;	sec;	37.6
note 0 cut	1556S	262582	264138	;	sec;	32.1

Example 68 A portion of the computer generated "note list" produced by the SPIRLZ algorithm, used in *Variation*.

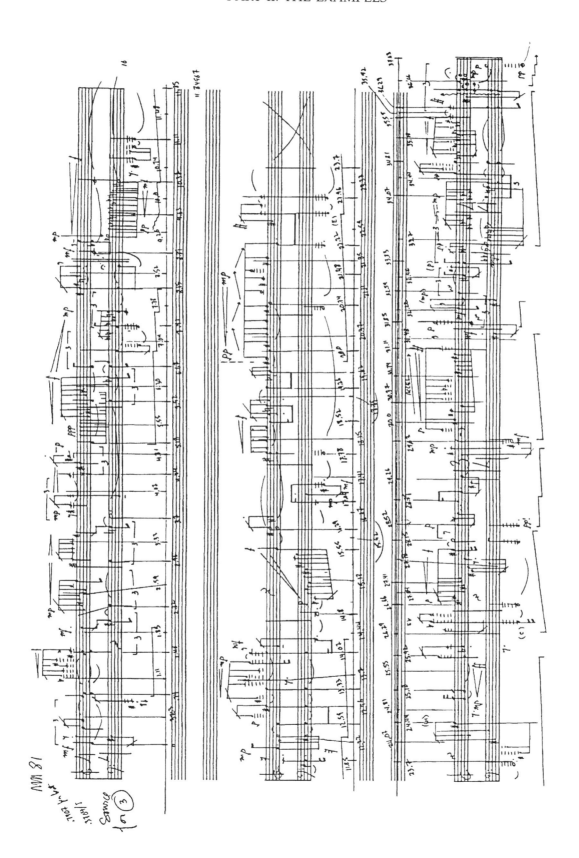

Example 69   The Linear core element from *Variation*, with superimposed timing for SPIRLZ extractions.

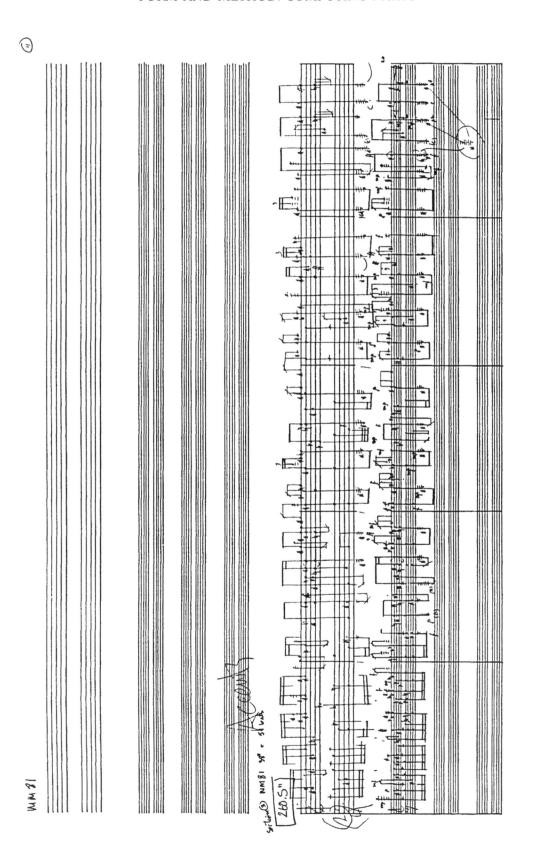

Example 70a   First of three pages from the sketch for *Variation*, showing the mediation from raw fragments to finished continuity.

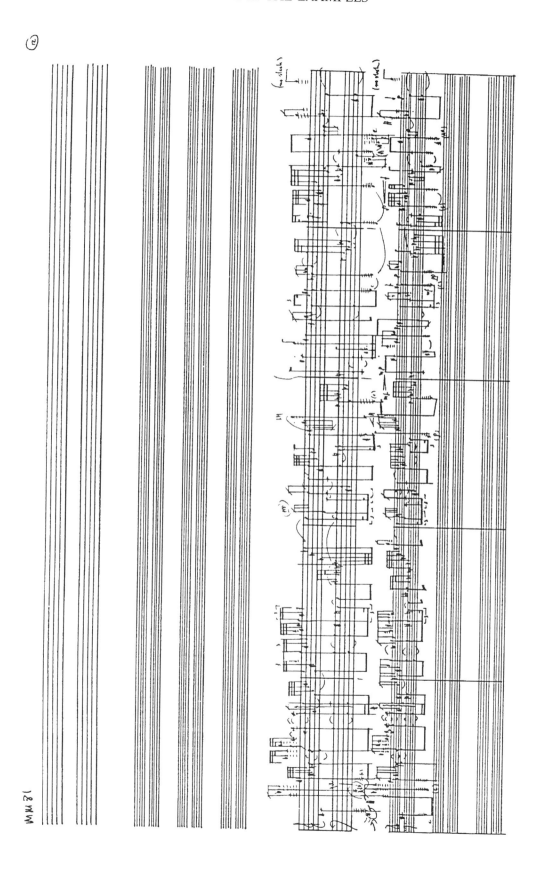

Example 70b Second page from the sketch for *Variation.*

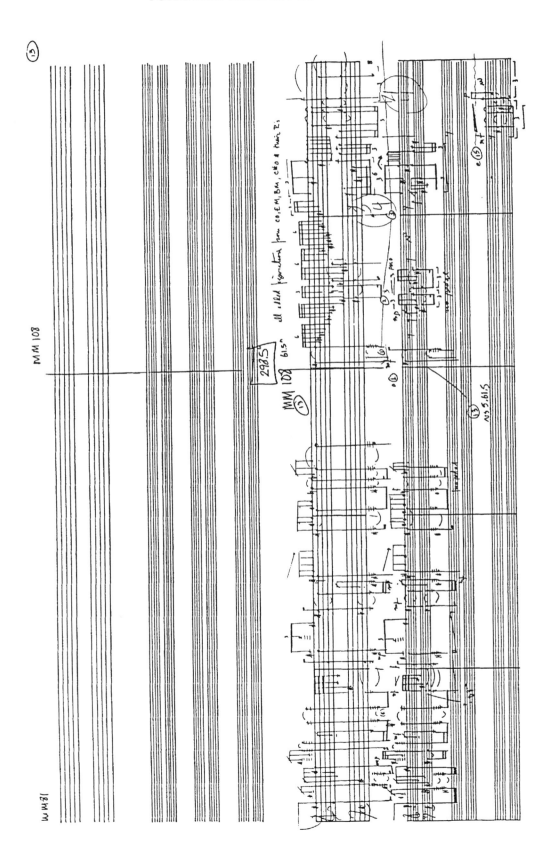

Example 70c Third page from the sketch for *Variation*.

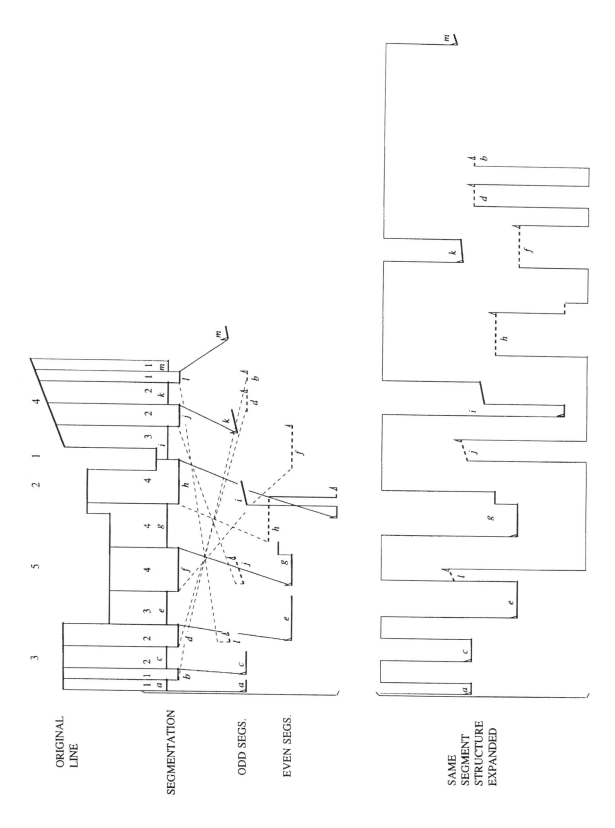

Example 71   A schematic view of the operation of the SPLITZ algorithm.

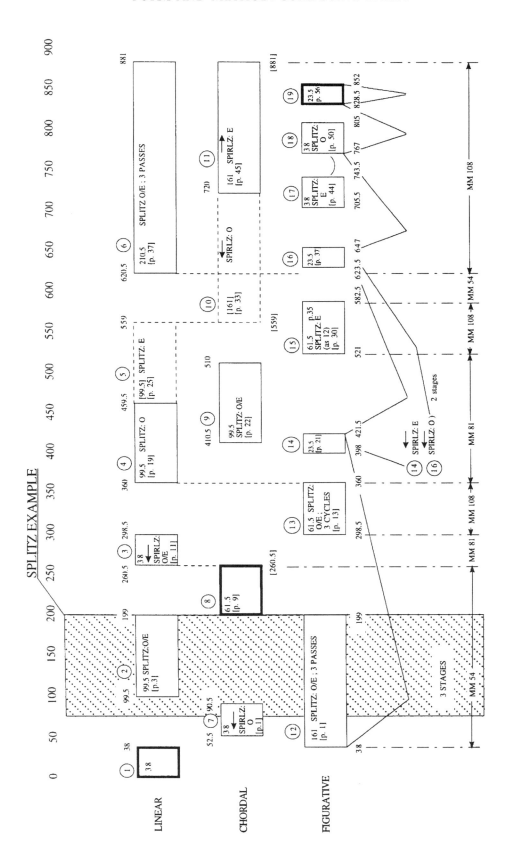

Example 72   The overall plan for *Variation*, highlighting a section which involves material derived from all three strata.

	position in seconds of extracted segment	seg. nos.	duration in seconds of extracted segment	sample numbers that define begin & end of extracted segment			position of segment in output recalculated in beats @ MM = 108
{odd	half-pass 1:		delay: 0.000000}				
note	0.000 1	1	0.280	0	2290	p4sec;	0.0
note	2.132 1	2	0.280	8020	10310	p4sec;	1.92
note	6.132 1	3	0.280	16040	18330	p4sec;	5.52
note	12.013 1	4	0.559	24060	28642	p4sec;	10.81
note	20.070 1	5	0.559	34372	38954	p4sec;	18.06
note	30.038 1	6	0.559	44684	49266	p4sec;	27.04
note	41.931 1	7	0.699	54996	60724	p4sec;	37.74
note	55.904 1	8	0.699	66454	72182	p4sec;	50.32
note	71.833 1	9	1.259	82496	92808	p4sec;	64.66
note	90.292 1	10	1.259	103122	113434	p4sec;	81.27
note	110.736 1	11	1.958	123748	139789	p4sec;	99.67
note	133.881 1	12	1.958	150103	166144	p4sec;	120.5
note	159.042 1	13	1.958	176458	192499	p4sec;	143.15
{even	half-pass 1:		delay: 11.601511}				
note	11.602 2	14	1.259	166145	176457	p4sec;	10.44
note	34.235 2	15	1.259	139790	150102	p4sec;	30.81
note	54.850 2	16	1.259	113435	123747	p4sec;	49.37
note	73.461 2	17	1.259	92809	103121	p4sec;	66.12
note	90.085 2	18	1.259	72183	82495	p4sec;	81.08
note	104.735 2	19	0.699	60725	66453	p4sec;	94.27
note	116.869 2	20	0.699	49267	54995	p4sec;	105.19
note	127.060 2	21	0.699	38955	44683	p4sec;	114.37
note	135.324 2	22	0.699	28643	34371	p4sec;	121.8
note	141.674 2	23	0.699	18331	24059	p4sec;	127.52
note	146.126 2	24	0.699	10311	16039	p4sec;	131.53
note	148.695 2	25	0.699	2291	8019	p4sec;	133.84
{odd	half-pass 2:		delay: 23.203022}				
note	23.203 1	1	0.280	0	2290	p4sec;	20.88
note	24.757 1	2	0.280	8020	10310	p4sec;	22.28
note	27.596 1	3	0.280	16040	18330	p4sec;	24.84
note	31.729 1	4	0.559	24060	28642	p4sec;	28.56
note	37.446 1	5	0.559	34372	38954	p4sec;	33.7
note	44.477 1	6	0.559	44684	49266	p4sec;	40.03
note	52.833 1	7	0.699	54996	60724	p4sec;	47.55
note	62.664 1	8	0.699	66454	72182	p4sec;	56.4
note	73.839 1	9	1.259	82496	92808	p4sec;	66.46
note	86.930 1	10	1.259	103122	113434	p4sec;	78.24
note	101.387 1	11	1.958	123748	139789	p4sec;	91.26
note	117.919 1	12	1.958	150103	166144	p4sec;	106.14
note	135.839 1	13	1.958	176458	192499	p4sec;	122.27
[even	half-pass 2:		delay: 34.804535}				
note	34.805 2	14	1.259	166145	176457	p4sec;	31.33
note	49.603 2	15	1.259	139790	150102	p4sec;	44.65
note	63.123 2	16	1.259	113435	123747	p4sec;	56.82
note	75.374 2	17	1.259	92809	103121	p4sec;	67.84
note	86.366 2	18	1.259	72183	82495	p4sec;	77.74
note	96.108 2	19	0.699	60725	66453	p4sec;	86.51
note	104.050 2	20	0.699	49267	54995	p4sec;	93.65
note	110.762 2	21	0.699	38955	44683	p4sec;	99.70
note	116.253 2	22	0.699	28643	34371	p4sec;	104.64
note	120.532 2	23	0.699	18331	24059	p4sec;	108.50
note	123.608 2	24	0.699	10311	16039	p4sec;	111.26
note	125.492 2	25	0.699	2291	8019	p4sec;	112.95
{odd	half-pass 3:		delay: 46.406044}				
note	46.406 1	1	0.280	0	2290	p4sec;	41.76
note	47.382 1	2	0.280	8020	10310	p4sec;	42.65
note	49.059 1	3	0.280	16040	18330	p4sec;	44.16
note	51.444 1	4	0.559	24060	28642	p4sec;	46.3
note	54.821 1	5	0.559	34372	38954	p4sec;	49.34
note	58.916 1	6	0.559	44684	49266	p4sec;	53.03
note	63.735 1	7	0.699	54996	60724	p4sec;	57.37
note	69.423 1	8	0.699	66454	72182	p4sec;	62.49
note	75.846 1	9	1.259	82496	92808	p4sec;	68.27
note	83.568 1	10	1.259	103122	113434	p4sec;	75.22
note	92.037 1	11	1.958	123748	139789	p4sec;	82.84
note	101.958 1	12	1.958	150103	166144	p4sec;	91.77
note	112.636 1	13	1.958	176458	192499	p4sec;	101.38
{even	half-pass 3:		delay: 58.007557}				
note	58.008 2	14	1.259	166145	176457	p4sec;	52.2
note	64.971 2	15	1.259	139790	150102	p4sec;	58.48
note	71.397 2	16	1.259	113435	123747	p4sec;	64.26
note	77.287 2	17	1.259	92809	103121	p4sec;	69.57
note	82.647 2	18	1.259	72183	82495	p4sec;	74.39
note	87.480 2	19	0.699	60725	66453	p4sec;	78.74
note	91.231 2	20	0.699	49267	54995	p4sec;	82.12
note	94.464 2	21	0.699	38955	44683	p4sec;	85.03
note	97.182 2	22	0.699	28643	34371	p4sec;	87.48
note	99.390 2	23	0.699	18331	24059	p4sec;	89.46
note	101.091 2	24	0.699	10311	16039	p4sec;	90.99
note	102.289 2	25	0.699	2291	8019	p4sec;	92.07

Example 73   A "note list" produced by the SPLITZ algorithm.

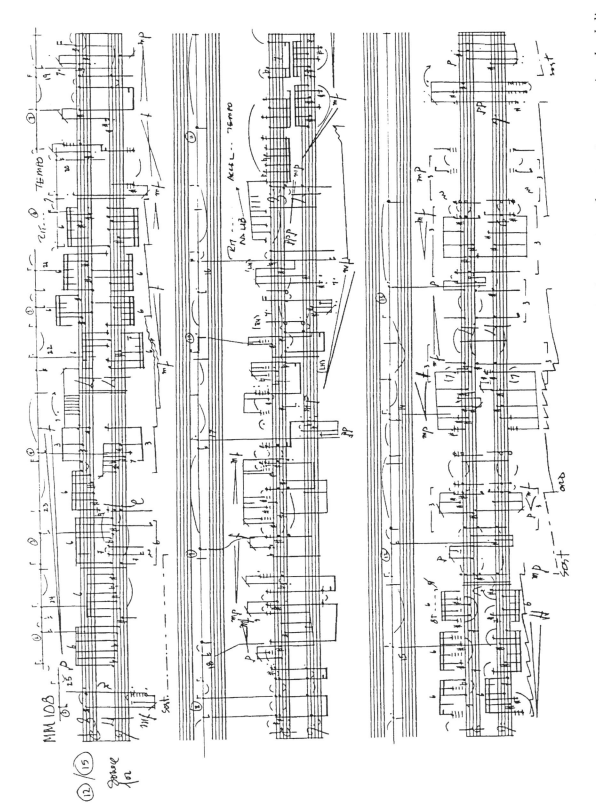

Example 74   The Figurative core element from *Variation*, with superimposed rhythmic values showing its proportional subdivision.

position in seconds of extracted segment	seg nos	duration in seconds of extracted segment				position of segment in output recalculated in beats @ MM = 81	position of segment in output recalculated in beats @ MM = 54
{odd half-pass 1: delay: 0.000000 }							
note 0.000 1	1	1.710	0	14007	p4sec;	0.0	0.0
note 2.189 1	2	1.710	35798	49805	p4sec;	2.95	1.97
note 4.861 1	3	1.710	71596	85603	p4sec;	6.56	4.38
note 8.016 1	4	1.710	107394	121401	p4sec;	10.82	7.22
note 11.659 1	5	0.950	143192	150973	p4sec;	15.74	10.5
note 15.032 1	6	0.950	164982	172763	p4sec;	20.29	13.53
note 18.897 1	7	0.950	186772	194553	p4sec;	25.51	17.0
note 23.257 1	8	0.760	208562	214786	p4sec;	31.40	20.93
note 27.924 1	9	0.760	222569	228793	p4sec;	37.70	25.13
note 33.091 1	10	0.760	236576	242800	p4sec;	44.68	29.78
note 38.761 1	11	0.760	250583	256807	p4sec;	52.33	34.89
note 44.936 1	12	0.380	264590	267701	p4sec;	60.67	40.45
note 51.240 1	13	0.380	273927	277038	p4sec;	69.18	46.12
note 58.054 1	14	0.380	283264	286375	p4sec;	78.38	52.25
note 65.381 1	15	0.380	289488	292599	p4sec;	88.27	58.84
note 73.225 1	16	0.190	295712	297267	p4sec;	98.86	65.91
note 81.397 1	17	0.190	300380	301935	p4sec;	109.89	73.26
note 90.092 1	18	0.190	305048	306603	p4sec;	121.63	81.09
note 99.310 1	19	0.190	309716	311271	p4sec;	134.08	89.39
{even half-pass 1: delay : 4.514350 }							
note 4.514 2	20	0.380	306604	309715	p4sec;	6.09	4.06
note 12.498 2	21	0.380	301936	305047	p4sec;	16.87	11.25
note 20.016 2	22	0.380	297268	300379	p4sec;	27.02	18.02
note 27.070 2	23	0.380	292600	295711	p4sec;	36.55	24.37
note 33.662 2	24	0.380	286376	289487	p4sec;	45.45	30.30
note 39.795 2	25	0.760	277039	283263	p4sec;	53.73	35.82
note 45.851 2	26	0.760	267702	273926	p4sec;	61.90	41.27
note 51.453 2	27	0.950	256808	264589	p4sec;	69.47	46.31
note 56.794 2	28	0.950	242801	250582	p4sec;	76.68	51.12
note 61.684 2	29	0.950	228794	236575	p4sec;	83.28	55.52
note 66.128 2	30	0.950	214787	222568	p4sec;	89.28	59.52
note 70.127 2	31	1.710	194554	208561	p4sec;	94.68	63.12
note 74.443 2	32	1.710	172764	186771	p4sec;	100.5	67.01
note 78.319 2	33	1.710	150974	164981	p4sec;	105.74	70.49
note 81.758 2	34	2.660	121402	143191	p4sec;	110.38	73.59
note 85.710 2	35	2.660	85604	107393	p4sec;	115.71	77.15
note 89.230 2	36	2.660	49806	71595	p4sec;	120.47	80.32
note 92.318 2	37	2.660	14008	35797	p4sec;	124.64	83.09

MM 81 ♩ = .7407

♪ = .1852 => .19

(14 x ♪) ♩_♩. = 2.66

(9 x ♪) ♩_♪ = 1.71

(5 x ♪) ♩_♪ = .95

(4 x ♪) ♩ = .76

(2 x ♪) ♪ = .38

♪ = .19

MM = 108

time	beats
0.00	
4.65	8.37
8.65	15.57
12.96	23.33
16.84	30.31
19.52	35.13
24.23	43.61
27.75	49.95
30.84	55.51

Example 75   A "note list" produced by the SPLITZ algorithm.

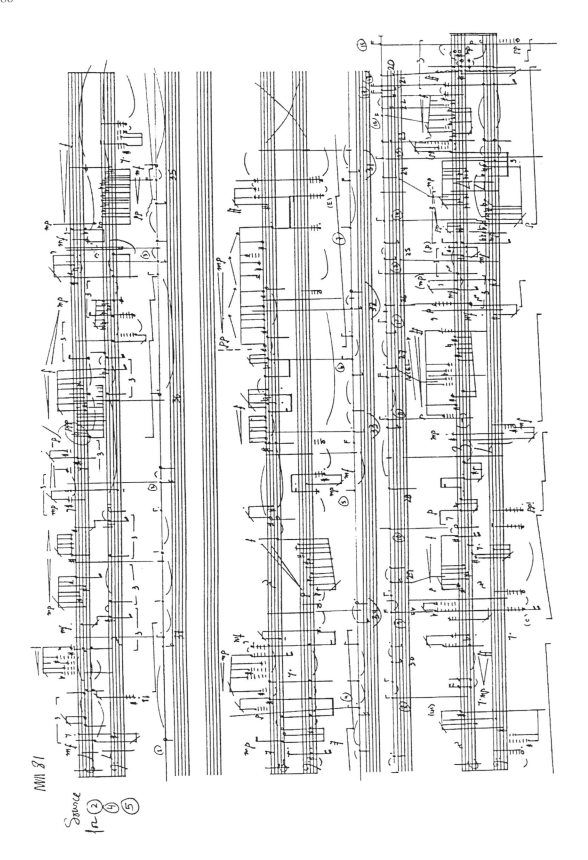

Example 76   The Linear core theme from *Variation*, with superimposed rhythmic values showing its proportional subdivision.

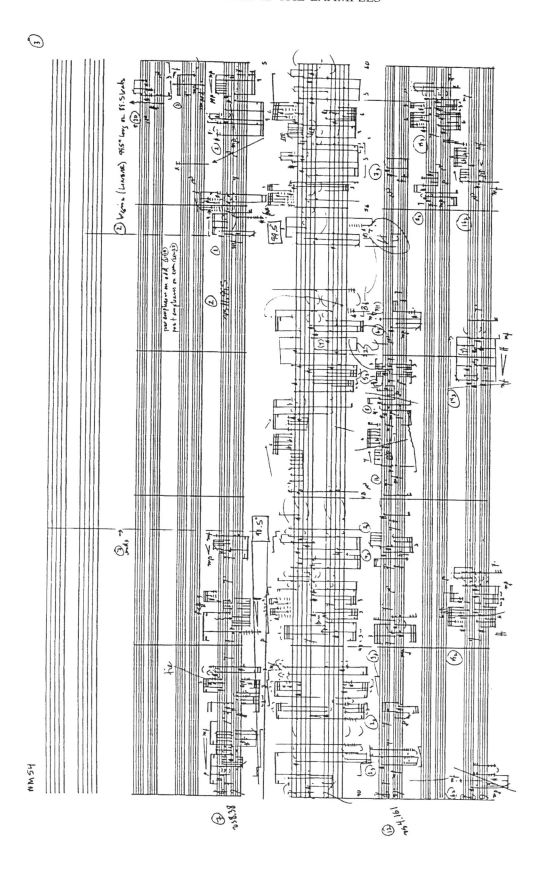

Example 77a   First of five successive pages from the sketch for *Variation*, showing the mediation from raw fragments to finished continuity.

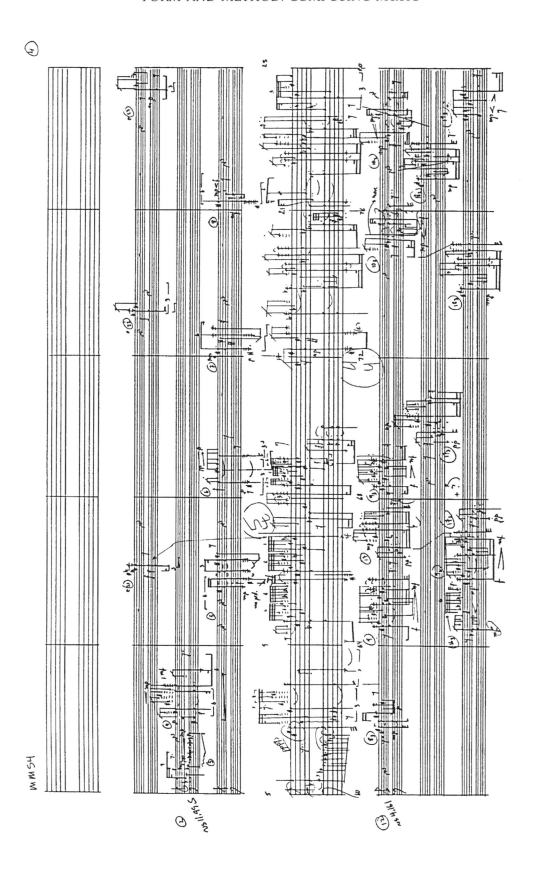

Example 77b   Second page from the sketch for *Variation*.

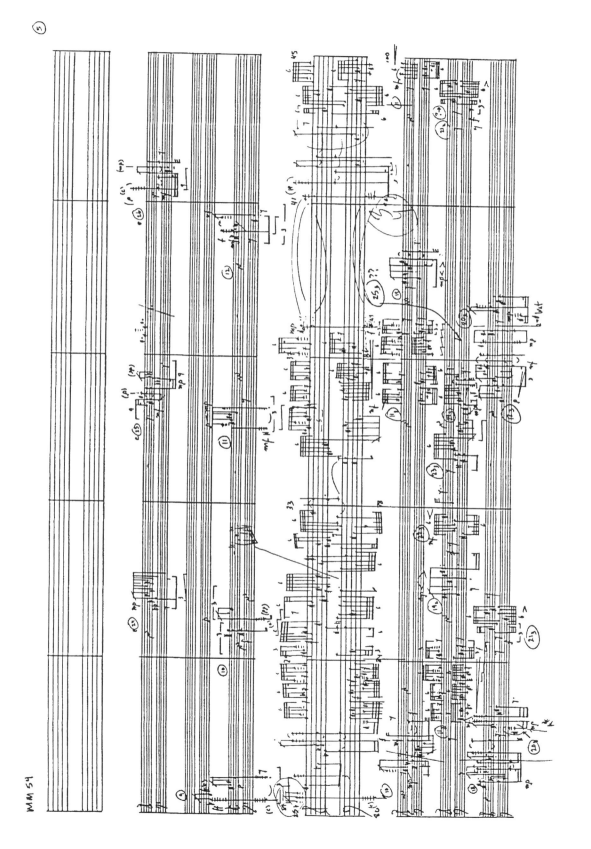

Example 77c   Third page from the sketch for *Variation*.

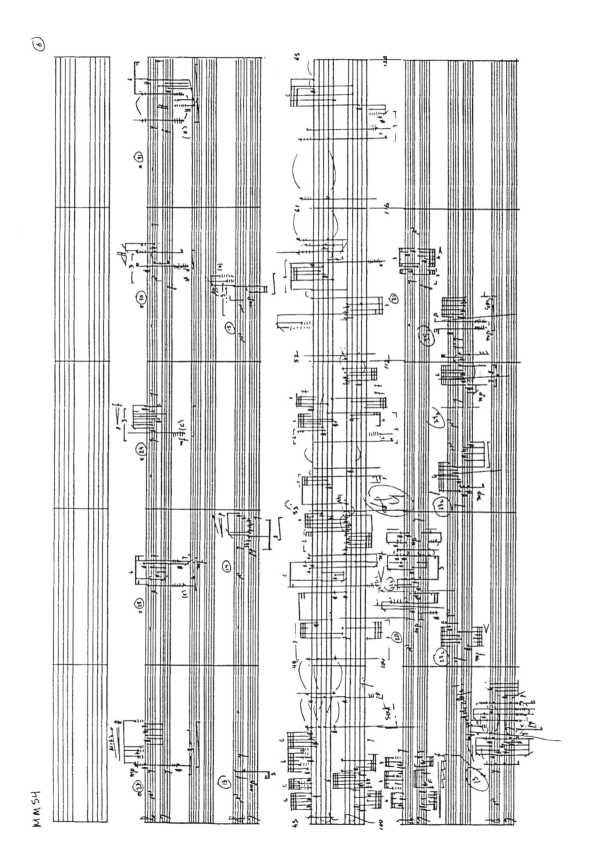

Example 77d   Fourth page from the sketch for *Variation.*

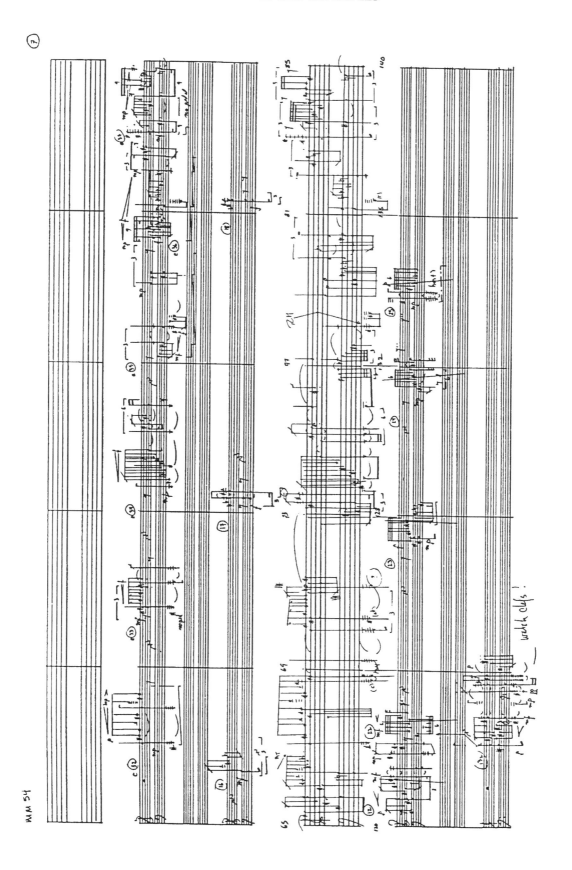

Example 77e   Fifth page from the sketch for *Variation*.

SPIRLZ	SPLITZ
continuous	discontinuous
overlapping segments taken in alternation	contiguous segments segments taken linearly
segment length automatically incremented (smaller or larger)	segment length specified by arbitrary series of proportions
begins in middle of subject file, works toward extremes	begins at outer extremes of subject file, works in opposing directions
terminates by concentrating on beginning or ending of subject file	terminates at both outer extremes of subject file
cyclical, redundant	canonic, parsimonious
monophonic	polyphonic

Example 78   A table comparing the SPLITZ and SPIRLZ algorithms.

SYMPHONY[MYTHS] (1990)

Example 79   The chart of row forms used in *Symphony[Myths]*.

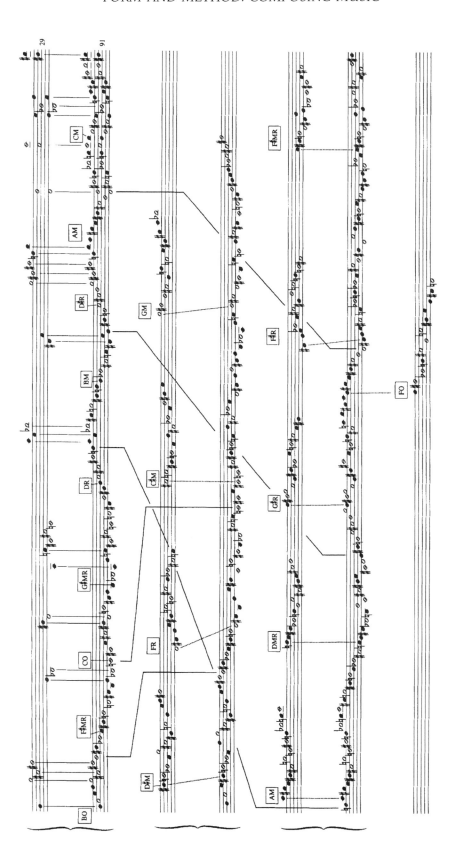

Example 80   Derivation from basic row forms of 91-note secondary pitch resource for *Symphony[Myths]*.

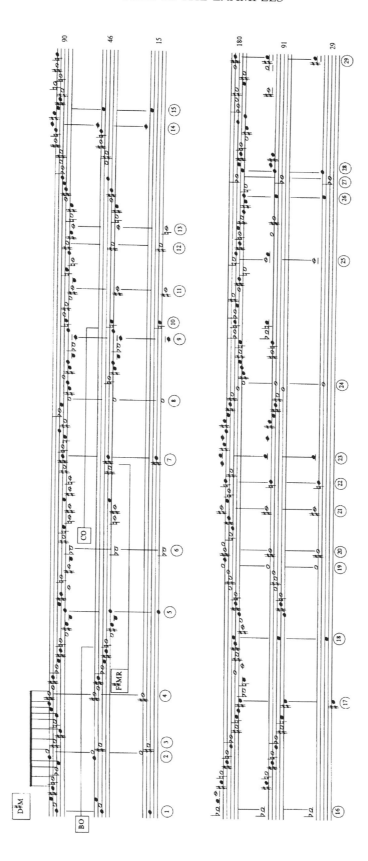

Example 81   The full secondary pitch resource with 29-, 91-, and 180-note sequences from *Symphony[Myths]*.

the two series: 1   2   4   7   13

                       1   3   5   9

29 & 13 come from measurement of *meoto iwa* pair

9 emerged as an attractive smaller number to
complete a basic "triad" of integers

13 is top number in "5" proportion, 9 in "4" proportion

5:4 is a nine element relationship	extrapolated from 13 - 180 series	Rounded off
	21.9	22
	19.7	20
	17.7	18
4 sources: - original series	15.9	15
(and its extension)	14.3	14
	13	13
- two rhythmic series	11.7	12
(5) 1 2 4 7 13	10.6	11
(4) 1 3 5 9	9.5	10
	8.6	9
- main proportions of	7.8	8
29:13:9	7	7
	6.3	
	5.7	
	5.2	

Example 82   First stage in the derivation of temporal control for *Symphony[Myths]*.

		Rounded off		
		180	180	
13x13	169	163	163	13
13x11	143	146.5	147	
13x10	130	131.5	132	
13x9	117	118	118	9
13x8	104	106	106	
13x7	91	95.3	95	
		85.7	86	7
13x6	78	77.2	77	
		69.5	70	
13x5	65	62.6	63	5
		56.3	56	
13x4	52	50.6	51	
		45.5	46	4
		41	41	
13x3	39	36.9	37	
		33.1	33	3
		29.9	30	
13x2	26	27	27	
		24.3		2
		21.9		
		19.7		
		17.7		1
		15.9		
		14.3		
		13		1

these 2 series
come from
dividing by 13

Example 83   Second stage in the derivation of temporal control for *Symphony[Myths]*.

of the primary number resources

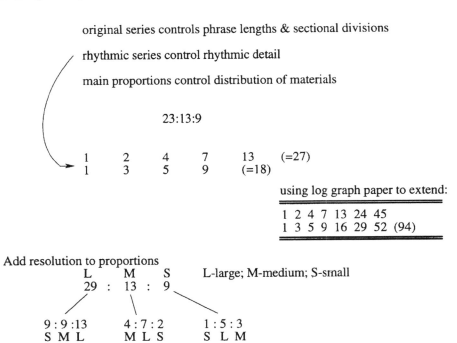

original series controls phrase lengths & sectional divisions

rhythmic series control rhythmic detail

main proportions control distribution of materials

23:13:9

| 1 | 2 | 4 | 7 | 13 | (=27) |
| 1 | 3 | 5 | 9 | (=18) | |

using log graph paper to extend:

1 2 4 7 13 24 45
1 3 5 9 16 29 52 (94)

Add resolution to proportions

        L   M   S   L-large; M-medium; S-small
       29 : 13 : 9

9 : 9 :13   4 : 7 : 2   1 : 5 : 3
S M L   M L S   S L M

Example 84   Third stage in the derivation of temporal control for *Symphony[Myths]*.

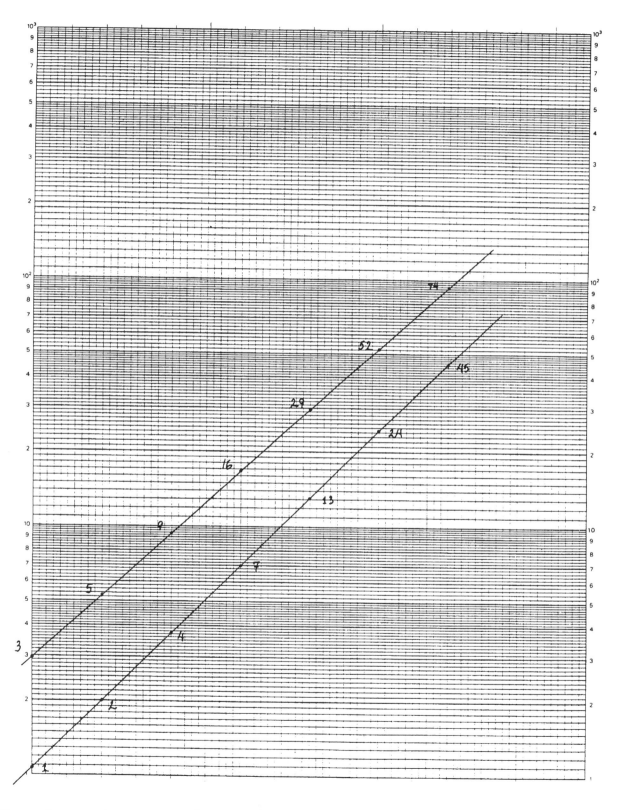

Example 85   Semi-log graph paper showing the *Symphony[Myths]* rhythmic sets.

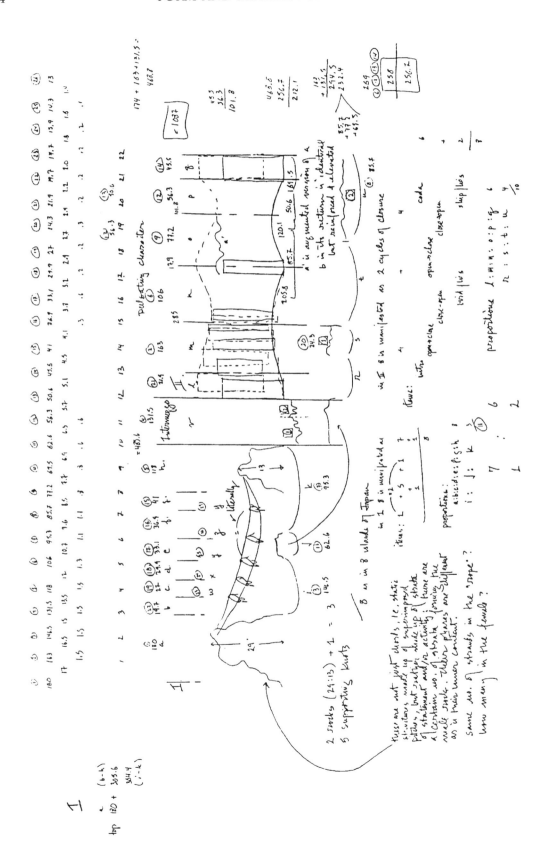

Example 86   A very early sketch of the possible application of the 26 + 3 proportional number series to the formal design of *Symphony[Myths]*.

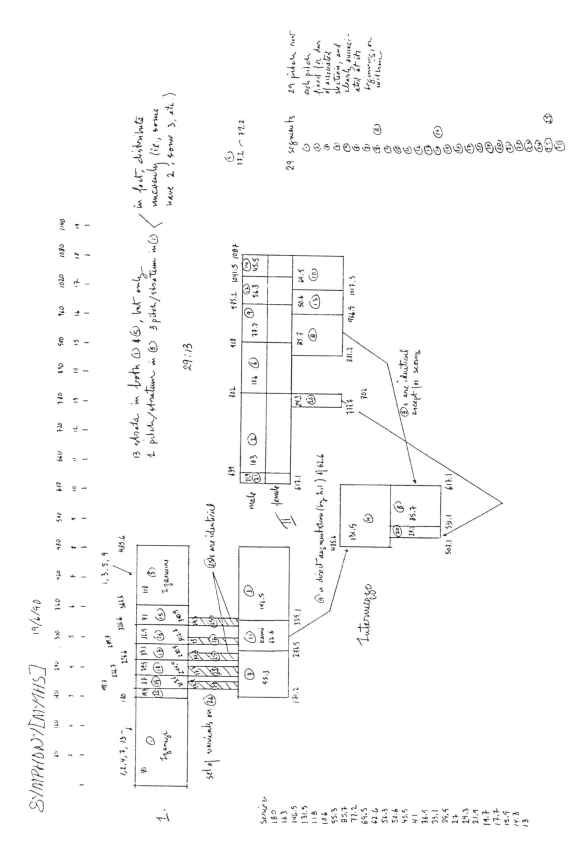

Example 87   Final overall plan for the sectional design of *Symphony[Myths]*.

13	VL I (MUTE) / PICC 1 / PNO
12	VL II (MUTE) / PICC 2 / HARP
11	2 FLS / E♭ CL
10	TRP (2-4) WA-WA MUTES
9	3 OB / VIB
8	VLA (MUTE) / TRP 1 (MUTE) / MAR
7	HN (1-3) / BSN 1 / MAR
6	CL (3&3) / TBN (MUTE) / VIB
5	CELLOS (MUTE)
4	CL 1 / 2 TBNS (MUTE)
3	HN (2&4) / BS CL
2	BSN (2&3) / BS TBN / HARP
1	TUBA / CBS / PNO

9	TRP (MUTE)
8	VIOLIN
7	ENG HN
6	CLAR
5	VC
4	VLA
3	TBN (MUTE)
2	BS CL
1	CONT BSN

I Strata of Rocks

(work out striking instrumentation for each layer)

13	PICCOLO / PIANO *	central flourishes
12	VL I / HARP *	initial flourishes
11	VL II / GLOCK	closing flourishes
10	FL (2) / E♭ CL / MARIMBA *	initial
9	CL (2) / OB (1)	central
8	TRP (3)	central
7	OB (2) / TRP (1) / HN (1)	initial
6	HN 3 / EH / TBN (1) / VC 1	central
5	VLA / TBN (2)	initial
4	B CL / HN (2&4) / BSN 1 / VC 2 / MAR	central
3	BSN (2&3) / BS TBN	closing
2	CB / HARP	central
1	CONT BSN / TUBA / PNO	central

* figures in emphasis instruments (pno, harp, mar) should originate in or descend to the areas they emphasize in their low-range complements

Example 88   The timbric design of the three "rock" elements for *Symphony[Myths]*, Movement I.

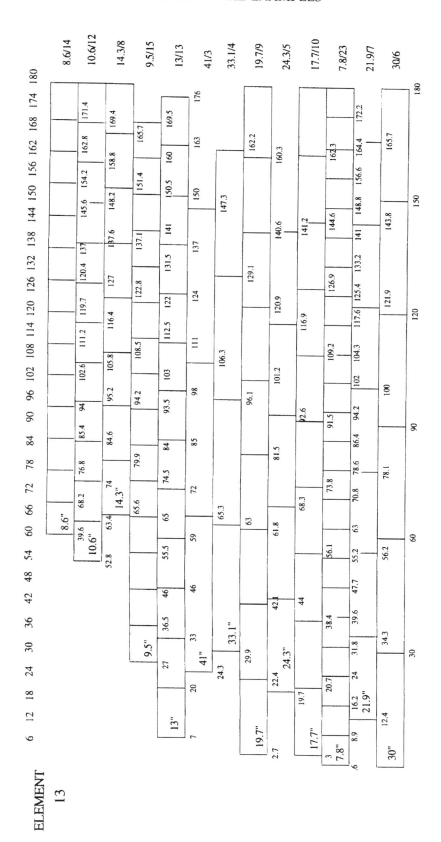

Example 89   The 13-layered structure of superimposed ostinati for element ① of *Symphony[Myths]*, Movement I.

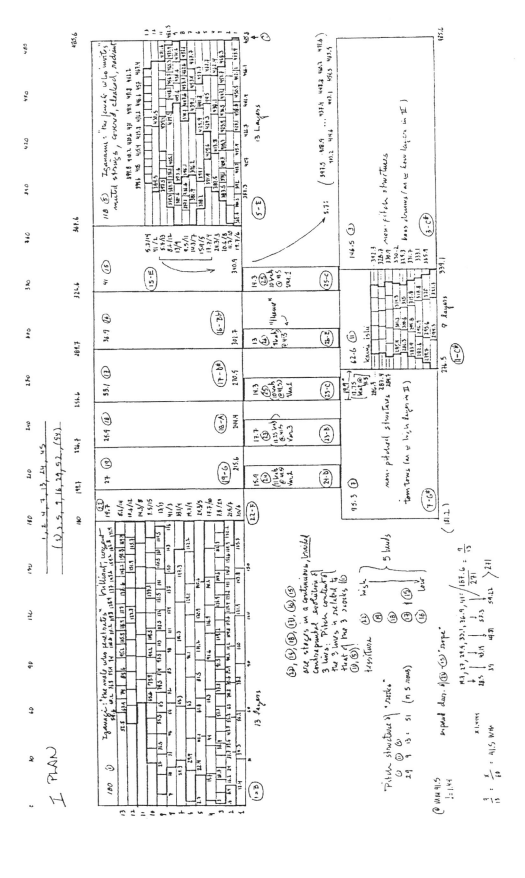

Example 90   Detailed temporal design for Movement I, *Symphony[Myths]*.

Example 91   The pitch content of the 13-layered, ostinatic strata of element ① , Movement 1, *Symphony[Myths]*.

Example 92   The extrapolation of element ①'s 29-note structure into the 13- and 9-tone forms *(Symphony[Myths])*.

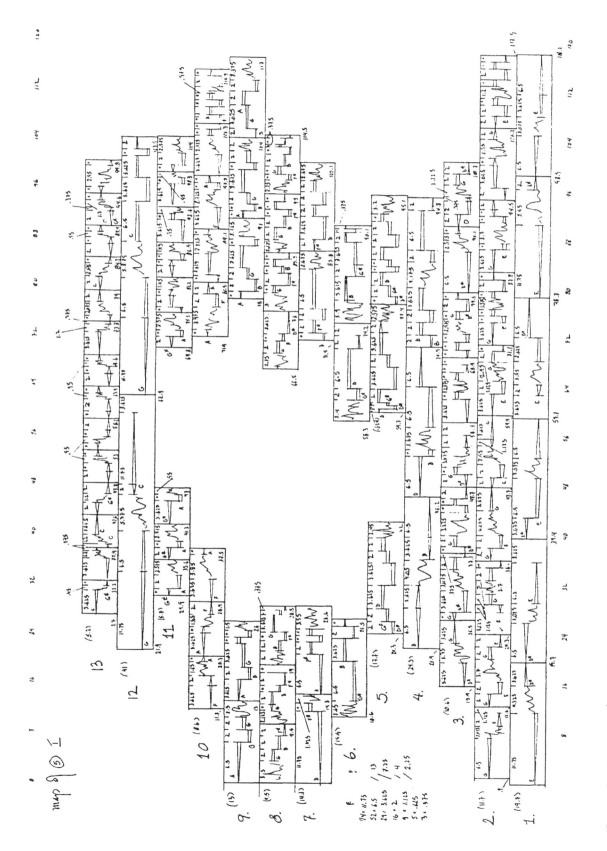

Example 93   A schematic plan for the structure of the female rock in Movement I of *Symphony[Myths]*.

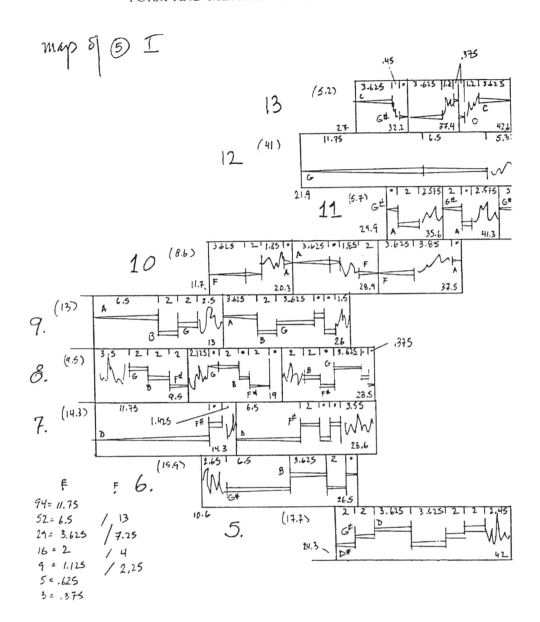

Example 94   A detail of the female rock textural design from Example 93.

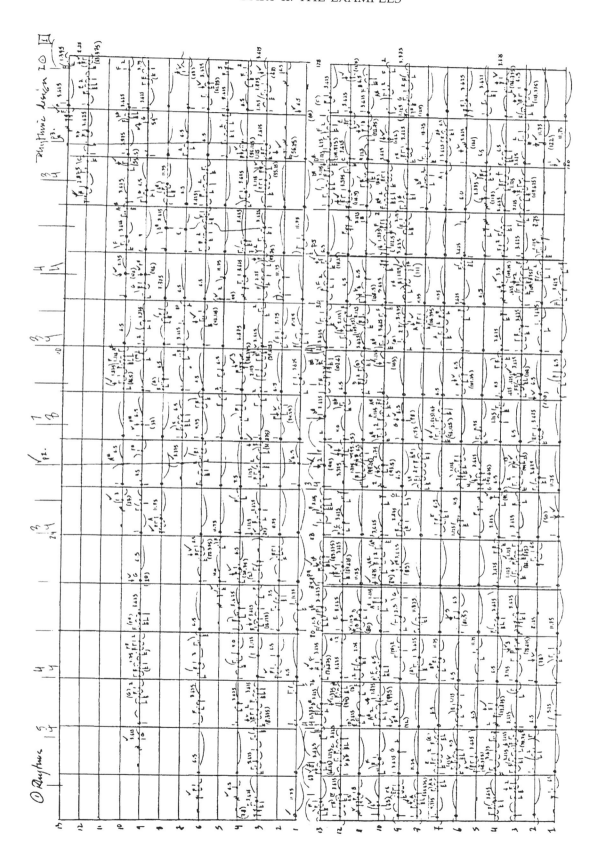

Example 95   The rhythmic structure of 13 ostinatic layers in element ① of Movement I, *Symphony[Myths]*.

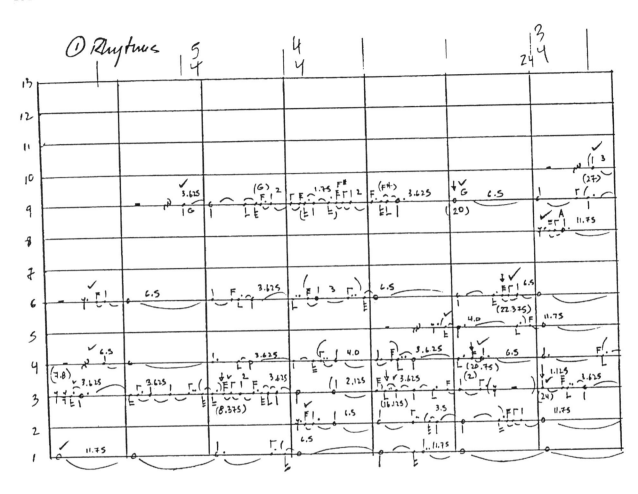

Example 96   A detail of the 13-layered rhythmic structure from Example 95.

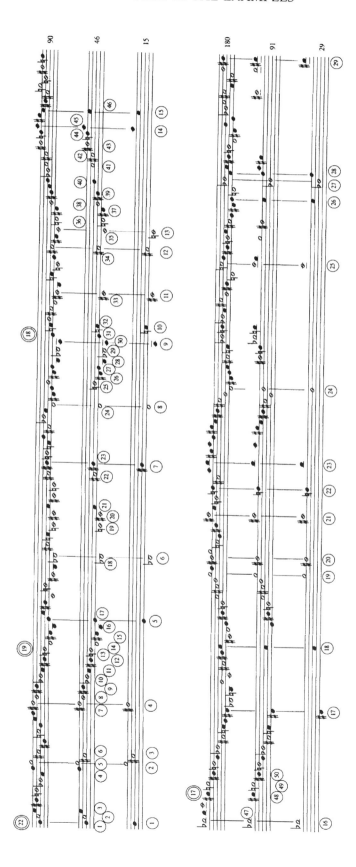

Example 97   The derivation of the 3-stranded central section of Movement I of *Symphony[Myths]* begins with a subdivision of the 3-level pitch resource first shown in Examples 80 and 81.

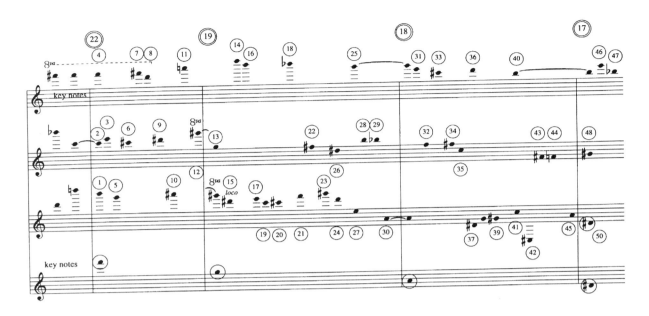

Example 98   Rough counterpoint is established in *Symphony[Myths]*, using a 3-part distribution of the 91-note central row composite.

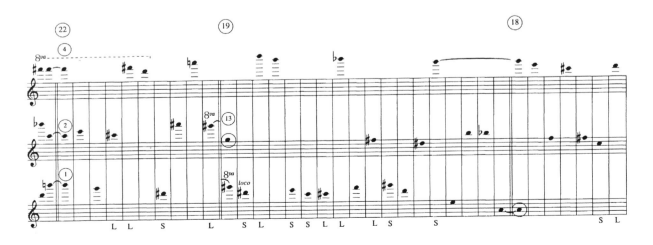

Example 99   Increasing precision of harmonic positioning (L = longer value and S = shorter), *Symphony[Myths]*.

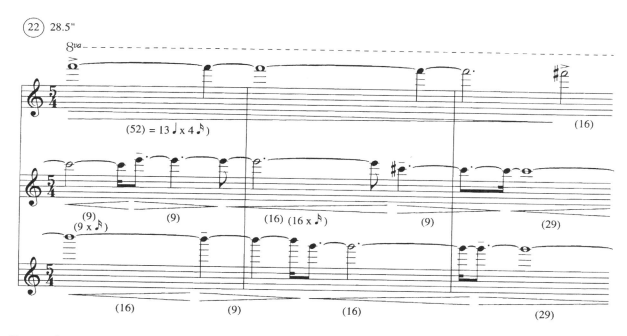

Example 100   A detail of the specific rhythmic values from *Symphony[Myths]* as they refine the relative temporal placement, drawing upon the rhythmic collection of integers.

Example 101   The completed voice-leading of elements ㉒ and ⑲, Movement I, *Symphony[Myths]*.

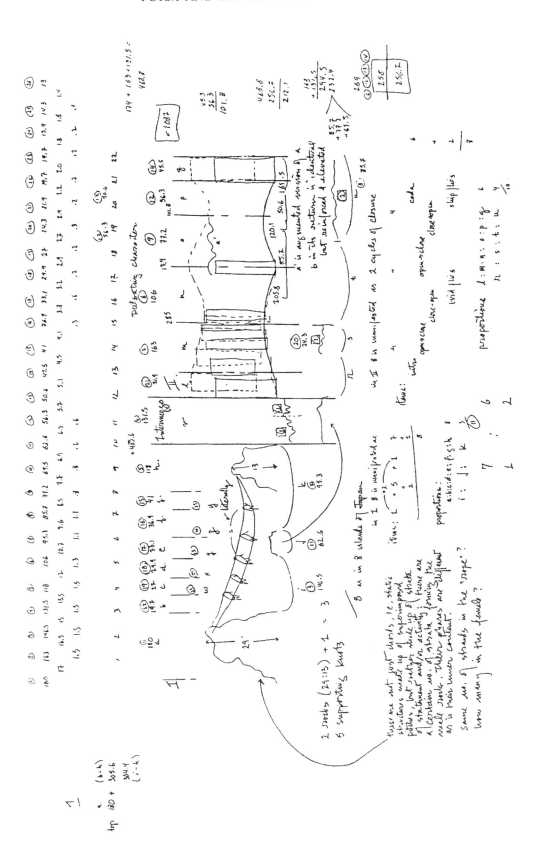

Example 102   The preliminary design for the overall structure of *Symphony[Myths]* suggests the design of Movement III.

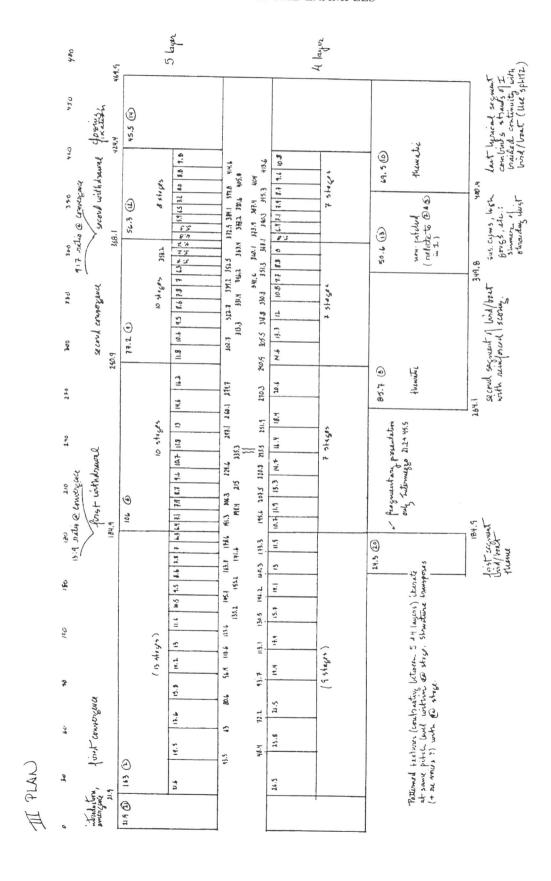

Example 103   The developed plan for Movement III of *Symphony[Myths]*.

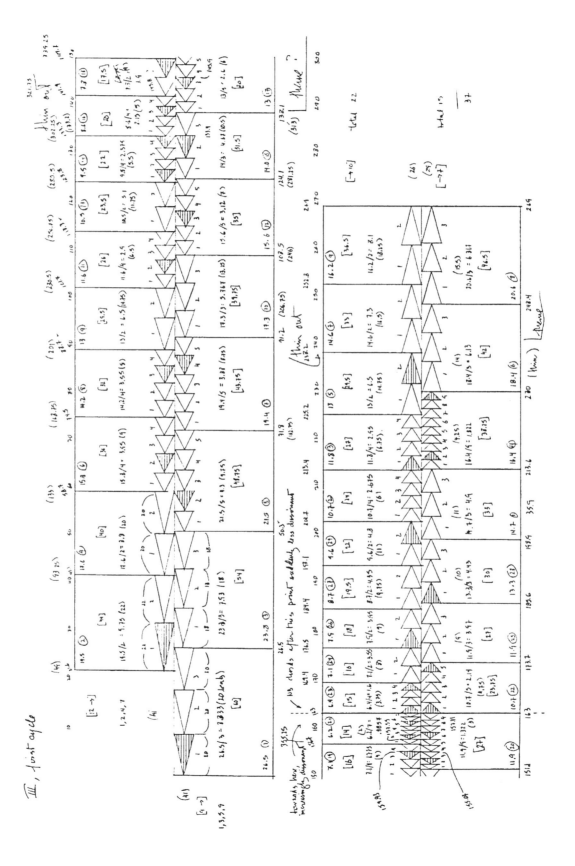

Example 104 *Symphony[Myths]*, Movement III, detailed plan for the first cycle of convergence.

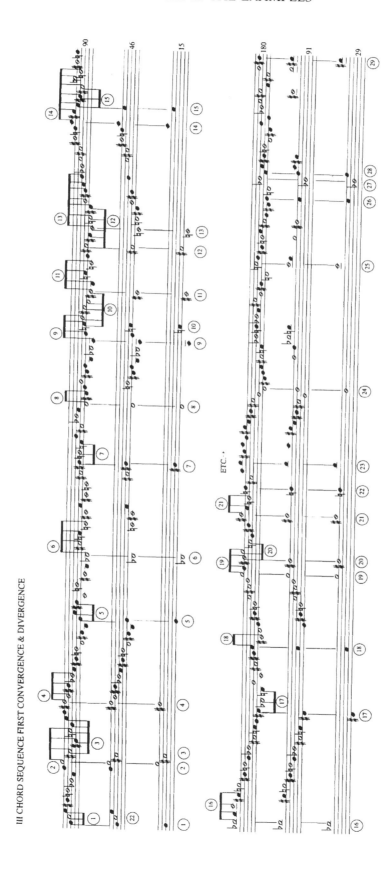

Example 105   The secondary pitch resource for *Symphony[Myths]* (as in Exs. 80 and 81), showing the chord sources for Movement III strata.

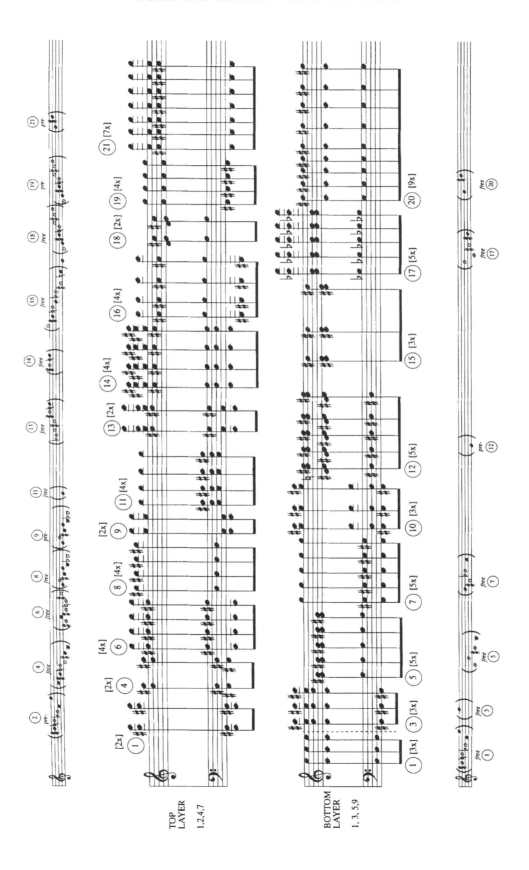

Example 106   The chordal structure for upper and lower strata, first convergence, Movement III, of *Symphony[Myths]*.

WHISPERS OUT OF TIME (1988)

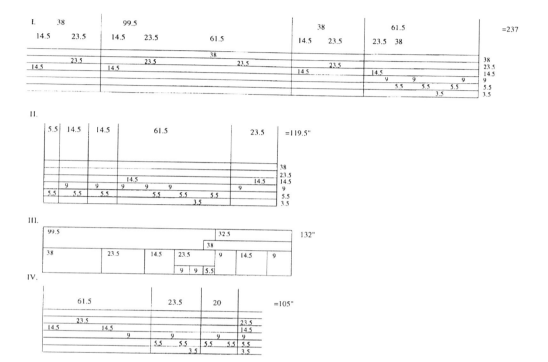

Example 107   The subsection proportionality for *Whispers Out of Time*.

PERSONAE (1990)

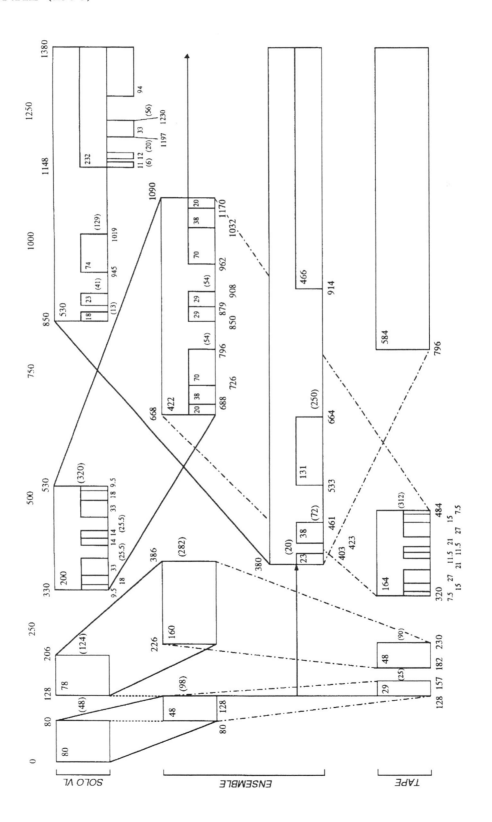

Example 108   The overall plan for *Personae*.

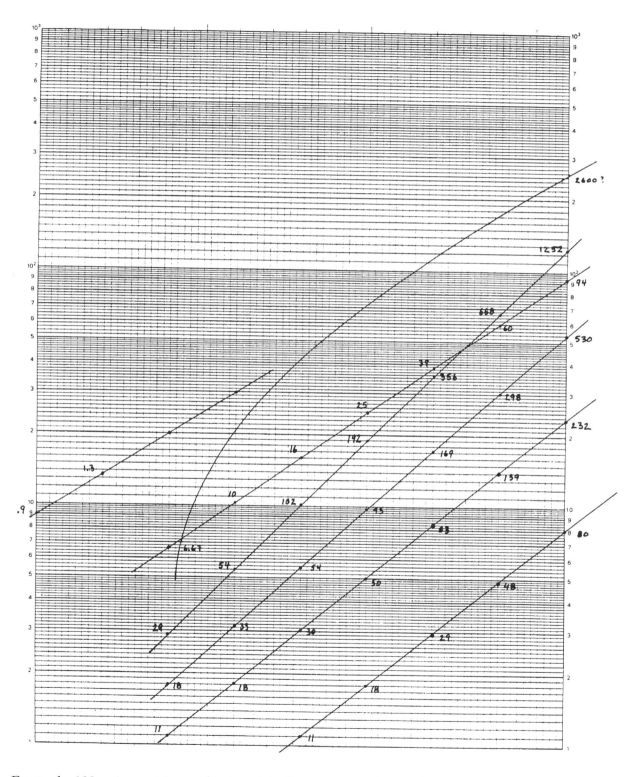

Example 109   A semi-logarithmic grid allows a set of straight lines at different slopes to establish the related numerical series necessary to shape the overall form of *Personae*.

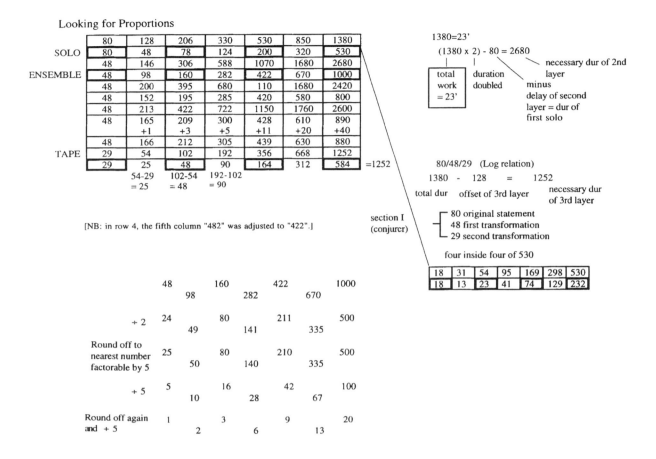

Example 110   Data from a page of the sketchbook for *Personae*, showing the derivation of proportional series relationships and of a set of integers for controlling rhythm.

	MEDITATOR III MM 44 1.3636	CONJURER I MM 66 .90909	ADVOCATE IV MM 88 .681818	DANCER II MM 132 .454545
2.73	𝅗𝅥			
1.918		𝅗𝅥		
1.36	♩	♩.	𝅗𝅥	𝅗𝅥.
1.023	♩.	♩ ♪	♩.	𝅗𝅥 ♪
.909	𝅘𝅥³	♩	♩ 𝅘𝅥³	𝅗𝅥
.6818	♪	♪.	♩	♩.
.606	⟨ 𝅘𝅥⁹ ♪ ⟩	𝅘𝅥³	⟨ 𝅘𝅥 ⁹ ♪ ⟩	♩ 𝅘𝅥³
.54	𝅘𝅥⁵			
.5114	♪.	⟨ ⟩	♪.	⟨ ⟩
.45	𝅘𝅥³	♪	𝅘𝅥³	♩
.303	⟨ 𝅘𝅥⁹:⁸ ⟩	𝅘𝅥³	⟨ ⟩	𝅘𝅥³
.34 / .27	𝅘𝅥 𝅘𝅥⁵	♪.	♪	♪. 𝅘𝅥⁵ ₁₃꜀ 𝅘𝅥.⁵
.2273 / .1948	𝅘𝅥⁶ 𝅘𝅥⁷	♪	𝅘𝅥³	♪
.1818		𝅘𝅥⁵		
.17045 / .1515	♪ 𝅘𝅥⁹	𝅘𝅥⁶	♪ 𝅘𝅥⁹:⁸	𝅘𝅥³
.1363	𝅘𝅥¹⁰	𝅘𝅥⁷	𝅘𝅥⁵	
.1299 / .1136	𝅘𝅥¹²	♪	𝅘𝅥⁶	♪

Example 111 Comparison of the absolute durations of rhythmic values at the four tempos used in *Personae*.

Example 112   The row chart for *Personae*.

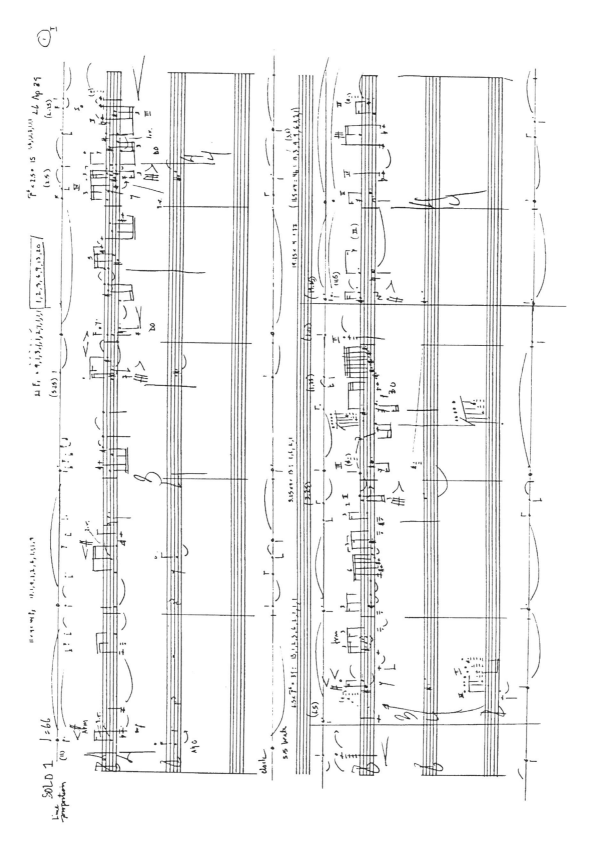

Example 113   The first page of the sketch for Solo I of *Personae.*

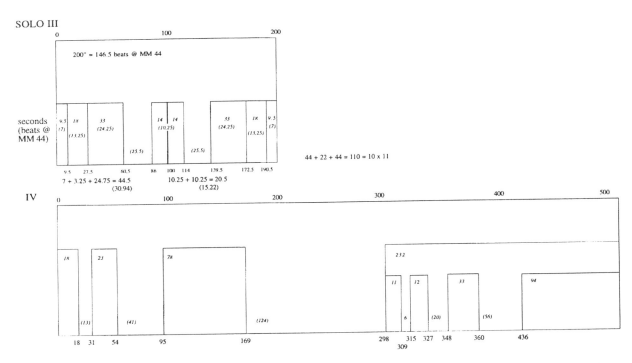

Example 114   Diagrams showing the internal proportional structure of Solos III and IV *(Personae)*.

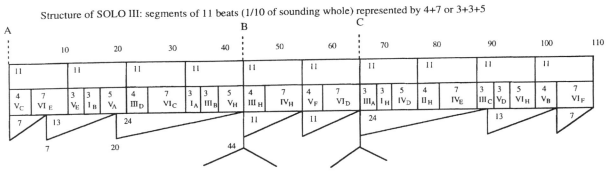

Example 115   Details of the inner structure of Solo III, including the distribution of harmonic content *(Personae)*.

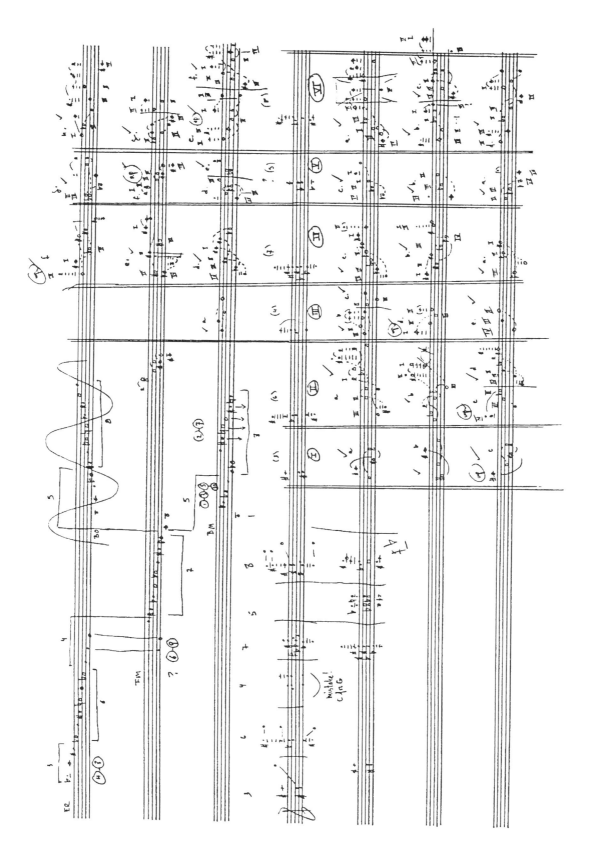

Example 116   The initial derivation of the harmonic resource for Solo III (*Personae*).

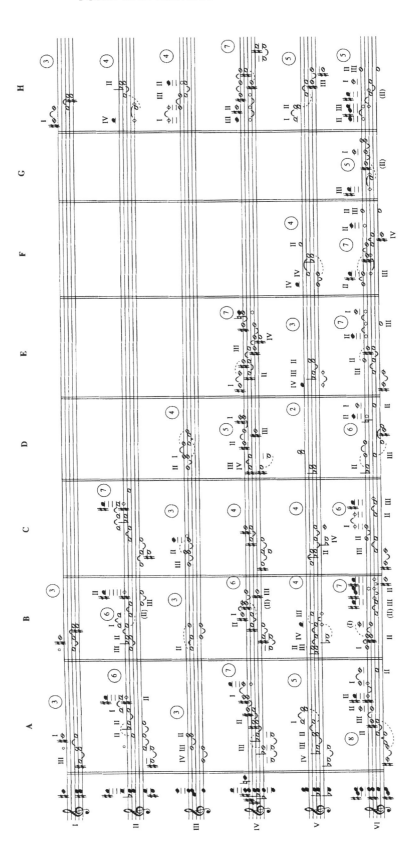

Example 117   A more advanced stage of categorization for the dyad content of Solo III (*Personae*).

Example 118   The dyadic successions specified in Example 115 are realized as actual progressions.

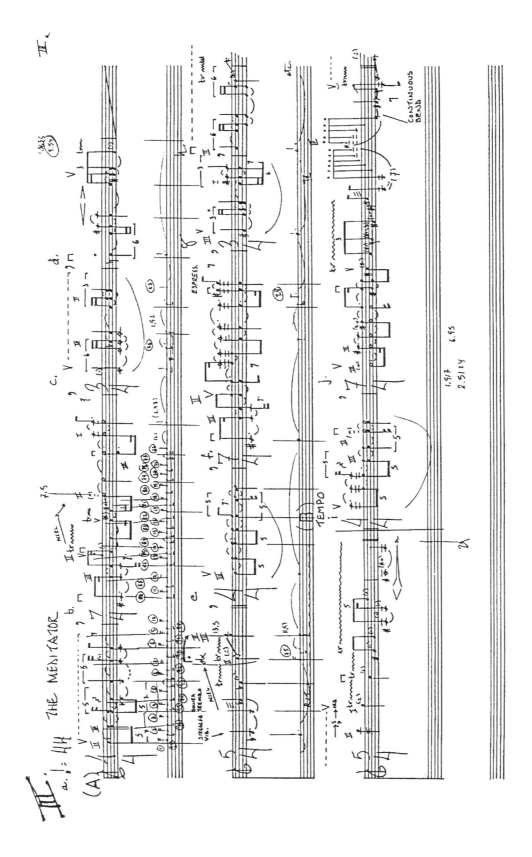

Example 119   The sketch from the beginning of Solo III (The Meditator) in *Personae*, showing the harmonic successions of Example 118 combined with the temporal proportions indicated in Example 115.

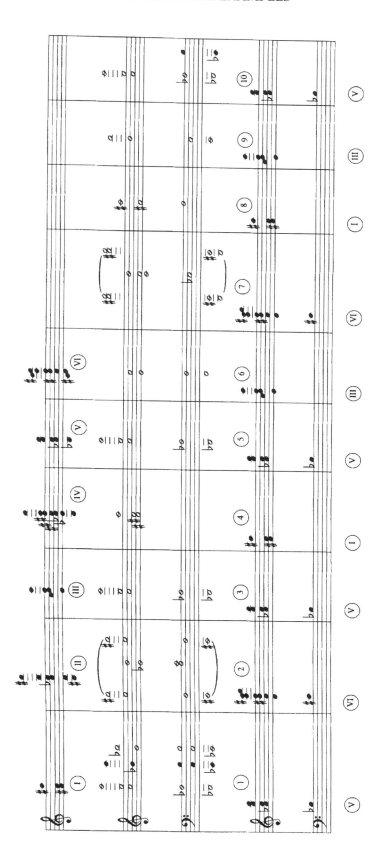

Example 120   A derived harmonic structure for use in the Ensemble response to Solo III (*Personae*).

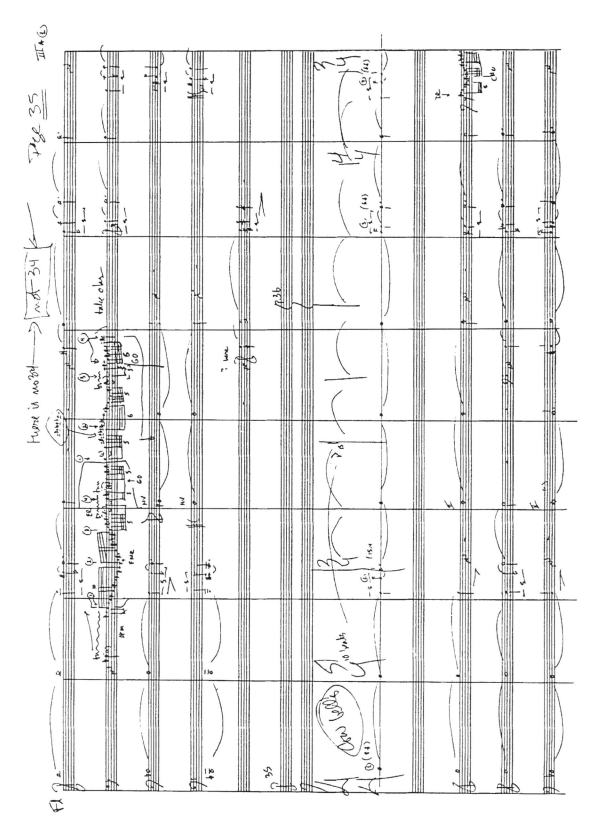

Example 121   A sketch page for the Ensemble response to Solo III corresponding to Example 120.

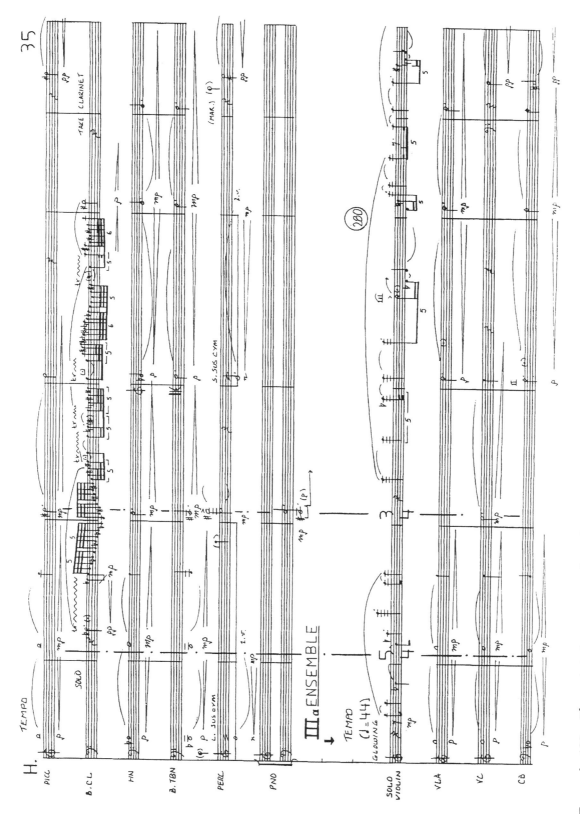

Example 122   The printed score page from *Personae* corresponding to the Example 121 sketch (reproduced with the permission of C. F. Peters Corporation, New York).

total *out* dur. 945" - 1230 = 285" from *in* dur. of 200";

SOLO III   3 passes; moderate lengths for even 1/2-pass (29 ...) &
            slightly shorter lengths (20 ...) for odd 1/2-pass

proportions : 20:29:38:70 [from ENSEMBLE IV$_{IV}$ proportions

of overall plan (850"-1090")]

200/17746 = .01127
.01127 x 20 = .2254
.01127 x 29 = .3268
.01127 x 38 = .42826

(49) 20 20 20 20 20 20 20 20 20 20 38 20 20 20 20 20 20 20 20 20 20 20 20 304 841 4900 70 ⎛ 4900 841...
(48) 29 29 29 29 29 29 29 29 29 29 29 29 29 29 29 29 29 29 29 29 29 29 29 232 1444 70 ⎝ 70 1444 232... ⎞ = 17746
97 terms

(38x8) (29x29) (70x70)

(8x29) (38x38)

Example 123   Basic exploration of "proportional series" characteristics in preparation for applying the SPLITZ algorithm to Solo III material from *Personae*.

	position in seconds of extracted segment		duration in seconds of extracted segment		seg. nos.			position of segment in output recalculated in beats @ MM = 44
{odd	half-pass	1:	delay: 0.000000 }					
note	0.000	1	0.225	0	1	1845	p4sec;	0.0
note	0.308	1	0.225	4523	2	6368	p4sec;	.226
note	0.701	1	0.225	9046	3	10891	p4sec;	.51
note	1.180	1	0.225	13569	4	15414	p4sec;	.86
note	1.747	1	0.225	18092	5	19937	p4sec;	1.28
note	2.404	1	0.225	22615	6	24460	p4sec;	1.76
note	3.154	1	0.225	27138	7	28983	p4sec;	2.31
note	3.996	1	0.225	31661	8	33506	p4sec;	2.93
note	4.935	1	0.225	36184	9	38029	p4sec;	3.62
note	5.971	1	0.225	40707	10	42552	p4sec;	4.38
note	7.106	1	0.428	45230	11	48737	p4sec;	5.21
note	8.547	1	0.225	51415	12	53260	p4sec;	6.27
note	9.888	1	0.225	55938	13	57783	p4sec;	7.25
note	11.335	1	0.225	60461	14	62306	p4sec;	8.31
note	12.890	1	0.225	64984	15	66829	p4sec;	9.45
note	14.555	1	0.225	69507	16	71352	p4sec;	10.67
note	16.333	1	0.225	74030	17	75875	p4sec;	11.98
note	18.226	1	0.225	78553	18	80398	p4sec;	13.37
note	20.237	1	0.225	83076	19	84921	p4sec;	14.84
note	22.367	1	0.225	87599	20	89444	p4sec;	16.40
note	24.619	1	0.225	92122	21	93967	p4sec;	18.05
note	26.996	1	3.426	96645	22	124710	p4sec;	19.80
note	32.701	1	9.478	146130	23	223774	p4sec;	23.98
note	44.587	1	55.224	357092	24	809483	p4sec;	32.70
note	102.352	1	0.789	815946		822407	p4sec;	
note	105.818	1	55.224	828870		1281261	p4sec;	
note	163.856	1	9.478	1414579		1492223	p4sec;	
note	176.290	1	3.426	1513643		1541708	p4sec;	
note	182.816	1	0.225	1544386		1546231	p4sec;	
note	186.287	1	0.225	1548909		1550754	p4sec;	
note	189.909	1	0.225	1553432		1555277	p4sec;	
note	193.683	1	0.225	1557955		1559800	p4sec;	
note	197.614	1	0.225	1562478		1564323	p4sec;	
note	201.704	1	0.225	1567001		1568846	p4sec;	
note	205.956	1	0.225	1571524		1573369	p4sec;	
note	210.374	1	0.225	1576047		1577892	p4sec;	
note	214.962	1	0.225	1580570		1582415	p4sec;	
note	219.723	1	0.225	1585093		1586938	p4sec;	
note	224.660	1	0.428	1589616		1593123	p4sec;	
note	229.980	1	0.225	1595801		1597646	p4sec;	
note	235.281	1	0.225	1600324		1602169	p4sec;	
note	240.769	1	0.225	1604847		1606692	p4sec;	
note	246.449	1	0.225	1609370		1611215	p4sec;	beats before 285" (12 30")
note	252.324	1	0.225	1613893	44	1615738	p4sec;	47.93
note	258.399	1	0.225	1618416	45	1620261	p4sec;	39.06
note	264.677	1	0.225	1622939	46	1624784	p4sec;	29.81
note	271.163	1	0.225	1627462	47	1629307	p4sec;	20.30
note	277.861	1	0.225	1631985	48	1633830	p4sec;	10.47
note	284.775	1	0.225	1636508	49	1638353	p4sec;	.33
{even	half-pass	1:	delay: 3.344492 }					
note	3.344	2	0.327	1633831	50	1636507	p4sec;	2.45
note	14.765	2	0.327	1629308	51	1631984	p4sec;	10.83
note	25.822	2	0.327	1624785	52	1627461	p4sec;	18.94
note	36.523	2	0.327	1620262	53	1622938	p4sec;	26.78
note	46.876	2	0.327	1615739	54	1618415	p4sec;	34.38
note	56.886	2	0.327	1611216	55	1613892	p4sec;	41.72
note	66.562	2	0.327	1606693	56	1609369	p4sec;	48.81
note	75.910	2	0.327	1602170		1604846	p4sec;	
note	84.936	2	0.327	1597647		1600323	p4sec;	
note	93.647	2	0.327	1593124		1595800	p4sec;	
note	102.050	2	0.327	1586939		1589615	p4sec;	
note	110.150	2	0.327	1582416		1585092	p4sec;	
note	117.954	2	0.327	1577893		1580569	p4sec;	

Example 124   The results from a computer run of the SPLITZ algorithm used to generate material for Solo IV from *Personae*.

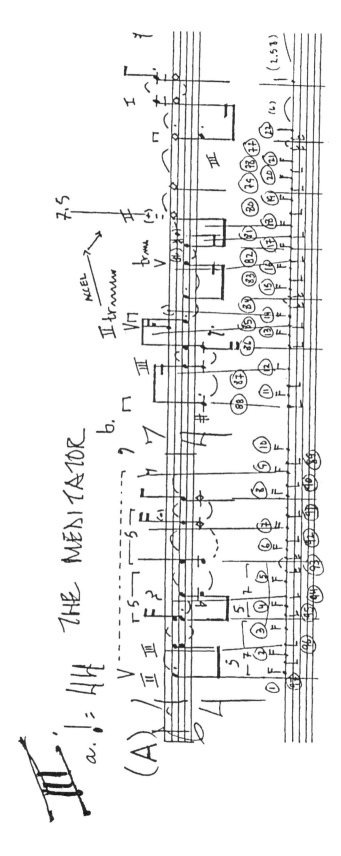

Example 125   A detail from the beginning of the sketch for Solo III from *Personae*, showing the rhythmic points at which segments were extracted by the SPLITZ algorithm.

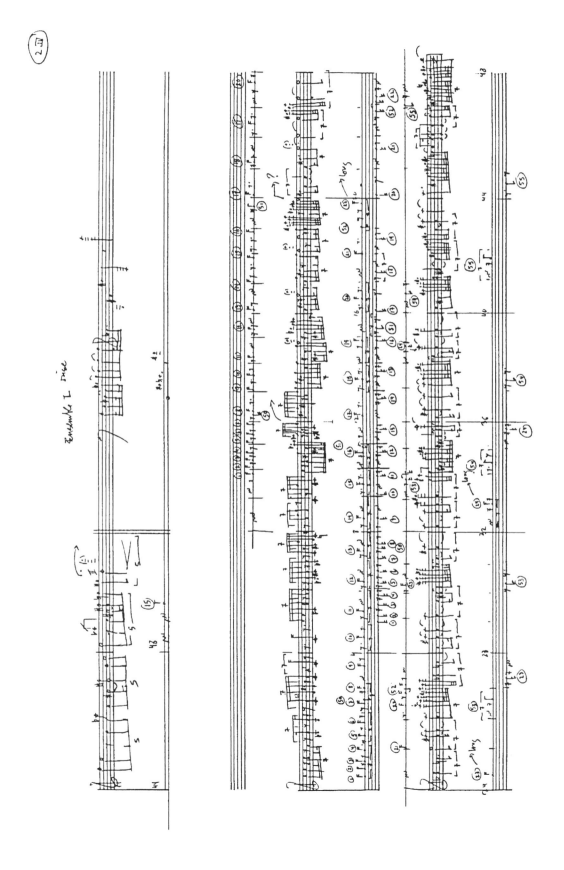

Example 126   The beginning of the sketch for Solo IV from *Personae*, showing the laying out in a new continuity of the small segments of Solo III that have been algorithmically identified and repositioned.

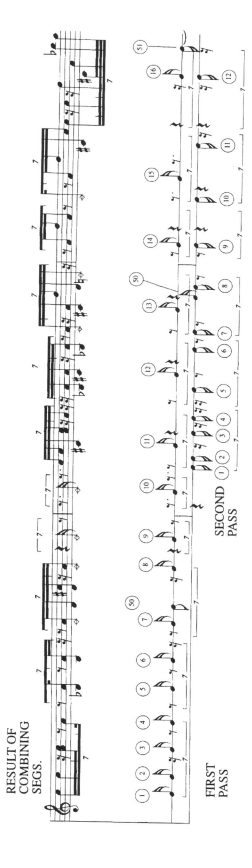

Example 127 Detail of Example 126.

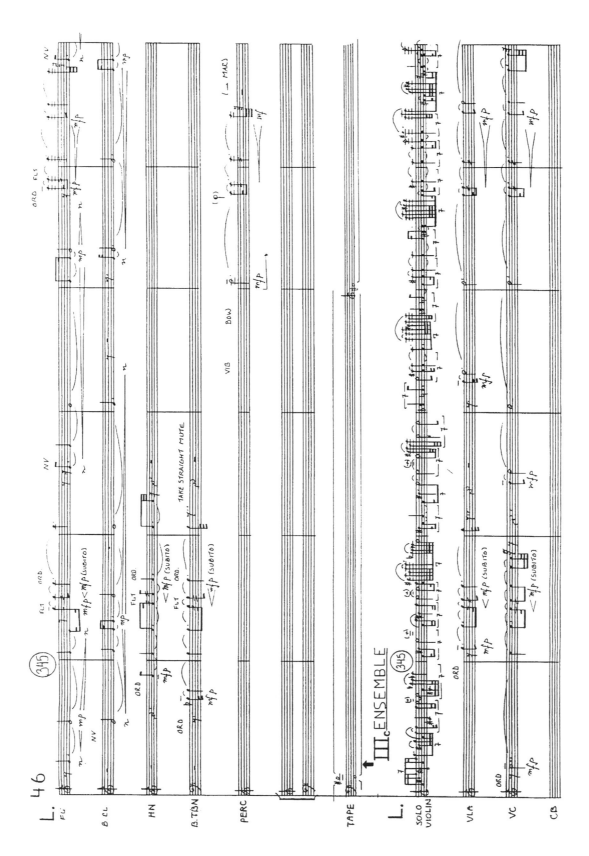

Example 128   Page 46 from the published score of *Personae* (reproduced with the permission of C. F. Peters Corporation, New York).

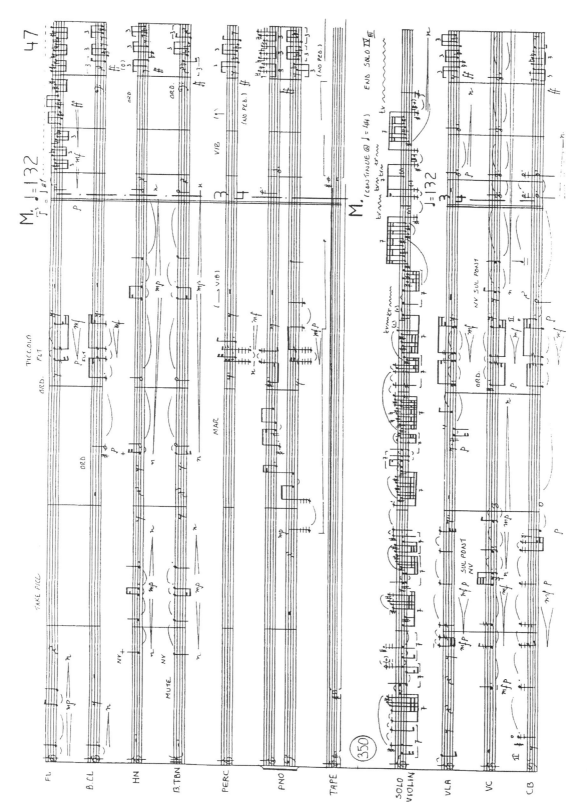

Example 129   Page 47 from the published score of *Personae* (reproduced with the permission of C. F. Peters Corporation, New York).

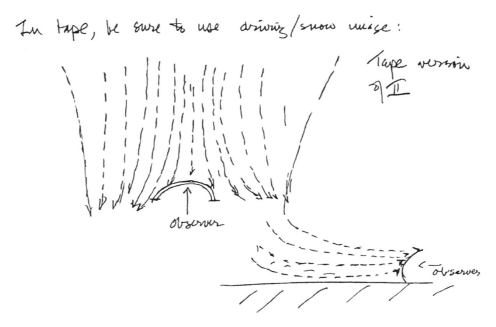

Example 130   The original sketch for a particular spatialization effect included in the computer part of *Personae*.

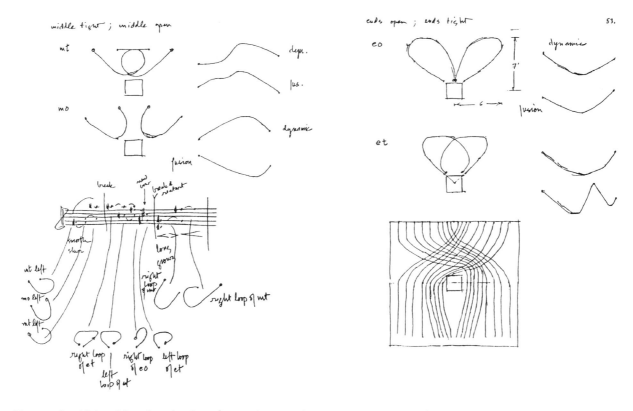

Example 131   Notebook sketches of spatialization strategies for *Personae*.

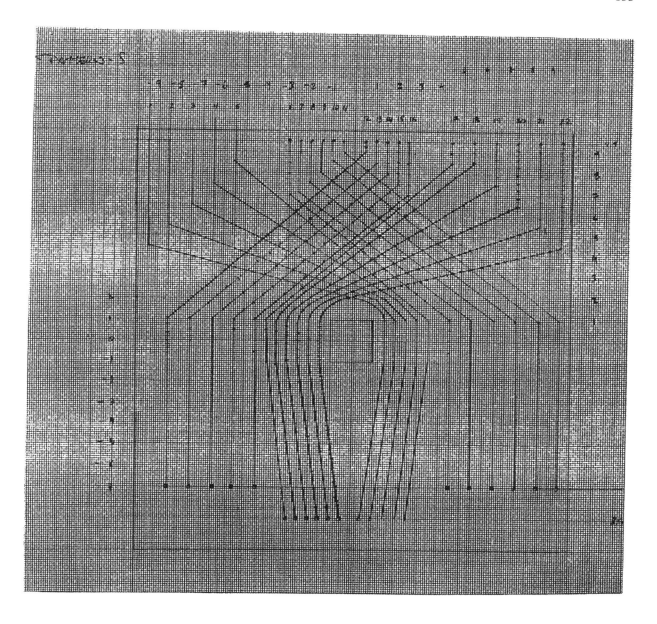

Example 132   The final design of the spatialization image sketched in Example 130.

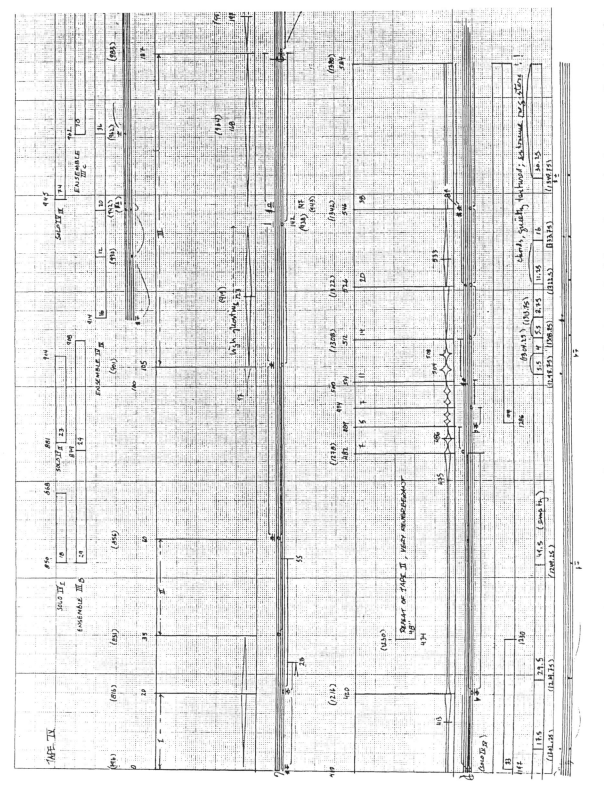

Example 133a A portion of the detailed plan for the final section of the last Solo (The Advocate) of *Personae* (beginning).

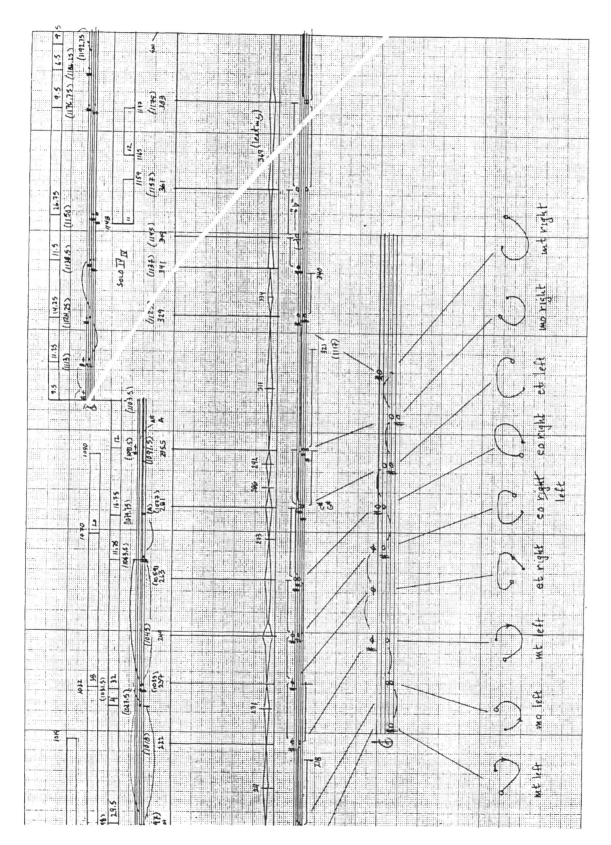

Example 133b A portion of the detailed plan for the final section of the last Solo (The Advocate) of *Personae* (end).